D1517810

Protestant Reformers loved to quote the ancient proverb, "Where God builds a church, the devil builds a chapel." Ed Stetzer and Jerry Rankin have challenged the church's prevailing devil-may-care attitudes with counterstrategies for opposing evil's obstruction and construction projects. I know of no better book to get your church from defense to offense against "your enemy [who] . . . prowls around" (1 Pet. 5:8).

—Leonard Sweet, E. Stanley Jones Professor of Evangelism
Drew Theological School
Madison, New Jersey

The local church was established by Christ to complete a mission; but in order to complete that mission, we must understand our adversary. Take the journey with Ed and Jerry as they reveal the plans of our enemy and the simple, yet powerful truths that will allow authentic Christ followers to overcome their distractions and win today's most critical battles.

—Brady Boyd, Senior Pastor
New Life Church, Colorado Springs, Colorado

Ed Stetzer and Jerry Rankin have a great heart for missions. That passion is reflected in this book that exposes the devices of the devil in trying to keep us from being a Great Commission people. Thanks, my brothers, for the insights and the challenge.

—Danny Akin, President
Southeastern Baptist Theological Seminary
Wake Forest, North Carolina

Anyone who wants to see the gospel advance in the culture through the church needs to know how Satan opposes that effort. This book is a great contribution to our understanding of what it means to be missional Christians and churches.

—Mark Driscoll, Preaching Pastor
Mars Hill Church, Seattle, Washington

A book explaining the contours of battle on the cutting edge of international missions, from two of the finest missiologists alive, *Spiritual Warfare and Missions* combines biblical exposition, an acute awareness of the progress of worldwide mission work and insight from two seasoned field workers. This book is an introduction to the battle and a call to arms.

—J. D. Greear, Pastor
The Summit Church, Durham, North Carolina

Jerry Rankin and Ed Stetzer have produced a veritable handbook on spiritual warfare and missions. If you've ever wondered why the unreached remain unreached, read this book.

—Peter J. Iliyn, Director
North America, Youth With A Mission

Jerry Rankin and Ed Stetzer speak out of life experiences, addressing what we all know too well—Christians and churches allow Satan's lies to hinder the mission. In this helpful book, they expose the lies, unpack Biblical instruction, and clearly present God's plan to overcome. This is a timely and needed book.

—Al Gilbert, Senior Pastor
Calvary Baptist Church, Winston-Salem, North Carolina

SPIRITUAL
WARFARE
AND
MISSIONS

SPIRITUAL
WARFARE
AND
MISSIONS

THE BATTLE FOR GOD'S GLORY
AMONG THE NATIONS

JERRY RANKIN
AND ED STETZER

PUBLISHING GROUP
NASHVILLE, TENNESSEE

978-0-8054-4887-0

Published by B&H Publishing Group
Nashville, Tennessee

Dewey Decimal Classification: 269.2
Subject Heading: INTERNATIONAL MISSIONS \ SPIRITUAL
WARFARE \ EVANGELISTIC WORK

DEDICATION

This book is dedicated to the pastors who are catching a global vision and have a passion for leading their church to be aligned with God in reaching the people of the world for His glory. Resisting the temptation of Satan to focus on their own provincial world and build their local kingdom, growing numbers are leading their people to pray for unreached people groups, providing opportunities for strategic short-term involvement around the world and encouraging their churches to give generously and sacrificially to missions. They have discovered the key to spiritual vitality and local impact is a heart for God's kingdom work to the ends of the earth.

CONTENTS

FOREWORD

There is a spiritual battle presently raging for the souls of billions of men and women around the world.

The scope of this spiritual battle is universal. It covers and comprises every tongue, tribe, language, nation, person, and people group. There is no place on this earth where this war is not being waged.

The stakes in this spiritual battle are eternal. There is a true God over this world who desires all people to experience everlasting joy in heaven. There is a false god in this world who desires all people to experience everlasting suffering in hell.

The enemy in this spiritual battle is formidable. He is like a lion looking for his kill, and he is dead set on defaming God's glory and destroying God's people. Where the church exists, he works to draw us in through temptation and discourage us in trial. He lures us with possessions and prosperity, and he lulls us to sleep with comforts and complacency. He deceives, deters, and distracts the church from knowing the wonder of Christ and declaring the worth of Christ to the ends of the earth.

Meanwhile, he holds thousands of unreached people groups captive through deceptive philosophies, hollow worldviews, and false religions. These people groups are virtually untouched by the gospel of the glory of God, and this is where the adversary's stronghold is fiercest. Any Christian and any church that desires to proclaim the gospel among the unreached people groups of the world can expect to be met with the full force of hell in the process.

This is the picture that Jerry Rankin and Ed Stetzer put before us in this book. They faithfully demonstrate how God has created His people to declare His glory to the ends of the earth. Then they skillfully explicate the schemes Satan uses to defame God's glory among the peoples of the world. Their exegesis is precise, their application is pointed, and their analyses of Satan's strategies sound a poignant call for Christians and churches alike to move with haste to the front lines of this battle.

We do not have time to waste. We do not have time to play artificial games in contemporary culture or wage artificial wars in comfortable churches. We have been captured by a God-centered passion and we have been commissioned with a global purpose. Every Christian and every church has been called to engage in this war. It may not be easy, it might not be safe, and it will likely involve great cost; but in the end we can take heart: the outcome of this spiritual battle is irreversible. Satan has been defeated, and he will be destroyed. We do not fight this battle for victory; we fight this battle from victory. We stand on the merits of the Lamb who was slain and the Lamb who has already won the ultimate battle; and we sacrifice our lives in death-defying obedience to His commands, confident that one day soon we will gather with a ransomed people from every nation, tribe, tongue, and language, and together we will declare His praises for all of eternity.

May God help us to fight the battle and to be found faithful until that day.

—David Platt, Senior Pastor
The Church at Brook Hills, Birmingham, Alabama

PREFACE

We share a passion for the mission of God! Both of us have sought to be obedient to God's leadership in our lives with regard to personal involvement in reaching a lost world. From the perspective of our own witness and ministry in positions of denominational leadership, our callings have taken divergent paths. We come from different backgrounds and experiences, but all that we have done reflects a shared focus on the Great Commission. We believe God is moving in providence and power toward that coming day when representatives from every tribe, people, language, and nation will be gathered around the throne of God. Praise for the Lamb that was slain and the ushering in of the kingdom of God will result in the worship and praise of the One to whom all glory is due.

Our conviction is always that the task of discipling the nations is not the responsibility of an elite group of missionaries sent out on behalf of the church, but this is a mandate given to all the people of God. No one is exempt from the task of bearing witness to the ends of the earth, of the salvation that can be found in Jesus Christ alone. We have each sought to mobilize and channel the potential of local churches toward fulfillment of the Great Commission. In recent years our roles have merged at times as opportunities for coordinated collaboration in meeting this challenge have surfaced.

God is moving in unprecedented ways to penetrate nations and peoples long deprived of the life-changing message of the gospel. As we move further into the twenty-first century, a sovereign God is using global events to open doors of opportunity in response to the pervasive spiritual hunger of a sinful and fallen world. Yet an enemy exists who is jealous of God's glory and is doing everything he possibly can, using his devious and evil schema, to barricade the spread of the gospel and hinder the proclamation of God's glory.

Satan is identified as the deceiver of the nations. His subtle tactics as an angel of light are powerful as he seeks to weaken and distort the witness of God's people. The powers of darkness create distorted religious worldviews, cause totalitarian governments to restrict a Christian witness, and seek to squelch the advance of the kingdom through persecution of believers. However, proving to be even more successful is Satan's ability to use our self-centered, fleshly nature and inclination to compromise with worldly, carnal influences that continue to divert God's people from the priority of God's mission.

I (Jerry) wrote an earlier volume, *Spiritual Warfare: The Battle for God's Glory*. This was an effort to expose the tactics of our enemy who is seeking to rob Christians of the victory and life of holiness we have been given in Jesus Christ that God might be glorified in our lives personally. Because Satan's success demands secrecy and anonymity, we have sought to expose his strategies that are designed to deprive God of His intended purpose of being exalted among the nations and all the peoples of the world. Satan's most effective strategy is not the opposition to the kingdom on mission fields around the world but the indifference of churches and God's people who have become self-centered and lost a passion for reaching a lost world.

As I (Ed) travel and speak among God's people, I also pray that God will awaken them to the spiritual battle that is taking place around us. If God's people, especially in North America, would become energized about reaching the nations with the gospel, then God's glory would be proclaimed like never before. The reason—God's people in North America have the resources, both the people and money, to make a significant impact. We hope that in the days ahead we will see such a movement. It is the reason why we have partnered together to write on this subject in particular. We see the unlimited potential that resides in the body of Christ.

We are grateful for the widespread influence and support of colleagues at the International Mission Board and LifeWay Christian Resources, who are an inspiration in their commitment to the Great Commission. Thousands of missionaries serving faithfully around the world are our heroes; they are on the cutting edge of pushing back the frontiers of lostness. Our vision of the ultimate victory of our Lord is stirred by their reports and the testimonies of the powerful way God's Spirit is moving to engage the peoples of the world with the gospel and turn hearts to Jesus Christ in saving faith.

However, the message of this book has grown out of seeing thousands of churches beginning to catch the vision and be shaped by a passion for involvement in global missions. What could happen if every church and every Christian became obedient to what God has called us as His people to do? The potential of the kingdoms of the world becoming the kingdom of our Lord is evident. But Satan doesn't want that to happen. We pray this book will expose our enemy's tactics and challenge the people of God to become focused on declaring His glory among the nations.

We want to express appreciation to many who provided resources for our writing, including the communication staff and Global Research Department of the International Mission Board and LifeWay Research. We are grateful for the editorial service provided by Russell Rankin. It has been a joy to work with Thomas Walters and the staff at B&H Publishing Group; their encouragement and support of this project has encouraged us to prevail in our collaboration and effort to share these insights and challenges with you.

—Jerry Rankin and Ed Stetzer

CHAPTER 1

GOD'S PURPOSE: TO BE EXALTED AMONG THE NATIONS

I had been traveling for almost eight hours over winding dirt roads, sections of which were more appropriate for an all-terrain vehicle. The rainy season had left the narrow motor-way a gully as water from the surrounding hills converged into cascading streams, washing away the gravel and leaving a patch-work of potholes in the occasional sections of deteriorating pave-ment. Ten-wheel, open-bed trucks, heavily laden with goods being transported to the isolated market towns of the interior, had left deep trenches, which the driver of our lightweight sedan found difficult to navigate.

It was 1982, and I (Jerry) had been in charge of creating a grow-ing network of indigenous partners throughout India to expand mission initiatives in the country. We envisioned volunteer teams and itinerant missionaries making connections for the sake of min-istry through humanitarian projects, training church leaders, and facilitating church growth. Contacts with Baptist leaders in other parts of the country had alerted me to a remnant of Baptists in the Khond Hills of the State of Orissa. Subsequent communication with this group resulted in an invitation to come and speak at their annual associational gathering.

I had taken a flight from Calcutta south to Bhubaneswar, a city I had never heard of and could not even pronounce. The remote location and isolated landing strip gave me the impression that I had arrived at my destination, only to be met by my hosts and informed we faced an eight-hour drive to the site of the meeting.

Crammed into the overloaded vehicle with my traveling companions, I had images of riding in Jehu's chariot as the driver asserted total authority over the roadway and anything that dared to infringe on his right-of-way. Approaching a village, he seemed to accelerate with horn blaring as chickens, goats, and children scattered. The populated communities grew sparse as the road wound higher and higher around barren hills that for generations had been stripped of trees out of necessity for fuel and land for farming.

As we would dip into an occasional valley, the road would be totally enveloped in a jungle canopy of overhanging trees. Monkeys scurried into the underbrush as we rounded a bend, and we found ourselves braking to avoid running into the back end of an elephant ambling leisurely with his *mahout* perched high on his swaying shoulders.

Three flat tires lengthened the trip as each time the inner tube had to be removed, the puncture found and repaired, and then the tire reinflated through arduous efforts using a malfunctioning hand pump. I began to get a little anxious as the shadows began to lengthen and the security of civilization seemed to be left far behind. A pastor, who was to be my translator, told me about the Kui people with whom we would be meeting.

A generation ago they had never heard the gospel. They were among tribal groups so isolated that they had never been reached with the message of God's love and salvation until some British missionaries established contact soon after World War II. In fact, these people were so pagan in their syncretistic Hindu and animist beliefs, I was told, that they would sacrifice one of their children and sprinkle his blood on their fields at planting time, believing the gods would give them a favorable harvest.

I began to see half-clothed people with scars and tattoos on their faces and bodies, unlike I had seen elsewhere in my travels throughout India. I have been many places in subsequent years that could be identified as the ends of the earth—remote villages in Mali, West Africa, indigenous Indian enclaves in the Amazon jungles of South America, the desert of southern Algeria, and isolated valleys of the Himalayas in Nepal. I have found myself incredulous to be standing in places like North Korea, Afghanistan, and Iran, but never had I sensed we were reaching beyond the fringes of the Great Commission as I did in penetrating the Khond Hills of India.

Topping a ridge, we suddenly caught sight of a massive crowd milling around an intersection ahead. My initial impression was that there had been a terrible accident, but then I was informed we had finally arrived at our destination and the crowd had come to welcome us. We disembarked from the car and walked the final kilometer to the sight of the annual meeting. We were escorted by a band of men adorned in grass skirts and feathers in their headdresses, dancing to the beat of drums and bamboo flutes. Their tongues trilling in traditional greeting, women lined the side of the road in saris of bright tribal colors of yellow, orange, red, and chartreuse.

More than three thousand people had gathered from every village in the Khond Hills. With their families and village clans, they were camped all across the hillsides surrounding a huge brush arbor. They weren't very time conscious, waiting for us to arrive to gather and begin the program. They sat on the ground underneath a lacy pattern of sunlight and shadows dancing through the leaves and branches laid across low-hanging poles.

When everyone was settled, the man who seemed to be in charge shouted something, and all the people responded with a shout. Once again the leader shouted, and in antiphonal response the people replied. Not understanding the local dialect, I presumed this was simply a customary way of beginning a public ceremony or perhaps a way of greeting us as the honored guests.

My interpreter nudged me and asked if I knew what they were saying, which, of course, I didn't. He said, "The leader is shouting, 'Who is the Lord?' And all the people are responding, 'Jesus is Lord.'" As this was repeated several times, goose bumps appeared on my arms, and a chill went up my spine. Here were a people that were not a people, a people who had lived in darkness but had now become the people of God. This is what Paul referred to as he quoted the prophet Hosea in Romans 9:26, "You are not My people, [but] they will be called: Sons of the living God" (Hos. 1:10). These were a people in darkness who had now come to the light as Isaiah prophesied, "Darkness covers the earth, and total darkness the peoples; but the LORD will shine over you. . . . Nations will come to your light" (Isa. 60:2–3).

As I heard the Kui people of the Khond Hills declaring "Jesus is Lord," I immediately thought of Philippians 2:10–11 and the awesome implications of what I was witnessing. "So that at the name of Jesus every knee should bow . . . and every tongue should confess that Jesus Christ is Lord, to the glory of God the Father." Just as these Kui people, geographically isolated and separated from God, living in spiritual darkness, had now become the people of God, one day all people will recognize Jesus as Lord. God will be glorified by the confession of praise being declared by every tongue, "Jesus is Lord" to the glory of God the Father!

> *Everything created in the world should be seen in the context of existing for God's glory.*

God's ultimate purpose and desire is clear: to be glorified through His redemption of the nations. He alone is worthy of all praise and honor. His purpose is to be known and worshipped and exalted by the nations and peoples of the earth. The culmination of His divine activity in the world is expressed in the book of

Revelation: "Our Lord and God, You are worthy to receive glory and honor and power, because You have created all things, and because of Your will they exist and were created" (Rev. 4:11). Everything created in the world should be seen in the context of existing for God's glory. Every activity and endeavor should be to glorify Him not only in our lives and community but among all peoples, even to the ends of the earth.

Unwinding from the Triumphant Conclusion

The movement and mission from God can be traced through a linguistic thread woven throughout Scripture. The thread began under the rebellious circumstances in Babel and became the platform for God's mission through Pentecost and His glory in Revelation. By following the linguistic thread, we can better understand our mission with Him and for Him. The thread throughout the biblical record also traces God's relentless pursuit of a people for His glory. Rewinding God's story from Revelation 7, a picture of the missionary heart of God is clear. As people gather at the end of the age, we read in Revelation 7:9–10, "After this I looked, and there was a vast multitude from every nation, tribe, people, and language, which no one could number, standing before the throne and before the Lamb. They were robed in white with palm branches in their hands. And they cried out in a loud voice: Salvation belongs to our God, who is seated on the throne, and to the Lamb!" What will that sound like? Will everybody praise in a different language? Our information about the details is limited, but we do know it will be one voice. In unity brought about by God's presence and kingdom, from distinct people groups, His people will worship in the many languages they spoke during their mortal lives, giving praise to the Lord and glory to the Father.

Perhaps God retains languages in heaven because of their usefulness during the mission to deliver people there. When the Holy Spirit arrived to indwell believers in Acts, we see a picture of the "beginning of the end" in God's plan. For God's purposes, the early church was given the supernatural ability to speak in tongues (foreign languages), and thus, they were understood as the gospel was proclaimed at Pentecost. Through the person of the Holy Spirit, God's purposes were accomplished like no other time in history. When God's power is manifested, no arguments of man or principality can stand against it.

God's supernatural power and purpose were at work for the church in perfect harmony. The incredible aftereffect was seen through transformed lives: at least three thousand saved and baptized in Acts 2. God's ultimate glory is best manifested when people from every tongue, tribe, and nation sing praise to His name. At no other time in history has the power of God been experienced by representatives of the known world in such an intensely multicultural incident. Notice the linguistic thread.

The birth of the Christian movement was multiethnic and multicultural. Our current experience of Christianity in America is painfully monocultural. We can have the knowledge and practice of Christianity perfect. But until there is a clear embrace of the multicultural, multiethnic roots of Christianity, we will miss the greater blessing of God and cover of God's glory. Dr. Martin Luther King Jr. called the eleven o'clock worship hour on Sunday morning the most racially segregated hour in America. The picture that was bothersome to Dr. King, in light of Pentecost, should be equally appalling to missionary Christians. When God's supernatural power is evident, no segregation exists. He speaks a singular message to diverse people, and they embrace the true God when hearing of Him in their heart language.

Globalization was at its finest hour at Pentecost. Globalization is commonly used as an economic term. Mainly due to the rapid growth of technology, geography is no longer an obstacle to buying and selling. The result is a more competitive environment. When the world competed for positions of power, God produced global Christians at Pentecost by producing level ground for all people. God was glorified by this amazing, supernatural act of tongues. If only one nation had experienced Pentecost, that one nation could have felt favored. But God favors every tribe equally. There is no one guardian of special faith, knowledge, or mystical experiences. No skin color or people group can elevate themselves over the rest. God is the great gift giver partially because all of us are the blessed receivers of His gift. Luke described the scene in Acts:

> There were Jews living in Jerusalem, devout men from every nation under heaven. When this sound occurred, the multitude came together and was confused because each one heard them speaking in his own language. And they were astounded and amazed, saying, "Look, aren't all these who are speaking Galileans? How is it that we hear, each of us, in our own native language? Parthians, Medes, Elamites; those who live in Mesopotamia, in Judea and Cappadocia, Pontus and Asia, Phrygia and Pamphylia, Egypt and the parts of Libya near Cyrene; visitors from Rome, both Jews and proselytes, Cretans and Arabs—we hear them speaking in our own languages the magnificent acts of God." (Acts 2:5–11)

The purpose and desire of our missionary God is demonstrated again through the linguistic thread.

Millions were in Jerusalem for Pentecost. God appointed a gathering place three times a year for His people to "appear before" Him (Deut. 16:16). The Holy City, established by King David, was the place for pilgrims to experience deeper life with God. Small, diverse people groups experienced the power of God through an encounter with Jesus Christ at Pentecost. Priests who witnessed the historic event of the temple veil being torn in two a few months earlier would experience more history. "Suddenly a sound like that of a violent rushing wind came from heaven, and it filled the whole house where they were staying. And tongues, like flames of fire that were divided, appeared to them and rested on each one of them. Then they were all filled with the Holy Spirit and began to speak in different languages, as the Spirit gave them ability for speech" (Acts 2:2–4). God miraculously reversed what happened at Babel for the moment. Tongues once again appear but in everyone's heart language. Pilgrims experienced the power of God for the first time. Immediately they became colaborers in the mission of God.

Before Pentecost the mission of God was given exclusively to Israel. Being chosen bore an incredible worldwide mission responsibility to be a light to the nations. In Isaiah, God makes clear the missionary purpose of Israel. God's people struggled with the mission because of their contempt for people other than their own. "I, the LORD, have called you for a righteous purpose, and I will hold you by your hand. I will keep you, and I make you a covenant for the people and a light to the nations, in order to open blind eyes, to bring out prisoners from the dungeon, and those sitting in darkness from the prison house" (Isa. 42:6–7). God's promise to Abram, to bless all nations through him, is further fulfilled at Pentecost. No longer is the mission of God through Israel only. No tribe is more called or less called than the other. Christians in Africa have as much responsibility for the mission of God to the nations as Christians in Asia. North American Christians have as much responsibility for the mission of God as do Christians in Europe. We are all called to go to the nations. Why? To live out the missionary heart of God who is telling all Christians, everywhere, to go some place else with the gospel!

Peter rewound the story further by connecting the event with a prediction from Joel the prophet of the pouring out of the Spirit. Miracles seen long ago were demonstrated once again. The miracle of seeing and embracing Jesus among a diverse people with diverse belief systems is undeniable. As told to Joel by God, the sign would be a great outpouring on "all flesh." The power of God is not limited to Jewish flesh or Gentile flesh. Without the power of the Spirit of God, it would be impossible to engage the diversity of the world and its many languages. Global conversion to Christ does seem impossible. Suddenly we see the only way to touch the diverse nations of the world with the gospel of Jesus is through the power of the Holy Spirit. Everyone had equal access to all of God, instantly. Priests or institutional religious ceremonies were no longer obstacles to a love relationship with God.

Jerusalem was a sacred place to those who sought the God of Abraham. As we trace the linguistic thread throughout the story of God, we see two forces around the Holy City. Until Pentecost the epicenter of life with God was the pilgrimage to the temple and the Holy City. Pilgrims went up to Jerusalem to find and follow God. Centripetal force pulled inward. The nations came up to Jerusalem. Historians estimate more than two million people visited for Pentecost. Much to the disappointment of God, pilgrims would not only abuse the journey, but they would reduce God and their experience with Him to one place. The pilgrimage itself led to moral and spiritual abuses of the commands of God. Pentecost literally released the Christian movement from an inward movement around a geographical location to an outward movement to every tongue, tribe, and nation. Now from Jerusalem, divine centrifugal force would move missionary Christians from everywhere to everywhere. Pentecost was a centripetal force or action that led to a centrifugal explosion.

The world is now flat. People travel from people group to people group with the gospel. The testimony of God's power and purpose is left every place they go. We often use Acts 1:8 as an inspirational message to explain the geographical responsibility of every Christian. If you are looking for a "missions begins at home" text, try the Great Commandment or the story of the Good Samaritan. Although the principles may be supported in Acts 1:8, a larger story is often missed. Any desire to evangelize that causes someone to focus only on their own type of people is the greatest hindrance to the multicultural, multiethnic vision of God. Acts 1:8 is first prophetic in nature. Jesus informed disciples of what was about to happen before their eyes. Jesus explained to them exactly what a movement of God would look like. The Holy Spirit with incredible centrifugal force would thrust them outward. The same Holy Spirit who drew them into the kingdom would send them to the nations. Progress can be traced through languages. Jim Slack, a research strategist in global evangelism and church growth, addressed the danger of misunderstanding Acts 1:8:

"To see Acts 1:8 as 'my own kind first' would lead the follower to make the same mistake that Israel made over and over again—Israel first in ministry and maybe the others after them. To treat Acts 1:8 as meaning 'go to my people first' would run the risk of committing Jonah's ethnocentric sin over again."[1]

Pentecost displayed the missionary heart of God. People who experienced the power of God became one. Diverse cultures experienced God in identical ways. God is revealed as one God. One God is talking; one God is working. The reality described in Ephesians is demonstrated at Pentecost: "There is one body and one Spirit, just as you were called to one hope at your calling; one Lord, one faith, one baptism, one God and Father of all, who is above all and through all and in all" (Eph. 4:4–6). Often we struggle in churches of the same tongue, tribe, or nation. Disunity is a clear sign that God is not involved. How much more does racial prejudice or bigotry become anti-God? God loves diversity because He created diversity.

Satan does not want us to know how eager the nations are to hear God's message, so he builds attitudes of racism, bigotry, and superiority in our hearts. Yet people all over the world are much more willing to hear than we are to tell. God had to change the heart of Simon Peter in Acts 10. He was to be a missionary to the Gentiles. Peter was influenced by a religious background that did not like Gentiles or consider them equals. The barrier to the gospel was not the ignorance of the Gentiles but the prejudice of Peter. God was already at work in the life of an Italian military leader named Cornelius. God began to change Peter's heart through a vision. The vision (a blanket with animals considered unclean) was God's way to reveal the prejudice in Peter's heart. The story in Acts 10 is filled with dramatic twists, but there was a turning point and a sincere confession. Peter visited Cornelius, his family, and his friends who were eager to hear the gospel. We read, "When

Peter entered, Cornelius met him, fell at his feet, and worshiped him. But Peter helped him up and said, 'Stand up! I myself am also a man.' While talking with him, he went on in and found that many had come together there. Peter said to them, 'You know it's forbidden for a Jewish man to associate with or visit a foreigner. But God has shown me that I must not call any person common or unclean'" (Acts 10:25–28). Peter went to a people of another tongue. At Pentecost, Satan witnessed the linguistic thread that foreshadowed his ultimate defeat. The tongues that praised the Lord at Pentecost would praise the Lord in celebration after his final defeat. The ultimate barriers of hatred and superiority used to divide mankind and hinder the gospel were removed for the glory of God.

Everyone at Pentecost knew something extraordinary happened. When God puts His glory on display, the enemy goes on the attack. All of us who have benefited from Pentecost have one purpose: to extend the invitation of God to every nation. "Nation" does not designate governments or geographic borders. *Nation* refers to *ethne* or ethnolinguistic people groups of the world. If nations were city-states, we would have about 240 places to go and fulfill the Great Commission. Considering how many years we have been at it, we should not have many nations left to take the gospel. But "ethne" refers to languages and cultures or ethnic identities. The latest *Ethnologue* research catalogued 6,909 living languages in the world. When broken down by dialects and alternative language names, the list swells to more than forty thousand.[2]

Satan understands that his post-Pentecostal mission must change the focus of his opposition to the advance of God's kingdom. He only needs to accomplish one thing: cause us to depend on ourselves to fulfill God's missionary task. If Satan can accomplish this, nothing else matters. His most believable lie is "you can do this." Try harder, think smarter, send more people. The miracle at Pentecost that caught the attention of so many was more than an attractive mass evangelism meeting. Pentecost was an encounter with the power of God. The incredible barriers overcome on the birthday of the church could only have been overcome by God Himself. The barriers to evangelize our own neighbors are great enough, but even greater are the barriers to evangelize a remote village on the other side of the world that speaks another language. Perhaps this is why Jesus described Satan this way in John 8:44: "When he tells a lie, he speaks from his own nature, because he is a liar and the father of liars." He convinces us of our ability and great commitment to the cause. We go out to make a name for ourselves as missionaries and fail miserably. The native language of our adversary is deception, duplicity, and lying. Whereas God always speaks the language of truth because it is His nature, Satan always speaks the language of falsehood because it is his nature.

> *The language of our adversary is deception, duplicity, and lying whereas God always speaks the language of truth.*

The final rewind of God's story goes back to Genesis 11. The episode was the Tower of Babel. The scene was the birth of heathenism (self-glory) as the result of one tongue among men. Satan is alive and well. His desire for fame and glory is passed on to man. God's postflood plan was for the descendents of Noah to scatter and populate the earth. Genesis recounts God's plan: "God blessed Noah and his sons and said to them, 'Be fruitful and multiply and fill the earth'" (Gen. 9:1). Yet the nature of man was seen in his desire to create another plan: "And they said, 'Come, let us build ourselves a city and a tower with its top in the sky. Let us make a name for ourselves; otherwise, we will be scattered over the face of the whole earth'" (Gen. 11:4). In only two chapters after the Flood, man began not only to sin alone but to sin in groups. God, as before the Flood, and in the garden found Himself set aside by humanity. God was distant from the minds and hearts of self-absorbed men yet relentless in His pursuit of them.

What was the issue? Notice this—"Let us make a name for ourselves." The very thing rightfully belonging to God, man immediately claimed for himself—a famous name. Man wanted the glory only belonging to God. Man, since the garden, chose to go east, away from God, setting his own course. But God's fame is seen as every tongue, tribe, and nation returns to His name, His glory, and His worship. It was lost at Babel but returns via Pentecost and is consummated at the end of the age in the book of Revelation. God scattered the people of Babel, changing one language to multiple languages. Man's desire to make a name for himself had terrible consequences. Was God intimidated by the potential of man to accomplish things with one tongue? God is omnipotent, which means never intimidated. God knew that Babel would become a civilization of frustrated, godless people if He did not intervene. Never for a moment did He fear their potential to overthrow Him and actually supplant His glory.

Notice the fingerprints of Satan all over the crime at the Tower of Babel. Satan wanted to be equal to God. He tempted Eve with equality with God. Although Satan is not specifically mentioned, the people at Babel desired to reach heaven and make themselves famous. Like taking something away from children because of the damage they can do to themselves, God took away man's ability to communicate freely with every other person on the planet. Language is God's gift to man. Different languages are a demonstration of God's relentless love of man. Every time you hear a conversation in another language that you cannot understand, praise God for His love. God saw that man would destroy himself and attempt to live life apart from Him. He lovingly gifted us with diverse tongues to slow us down. He gave us tongues to go deeper into relationships with less people. Tongues reveal our limitations and helplessness. What a creative and loving way to discipline a self-absorbed, self-promoting, sinful man!

Scripture Affirms God's Desire for Glory among All Peoples

God did not give up on His relentless pursuit of man, and neither will Satan. Not even to his bitter end (Rev. 13:7–10). Genesis 12 begins a new "chapter one" of God on mission through a man named Abram. He chose a new missionary. God told Abram, "I will bless those who bless you, I will curse those who treat you with contempt, and all the peoples on earth will be blessed through you" (Gen. 12:3).

So, when an empire has seemingly brought peace to the world, God comes as the Word to speak of true peace between His kingdom and ours. At Pentecost, He began regathering the nations under the banner of His rule. And we will see at the end of the age, all the nations will speak in their own languages in making His name great. Having rewound from the culmination of God's glory at the consummation of the ages, let us see how this is affirmed in the biblical narrative as the essence of His mission for His people.

Many recognize that Psalm 117 is the shortest chapter in the Bible—only two short verses. However, most people are not aware that it is also the middle of the Bible. There are an equal number of chapters from Genesis 1 to Psalm 117 as there are from Psalm 118 to Revelation 22! Not only is this little psalm the middle of the Bible, but those verses also reflect the central theme of the whole Bible. "Praise the LORD, all nations! Glorify Him, all peoples! For great is His faithful love to us; the LORD's faithfulness endures forever. Hallelujah!" (Ps. 117:1–2).

This psalm speaks of God's faithful love to us—a love that took initiative in providing salvation, not because of our merit but because of His mercy. It speaks of the eternal security that we have in Him, not because of our ability to persevere but because of His faithfulness. He alone is worthy of all praise and glory. We are often guilty of an egotistical theology as if our salvation is all about us. But our salvation is not just to save us from hell and give us assurance of going to heaven. Through God's redemptive act of sending Jesus to die on the cross, we can be cleansed of sin, made holy, and restored to the image of Christ, but ultimately it is for His glory.

Asked why Jesus died on the cross, most Christians would reply in an obvious self-centered response, "To save me from my sin." Praise God; that is correct. When one accepts Jesus Christ as Savior in repentance and faith, what He did on the cross does atone for one's sins. But Jesus Himself put this question in proper perspective in explaining His death and resurrection to His disciples. "He also said to them, 'This is what is written: the Messiah would suffer and rise from the dead the third day, and repentance for forgiveness of sins would be proclaimed in His name to all nations, beginning at Jerusalem'" (Luke 24:46–47). Jesus didn't die just for us but to give us a message of salvation and forgiveness for all nations. We need to be reminded that "God so loved the world" (John 3:16 KJV); that does not mean just our world of beautiful homes, shopping malls, and expressways but the whole world—all peoples, tribes, languages, and nations. Massive people groups of China and diverse tribes of Africa are part of the world God loved. People in the megacities of Asia and Latin America, refugees in Darfur and people living in hopelessness and despair in the war-torn countries of Iraq, Gaza, and Afghanistan are included. The mission of God is for you, but it does not end with you.

This is what Psalm 117 is saying: "Praise the LORD, all nations! Glorify Him, all peoples!" His glory among all peoples is a theme that resonates throughout the Psalms. "Know that I am God, exalted among the nations" (Ps. 46:10). He foresees the day revealed in Revelation in Psalm 22:27–28, "All the ends of the earth will remember and turn to the LORD. All the families of the nations will bow down before You, for kingship belongs to the LORD; He rules over the nations." Again,

> *Jesus didn't die just for us, but to give us a message of salvation for all nations.*

His glory among the nations is affirmed, "All the nations You have made will come and bow down before You, Lord, and will honor [glorify] Your name. For You are great and perform wonders; You alone are God" (Ps. 86:9–10). As the book of Psalms approaches conclusion, we are told, "Kings of the earth and all peoples, princes and all judges of the earth, young men as well as young women, old and young together. Let them praise the name of the LORD, for His name alone is exalted. His majesty covers heaven and earth" (Ps. 148:11–13).

God's glory among the nations is the compelling task of missions. The primary objective for which He calls a people to Himself is to be His possession and serve Him. Peter quotes several Old Testament passages in reminding us, "You are a chosen race, a royal priesthood, a holy nation, a people for His possession, so that you may proclaim the praises of the One who called you out of darkness into His marvelous light" (1 Pet. 2:9). Becoming the people of God is not just for our blessing and benefit; it is to declare His glory and to be an instrument of praise so that all the earth will exalt His name. David declared, "I will praise You, Lord, among the peoples; I will sing praises to You among the nations. . . . God, be exalted above the heavens; let your glory be over the whole earth" (Ps. 57:9, 11).

God's purpose to be glorified among the nations is a prominent thread woven throughout Scripture from Genesis to Revelation. It was reflected in His call to Abram to leave his home and family so that "all the peoples on earth will be blessed through you" (Gen. 12:3). This covenant with Abraham was referring to the promise of a Redeemer who would come providing the blessing of salvation for the nations. God's renewal of this covenant promise is recorded in Genesis 22:18, "And all the nations of the earth will be blessed by your offspring because you have obeyed My command." The covenant was confirmed with Isaac and then Jacob, "Your offspring will be like the dust of the earth. . . . All the peoples on earth will be blessed" (Gen. 28:14). The first reference to "offspring" is to Jesus Christ as a descendent of Abraham, but the second reference is to those who become the spiritual descendants of Abraham and Jacob. Paul explained, "It is not the children by physical descent who are God's children, but the children of the promise are considered seed" (Rom. 9:8). "So understand that those who have faith are Abraham's sons" (Gal. 3:7). God's purpose to be glorified among all nations began to be fulfilled in the call to Abraham and the creation of a chosen people, but it continues through us who are the spiritual sons of Abraham. In God's providence it will eventually be inclusive of those from every tribe and people.

God's People Are Called to Declare His Glory

The nation of Israel realized that they were chosen not because they deserved God's special favor and blessing, but they were to be an instrument to declare His glory among the nations. In the sixteenth chapter of 1 Chronicles, the occasion of bringing the ark of the covenant into the tabernacle was a day of celebration and praise. The ark represented the presence of God in the midst of His people. The people rejoiced in having a special relationship with God, but they recognized their responsibility to declare His glory and make Him known among all peoples. "Give thanks to the LORD; call on His name; proclaim His deeds among the peoples. Sing to Him; sing praise to Him; tell about all His wonderful works!" (1 Chron. 16:8–9). God's purpose extended beyond Israel as His chosen people. "Sing to the LORD, all the earth. Proclaim His salvation from day to day. Declare His glory among the nations, His wonderful works among all peoples. For the LORD is great and is highly praised. . . . Worship the Lord in the splendor of His holiness; tremble before Him, all the earth" (1 Chron. 16: 23–25, 29–30).

As God's people they were to proclaim His salvation and tell of His mighty works; they were to declare His glory among the peoples of the earth to the end that all nations would sing His praise. In fact, this was the purpose for their location. Generations earlier when God called Abraham "to the land that I will show you"

(Gen. 12:1) and eventually led his descendants to possess the land of Canaan, it was related to His glory among the nations. God had an ulterior motive in growing their numbers to be a great nation for four hundred years in Egypt and then giving them a land where they would prosper. He wasn't acting only on their behalf out of concern for their welfare and to give them a prosperous land. They were positioned on the trade routes of the world and in the heart of civilization for a particular reason—to be a witness for His glory. Ezekiel reminds them of this aspect of God's providence: "This is what the Lord GOD says: I have set this Jerusalem in the center of the nations, with countries all around her" (Ezek. 5:5).

Solomon recognized this twofold purpose of God, to bless Israel but also for that to result in the nations exalting Him. As he dedicated the temple, he prayed regarding Israel, "So that they may fear You all the days they live on the land You gave our ancestors" (1 Kings 8:40). But he goes on in the following verses: "Even for the foreigner who is not of Your people Israel but has come from a distant land because of Your name—for they will hear of Your great name, mighty hand, and outstretched arm" (vv. 41–42). When Solomon's reputation for wisdom began to spread, 1 Kings 4:34 tells us, "People came from everywhere, sent by every king on earth who had heard of his wisdom, to listen to Solomon's wisdom." What they heard was that the fear of the Lord is the beginning of wisdom (Prov. 9:10), and God's glory spread. David reflected a consciousness of their witness among the nations in his song of deliverance after being rescued from the hand of his enemies, "Therefore I will praise You, LORD, among the nations" (2 Sam. 22:50).

One of the first passages of Scripture many of us probably recall memorizing as a child was Psalm 100. The first verse in the familiar King James Version says, "Make a joyful noise unto the Lord, all ye lands!" It confirms God's purpose to be praised and glorified in all lands and among all people. Israel realized that this was why God had chosen them and blessed them as His people. In Psalm 67:1 they prayed, "May God be gracious to us and bless us; look on us with favor." But the next verse goes on to say why they should expect God to be gracious and bless them—"so that Your way may be known on earth, Your salvation among all nations" (Ps. 67:2). We should remember this as we pray for God to bless us, our family, our business, our nation, or our church. Why would God choose to look with favor on us and be gracious to us, to answer our prayers and bless us? He blesses us so we might serve Him by being His witnesses and making His way known throughout the earth. He does not arbitrarily bless us just so we can revel in a prosperous lifestyle and personally enjoy the benefits of His blessings.

> *God does not bless us so we can enjoy a prosperous lifestyle but to make His way known throughout the earth.*

However, we must not miss the purpose for which God wants us to make His way known upon the earth. It is so He will receive the praise and glory of the nations. "Let the peoples praise You, God; let all the peoples praise You. Let the nations rejoice and shout for joy" (Ps. 67:3–4). John Piper reflects on this passage in the opening paragraph of his book, *Let the Nations Be Glad!: The Supremacy of God in Missions.*

> Missions is not the ultimate goal of the church. Worship is. Missions exists because worship doesn't. Worship is ultimate, not missions, because God is ultimate, not man. When this age is over, and the countless millions of the redeemed fall on their faces before the throne of God, missions will be no more. It is a temporary necessity. But worship abides forever.[3]

Worship can become routine and somewhat perfunctory as Christians gather week after week and go through the litany of singing hymns, voicing prayers corporately, and listening to an exhortation from the Word of God. Certainly God is honored as we nurture our relationship with Him and focus our praise and worship on Him. However, most of our world does not gather to praise and worship our Lord. They know nothing of His mercy and grace that would elicit a song of praise in their hearts.

Dr. Tom Elliff, former pastor of First Southern Baptist Church, Del City, Oklahoma, related an experience of leading members of his church on a mission trip to Cambodia. They were amazed at the opportunities to witness openly and minister to the people in this Buddhist country. One afternoon their missionary host accompanied them to a Buddhist monastery where he had been teaching English to the monks. The missionary had arranged a meeting with the team from America. Dr. Elliff recounted that they were uncomfortable going into such an environment, but they found the monks hospitable and excited about meeting friends from America and being able to practice their English. They were gracious to listen to the testimonies of these Christians. As they warmed to the fellowship, the American team began to sing some of the praise songs common to their worship back home.

It was an informal time, and spontaneously, someone asked the monks to sing some of their songs for them, their guests. The group of saffron-robed monks with shaved heads gathered and began a dissonant chant. Apparently realizing how they sounded, and it bearing no resemblance to the songs just heard, the chant faded out after a few lines, and one of them said, somewhat apologetic, "We don't have any songs in our religion!" Those who have not experienced the love and mercy of God have nothing to sing about. Buddhists, striving for their eternal destiny through the futility of their own good works, do not sing about the wonder and grace of redemptive love. Millions of Muslims, fervent in their devotion, worship a distant, impersonal god in a fatalistic religion that offers no assurance of salvation. Fear is not something that elicits songs of joy. Multitudes in animistic cultures, living in bondage to superstition, do not celebrate their hopeless state with song.

But God's people sing! Even more, God's desire is that all the nations would rejoice and sing for joy—a joy that comes only in knowing Him and experiencing His mercy and redemption. This is why He blesses us. We, just like Israel, are to be instruments of His mission to make His way and His salvation known upon the earth until all nations rejoice and sing His praise. As Piper explained, "We will be worshipping and praising God for eternity, but we have only a limited time upon this earth to engage in missions so that the nations would rejoice and sing for joy."[4]

> *God's desire is that all the nations would rejoice and sing for joy!*

As noted in the book of Revelation, one day this will be a reality, but meanwhile we are to be on mission. God reminded Israel in Isaiah 49:6, "It is not enough for you to be My servant raising up the tribes of Jacob and restoring the protected ones of Israel. I will also make you a light for the nations, to be My salvation to the ends of the earth." The glory of God demands that we not become self-centered, focused on our own blessings and relationship with God. He calls us as His people to be engaged on mission to declare His glory among the nations. "Shout joyfully to God, all the earth! Sing the glory of His name; make His praise glorious. . . . All the earth will worship You and sing praise to You. They will sing praise to Your name" (Ps. 66:1–2, 4).

Everyone worships. We all find something to revere. People constantly watch one another to view those things that have their passion and allegiance. Why? We watch people's lives to discover what makes life worth living. For the Christian, worship becomes the most significant act because of a heart to glorify God. If our story is simply, "God has given me purpose and a better life," then good luck because there isn't much to go on there. In fact, that perspective offers nothing that cannot be discovered in dozens of other pursuits. A better life can be defined as anything slightly different than what I am experiencing now. The answer is relative. For a person who is bored and self-absorbed, a creative, upbeat worship service with a mission to help the needy provides purpose and a better life. The incredible danger in such a choice is that people choose an upgraded life of earthly purpose instead of a transformed, surrendered life through an eternal Lord. The end is death and eternal separation from God in hell.

Passionate worshippers demonstrate the only reason why man should find and follow God: He alone is worthy of our worship and our lives. Worship reveals a God who is bigger than us with a name that is eternally greater than ours. We read in Revelation, "Our Lord and God, You are worthy to receive glory and honor and power, because You have created all things, and because of Your will they exist and were created" (Rev. 4:11). Worship places the focus on the One who deserves the focus and delivers real life to His worshippers. True worship is the key to influence people to embrace our great God.

Israel's purpose was to relate to God and glorify Him through their faithful service. "May the Lord God, the God of Israel, be praised, who alone does wonders. May His glorious name be praised forever; the whole earth is filled with His glory" (Ps. 72:18–19). "The Lord is exalted above all the nations, His glory above the heavens" (Ps. 113:4). Recognizing the exalted nature of God and having confidence that His glory would be extended throughout the earth was expressed by the prophets generations later: "For the earth will be filled with the knowledge of the Lord's glory, as the waters cover the seas" (Hab. 2:14). Isaiah says, "For the earth will be full of the knowledge of the Lord as the waters cover the seas" (Isa. 11:9 nasb).

It is not uncommon for us to focus on specific aspects of the narrative history of Israel and miss the big picture. His intervention in the lives of His people was not just to hover over them dispensing blessings like a cosmic Santa Claus. His presence among them was not to get them beyond a local challenge with timely deliverance like a spiritual peace officer. In manifesting His sovereignty and power, He was focusing on the greater goal of bringing the nations and peoples of the earth to the point of exalting and fearing His name.

When Israel turned back from entering the promised land in faithlessness and rebellion against God's will, He threatened to destroy them. God proposed to create another nation greater and mightier than Israel. But Moses reminded God that Israel was already known as His chosen people; if He rejected them and they were defeated or destroyed, then it would reflect on His reputation. "If You kill this people with a single blow, the nations that have heard of Your fame will declare, 'Since the LORD wasn't able to bring this people into the land. . . . He has slaughtered them in the wilderness'" (Num. 14:15–16). God relented, because He was "slow to anger and rich in faithful love, forgiving wrongdoing and rebellion" (Num. 14:18). He declared that His power would be manifested, but don't miss the ultimate objective. He went on to say, "As surely as I live and as the whole earth is filled with the LORD's glory" (Num. 14:21).

After forty years in the wilderness and the faithless generation had been replaced, Joshua led Israel across the Jordan River. He reminded them that God had demonstrated His power to deliver them from Egypt, had rolled back the waters of the Red Sea, and now had dried up the waters of the Jordan that they might cross over. It wasn't just for their sake but as a testimony to all the nations. "For the LORD your God dried up the waters of the Jordan before you until you had crossed over, just as the LORD your God did to the Red Sea, which He dried up before us until we had crossed over. This is so that all the people of the earth may know that the Lord's hand is mighty, and so that you may always fear the LORD your God" (Josh. 4:23–24). Just as God's miraculous intervention in the affairs of His people was a testimony to the nations, so it was in other individual incidents.

Unfortunately we seldom see the trials and adversity we encounter as an opportunity to display and strengthen our faith in God. The moment of divine intervention is an opportunity for God to be glorified. There is a concerted appeal to pray for America to return to God and for a restoration of Judeo-Christian values to be reflected in our society. We pray that we might be relieved from a volatile and uncertain economic situation so that we can be assured of security and prosperity. God delivered Israel from many similar trials but for a greater purpose. God's plan was for His name to be exalted among the peoples of the earth. Perhaps we do not see the divine intervention we yearn for because we think it is only about us, our needs and our country rather than an impetus for the mission to which God has called us.

> *We do not see the divine intervention for which we yearn in our country because we think it is for us and our needs rather than an impetus for God's mission.*

Obviously Satan, seeking to deprive God of being glorified through His people, Israel, and hence to be made known and exalted among the nations, was behind Israel's failures and apostasy. From pride at Babel to the faithless generation at the time of Moses and continuous compromise and idolatry, the adversary successfully led them astray from fulfilling God's purpose. But, according to Revelation 20, we can celebrate his ultimate defeat when the enemy of every tongue, tribe, and nation and his devious mission will be terminated. "When the 1,000 years are completed, Satan will be released from his prison and will go out to deceive the nations at the four corners of the earth, Gog and Magog, to gather them for battle. Their number is like the sand of the sea. They came up over the surface of the earth and surrounded the encampment of the saints, the beloved city. Then fire came down from heaven and consumed them. The Devil who deceived them was thrown into the lake of fire and sulfur where the beast and the false prophet are, and they will be tormented day and night forever and ever" (Rev. 20:7–10).

Not only do we know that every language will be one voice to praise God, but the mission of God will be complete at this point. Truly we can spend eternity loving and enjoying God forever. He will be the receiver, and we will be the givers of worship. The Holy City, Jerusalem, will be new. The city with such a tumultuous history will now be a place of peace. No more fighting or politics will exist in the New Jerusalem. No more debate between the world's "great" religions will be heard. God gathers people back in Revelation for His glory. His plan was to spread out people through diverse languages at Babel so He could gather them back for His glory at Pentecost and in the New Jerusalem. God's people come up to Jerusalem one final time for eternity. In the unity brought about by God's presence and kingdom, His people will worship and praise God in the many languages they spoke during their mortal lives. God will be exalted among the nations!

The Linguistic Thread in the Story of God for Every Tongue, Tribe, Nation

	Babel (Genesis 11)	Pentecost (Acts 2)	Revelation (Revelation 7)
Setting	Scattered	Sent	Gathered
God	Distributor	Sender	Receiver
Motivation	Man's Fame	God's Mission	God's Glory
People	Self-Centered	Mission-Centered	Worship-Centered
Language	One to Multiple	Multiple, One Purpose	Multiple, One Voice
Mission	Distracted	Extended	Completed
Jerusalem	To Come	Out From	Comes Down

• **Babylon:** Seeking our own fame and self-promotion—our mission apart from God and an attempt to bless ourselves. Satan is in control of our destiny.

• **Pentecost:** God pours out His power on us in order that we might have relationship and purpose with Him. Satan's curse is lifted. Life with Christ is now our eternity.

• **Revelation:** We now have reached our ultimate purpose and destiny. Our eternal purpose is to give glory to God through worship. Satan experiences his final defeat.

--------- **Going Deeper** ---------

1. What new insight did you gain from the biblical overview of the glory of God and His heart for the nations? What will you do differently in the next thirty days as a result?

2. Your faith journey is a gift from God. List ways you can creatively share that gift with others for His glory. How can you encourage other Christians God has placed around you to do the same?

3. What kind of people and things do you find yourself praying about on a day-to-day basis? Does your prayer life reflect God's ultimate desire and purpose to be worshipped among the nations? Intentionally evaluate your prayer life for a week.

4. How does God want you to adjust your time and/or friends so that you can go on mission trips to help reach the nations or give more so that others can reach the nations with the gospel?

Overview of Chapter 2

Satan's External Obstacles to the Body of Christ and Mission of God

Every Man, Woman, and Child

Counterfeit Gospels	Closed Nations
People Groups Hidden	Persecuted Believers

The Glory of God is Hidden by Satan's Methodologies. (Ephesians 6:11)

Every Tongue, Tribe, and Nation

The Body of Christ must get through two lines of The Enemy in order to take the Gospel to Every Man, Woman, and Child in Every Tongue, Tribe, and Nation . . .

1) **The Internal Enemy Line**—Obstacles that keeps the Body of Christ inwardly focused and spiritually anemic.

2) **The External Enemy Line**—When the Body of Christ gets beyond the church, focused outward. The Enemy has created greater obstacles to intimidate and encourage the Army of the Lord to turn back or people far from the Lord to be blinded to the gospel.

CHAPTER 2

SATAN'S PURPOSE:
OPPOSE THE KINGDOM—
DEPRIVE GOD OF THE PRAISE
AND GLORY DUE HIM

Several years ago I (Jerry) accompanied a group of businessmen on a carefully arranged tour of a restricted Muslim country. The purpose of cultural tourism and a sincere effort to explore business opportunities put our itinerary at the discretion of the local tour company. After an elaborate late dinner and entertainment in the home of a local citizen, we were informed that we would be escorted to a nearby temple where we would observe a dervish worship. I recalled reading about whirling dervishes in comic books as a child but had always been under the impression they were imaginary.

We were seated in a gallery with several women and other interested spectators sparsely scattered about the bleachers. Down below men milled about the arena, and at the stroke of midnight, drums began a rhythmic beat. The group began to jump gracefully and turn in unchoreographed movements; but as the

drumbeat intensified, the twisting, swirling, leaping of the participants reached a frenetic pace. We sensed being in the presence of
an oppressive evil power as the dervish devotees, having danced
themselves into a trance, began to eat broken glass and slice sharp
knives across their bodies without any visible effect or appearance
of injury or blood.

I experienced similar feelings of being in an evil presence
on tours of Hindu temples in India. On more than one occasion
I observed Brahmin priests walking across a pit of glowing, white-
hot coals without pain, visible blisters, or burns on their feet.
Barbara Singerman tells about the common experience of encountering the demonic in the West African country of Benin in her
book, *Beyond Surrender.*

> One day while traveling from village to village
> we encountered a group of women walking to a
> ceremony. They were dressed in voodoo-worship
> attire with multiple strands of tiny beads on their
> necks and colorful cloth wrapped around their torsos.
> Powder covered their upper chests and exposed
> shoulders. The process of initiation into voodoo
> covens changes from sect to sect, but it always
> involves a common theme—the symbolic dying of
> the person and coming back to life possessed by the
> spirits. . . . During the ceremony the worshippers
> experience states of delirium, which cause them to
> act with animalistic impulses. They kill goats with
> their teeth and bathe themselves in the blood. To
> show their absolute dedication to the spirit, they
> tattoo their bodies with designs in which the scarring
> is permanent.[1]

Our newspaper headlines are filled with reports of Islamic
fanaticism while millions of devotees pray five times a day declaring Allah is God and Mohammed is his prophet. Their adherence to a fatalistic religion and allegiance to a distant, impersonal

deity gives them no assurance of salvation. Even though the word *Muslim* means "one who is submissive," it is not a commitment to a relationship that would recognize and honor the mercy of a loving God. With militant aggression, Muslims seek to dominate and force others into the faith through coercion and intimidation. Even suicide bombers are committed to the destruction of life in the distorted conviction it will bring them merit in the afterlife. It is a bloody sacrifice reaping no eternal reward.

The futility of the more than eight hundred million adherents of Buddhism was evident to me at funerals I attended in Thailand. I found the Thai people relational and hospitable. Believing their eternal destiny was determined by accumulating *karma*—good works—they were gracious and giving. Yet their religious devotion and acts of worship, which permeated all aspects of their everyday life, came out of a desire to reach enlightenment and, after numberless reincarnations, to escape the *cosmos* or worldly existence. Yet no concept of God or the reality of heaven as a possibility existed in their thinking. At their funerals Buddhist priests would encircle the casket of the deceased in a procession accompanied by incessant chanting of the litany:

> Dead, never to arise;
> asleep, never to awaken;
> gone, never to return.

They lived with a hope of ceasing their existence.

Cultural Catholicism is widespread throughout the world with the church dominant in Latin America, across many European countries, and firmly ingrained as a minority religious faith in many others. Many core teachings are consistent with our understanding of Scripture but contain basic teachings that hinder people from coming to a personal relationship with God through Jesus Christ alone. I am reminded of a friend who was seeking to plant an evangelical church in the heart of Mormon country in Utah. He had concluded that Satan's most effective strategy was not to create other religions that totally distorted the nature of God, but to create religious beliefs that were so close to the truth and resembled truth that they would easily lead people astray.

The Catholic Church, since Vatican II, has encouraged the reading of Scripture, but the teaching and authority of Scripture are obstructed by tradition, and the church is still viewed as essential to salvation. Encouraging people to pray to Mary and the saints, participating in the sacraments and assuming one can be born Christian, and salvation secured by infant baptism propagates a false way of works rather than salvation through Christ alone. In many parts of the world, the mixture of pagan practices and superstitious practices often looks more like animism than Christianity.

One particular evidence of satanic deception and power in the world is the spiritist practice of Santeria. Many would be shocked to know there are up to a hundred million practitioners of its various forms in the Americas, including the United States. Many ignore it as if it is just a syncretistic expression of Catholicism. The name comes from the Spanish word *santo* (saint) and literally means "the way of saints." It has been a powerful religious expression since African slaves were imported to the Caribbean and South America in the sixteenth century. Many of these slaves had been tribal leaders or religious priests in their home countries in West Africa, especially in what is now Nigeria and Benin. The slave trade brought many of these people to the shores of Cuba, Brazil, Haiti, Trinidad, and Puerto Rico. They were forced to convert to Catholicism and created Santeria as a way for their religious beliefs to survive by clothing them in the forms of the dominant Roman Catholic religion.

However, Santeria is not just a primitive religion carried over into the modern world; adherents are educated members of society who likely outnumber practicing Catholics in many modern societies. They believe in a powerful voodoo god that is the source of spiritual energy in the universe. Communication between these powers and humankind is accomplished through rituals, prayer, divination, and offerings, including sacrifices. Mediums, spirit possession, and trances in the midst of chants and rhythmic dancing and movements are not uncommon. The practice of magic and the impact of spells on individuals, whether for good or ill, is a recognized phenomenon. To the discerning Christian there is no question regarding the demonic nature of such widespread beliefs and practices and that it is in radical contradiction with that which would glorify God!

Why have so many rejected the path of truth that leads to God? Why have multitudes, for generations, been locked into religious worldviews that keep them from knowing Jesus Christ? When God offers the hope of eternal life and deliverance from the bondage of sin, why is the world embracing humanistic philosophies, arrogantly presuming that personal efforts are sufficient for all we desire? Why is God's truth being rejected in postmodern relativism? Prospects for God to be glorified among the nations and all the peoples of the world to sing His praise seem more distant than ever. Is this just a coincidence, a normal historical progression that affirms the irrelevance of the biblical revelation, or is there an adversary that is actively working against God's purpose?

God is not the source of any form of worship that does not exalt and lift up the name of Jesus!

I (Jerry) remember the informal discussions with seminary colleagues years ago regarding the origin and rationale for various world religions. We all acknowledged that man was created for fellowship with God, and there was a "God-shaped vacuum" within each heart that wasn't filled until one was personally restored to a relationship with Him. We also agreed that faith in Jesus Christ was the only way sinful man could relate to a holy and righteous God. Aware that most of the world had not come to faith in Jesus Christ and, in fact, were following the religious traditions of their culture, we sought to confront the issue of what gave rise to what each claimed as divine truth.

What was the source of their scriptures, such as the Qur'an or the Bhagavad Gita? Various rituals and worship forms are obviously designed to motivate the devotee to relate in some practical way to the power of deity. Religious practices are employed to satisfy the criteria for attaining a favorable afterlife with perceived spiritual powers. How have these ideas come about?

Obviously, all paths do not lead to God as there is only one true way that atones for sins and gives assurance of eternal life. The issue of our debate was whether or not other religions existed because of God's initiative, though without sufficient revelation to bring one to salvation, or if Satan was responsible for creating an alternative to the real thing in order to keep people from the kingdom of God. Do people worship and diligently perform rituals of sacrifice and devotion in other religions because God is at work, seeking to draw them to Himself? Could their sincere commitment to the only religious expression they know be used to enable them to understand faith in Jesus Christ? Or is Satan behind every false religious expression in order to blind people to the gospel?

My experience of working with Muslims in Indonesia, Buddhists in Thailand, and Hindus in India leaves no doubt that an adversary of the kingdom of God is leading the world astray as they put their hope in futile traditions. I have seen the empty ritual of cultural Catholics in the Philippines and Latin America and the multitudes in Africa still in bondage to the superstitions of their ancestors. Without question, God is not the source of any form of worship that does not exalt and lift up the name of Jesus! At His name every knee will bow in submission, and every tongue will proclaim His lordship, all to the worship and glory of God the Father.

Confrontation with the Enemy

I (Ed) am writing this on the plane returning from Taipei, Taiwan. While there, we saw many temples, altars, and offerings made to gods and ancestors. Well-educated and affluent Christians explained how some were possessed and others oppressed by the demonic. They saw it as real and told one another about it on cell phones—an interesting juxtaposition. Those in Taipei paid homage to ancient spirits while North Americans worship at the altar of technology.

Too often the average Christ follower in North America does not want to live with the knowledge of the great battle raging about them. We have lost our collective stomach for direct confrontation with the forces of darkness. Living in denial, the Western church remakes the images of spiritual warfare into cartoons and caricatures. Could it be possible that someone would really be at work to send people to hell? Satan would prefer us to be ashamed at his existence and put him in the category of mythology. We underestimate our enemy and accuser when God's Word is sadly embraced as a book of anecdotal, sweet stories with solid advice on how to make good decisions. Although on a macro level the Bible assures us we win, we skip the details of the gruesome confrontations along the way to victory.

The Bible is a book about a war. The war that began in a beautiful garden (Genesis) concludes on a bloody battlefield (Revelation). Who will emerge victorious is not at stake. We win—that has been settled by Christ. The stakes are the souls of men, women, and children of every tribe, tongue, and nation. The tactics or methods of Satan are to cause as much confusion as possible in the minds of believers and unbelievers alike. What is from God? What is from Satan? Oftentimes we are guilty of trying to figure things out on our own in the middle of the battle.

Jesus' followers attempted to sort out the rights and wrongs of confronting Satan early in their ministries. Spiritual warfare was so real in their day that there was never a question about its reality. But, as they did life with Jesus, they learned how to discern, confront, and defeat the work of the enemy. On at least three different occasions they failed in their understanding or response to demonic confrontations. As Jesus debriefed the three incidences with them, we can learn the danger of dealing with the devil. We can also see how close we can be to right responses and wrong responses. How do you guard against being completely over-whelmed and overmatched when confronting Satan? By remembering the need to depend on God and by taking Satan and his power seriously.

The first episode is found in Matthew 17: "Then the disciples approached Jesus privately and said, 'Why couldn't we drive it [the demon] out?' 'Because of your little faith,' He told them. 'For I assure you: If you have faith the size of a mustard seed, you will tell this mountain, "Move from here to there," and it will move. Nothing will be impossible for you. However, this kind does not come out except by prayer and fasting'" (Matt. 17:19–21).

Jesus' disciples had failed to assist a demonized boy because they had not prayed and sought God's presence. Confronting the devil's forces involves a lifetime of learning and maturity. When confronting darkness, nothing would be easy. Too much was at stake. Some confrontations were more difficult than others and required more faith. They learned that one size did not fit all in their confrontations with darkness. Faith in God gives a disciple authority to confront because he knows he does not fight Satan in his own strength. Our inappropriate fear of the devil can be traced to our lack of confidence in God's ability, not ours.

> *Our inappropriate fear of the devil can be traced to our lack of confidence in God's ability, not ours.*

In Luke, we discover another confrontation where the disciples were concerned about others who were successfully casting out demons in the name of Jesus. Luke records: "John responded, 'Master, we saw someone driving out demons in Your name, and we tried to stop him because he does not follow us'" (Luke 9:49). Even in his defeat, Satan caused Jesus' disciples to be distracted from their mission. Far too easily, they harbored a grudge against others who were on the same side of the battle. If Satan can make the enemy seem to be anyone but him, he has won the battle. Jesus taught a principle of spiritual warfare that cannot be overlooked. The principle is, "Do not think you are the only ones who can be successful." Often we feel that our tribe or group has special knowledge and superiority. Christians struggle from denomination to denomination with this tendency. But most groups struggle within denominations from church to church. Even worse, most churches struggle within from group to group. If the devil can make us feel superior to other Christians, then we reduce God's army to just a few. We often use protectionism and doctrinal purity as our universal permission to refuse cooperation for the glory of God. Hell is intimidated by Christians who work together in the power of the Spirit. Should we lock arms with all who "love Jesus" or claim to be "Christian"? Absolutely not. Yet there are times when we send wrong messages and hinder the work of God for a perceived higher good.

The third confrontation is seen in Luke 10. A large group of disciples were celebrating their apparent success over Satan through casting out demons. Jesus sensed they were on a dangerous path toward an inherent temptation. The disciples were reading too much into their success. He taught them, "However, don't rejoice that the spirits submit to you, but rejoice that your names are written in heaven" (Luke 10:20). Every Christian has a heart hungry to be successful for God. Our desire runs so deep that when it happens, it is difficult not to lose all perspective. If Satan cannot stop us from succeeding for God, his next step is to cause us to fail in our success. The disciples would succeed at the spiritual battle for Christ but could have an identity crisis regarding their identity in Christ. This is not uncommon for Christians. The real question is, How can I succeed for God, successfully? The disciples wanted Jesus' approval. Jesus told them they had His approval before they ever met a demon face-to-face. How encouraging and humbling at the same time! "Your spiritual destiny is a done deal," He told them. Jesus was teaching them a truth that should make them content all the time. In essence He was saying, "Some days you will cast out demons. Other days you will fail at casting out demons. Even other days you will have to stand and watch others cast out demons. But that isn't the point. The point is that you belong to Me. That will never, ever change." We must all learn how to succeed, successfully.

An important truth can be learned from all three stories of demonic confrontations. Success in defeating Satan will be in direct proportion to the depth of your personal relationship with Jesus. Your personal conversations with Him as you engage in spiritual warfare are critical. The real-time dialogue between you and Jesus opens us to the wisdom needed to make the strategic decisions He offers to win the battle. The battle can be confusing and difficult to discern at times. The real growth in understanding spiritual warfare among disciples came in the debrief time.

Not only does Satan deceive and lead multitudes astray with false religious and pagan worldviews, but he also offers counterfeit versions of Christian faith and the Christian life. To remain victorious, we must stand strong in our relationship with Christ as the only true way to life. Knowing we cannot win this battle alone, we remain in a position of humility with Christ. As Satan attempts to discredit Christians through influencing our own sinful and selfish choices, we fix our eyes on the presence of Christ's work in and around us. Our mission task of proclaiming His glory to the nations can be fulfilled by rejecting the temptations of dissension among the church and disobedience in our personal lives. Satan does not have to tempt us to embrace sinful living that would destroy our witness. All he has to do is divert our focus. To win the battle, we must value the advancement of God's kingdom instead of our own agenda.

> *Satan does not have to tempt us to embrace sinful living; all he has to do is divert our focus.*

Even six hundred years before Christ came, Isaiah envisioned the ultimate outcome which was quoted by Paul in

Philippians 2:10–11. "Turn to Me and be saved, all the ends of the earth. For I am God, and there is no other. By Myself I have sworn; truth has gone from My mouth, a word that will not be revoked: Every knee will bow to Me, every tongue will swear allegiance" (Isa. 45:22–23). As we make Christ known through our contemporary mission efforts and proclaim the gospel among unreached peoples and the remote corners of the earth, we can dwell in this assurance found in Isaiah. He envisioned people from every geographic area of the world knowing and worshipping the Lord. "They raise their voices, they sing out; they proclaim in the west the majesty of the LORD. Therefore in the east honor the LORD! In the islands of the west honor the name of the LORD, the God of Israel. From the ends of the earth we hear songs: the Splendor of the Righteous One" (Isa. 24:14–16). "I, the LORD, have called you for a righteous purpose, and I will hold you by your hand. I will keep you, and I make you a covenant for the people and a light to the nations. . . . I am Yahweh, that is My name; I will not give My glory to another. . . . Sing a new song to the LORD; sing His praise from the ends of the earth, you who go down to the sea with all that fills it, you islands with your inhabitants. Let the desert and its cities shout. . . . Let them cry out from the mountaintops. Let them give glory to the LORD, and declare His praise" (Isa. 42:6, 8, 10–12).

Isaiah envisioned the peoples living in darkness coming to the light and that time when His "house"—His temple and dwelling in the midst of His kingdom—would include not just Israel but all nations. "The people walking in darkness have seen a great light; on those living in the land of darkness, a light has dawned" (Isa. 9:2). "I will bring them to My holy mountain and let them rejoice in My house of prayer. Their burnt offerings and sacrifices will be acceptable on My altar, for My house will be called a house of prayer for all nations" (Isa. 56:7). The prophet Micah predicted, "His greatness will extend to the ends of the earth" (Mic. 5:4).

The Church Is Empowered
to Fulfill God's Mission!

God's purpose to be glorified and exalted among all peoples takes a significant paradigm shift toward fulfillment in the New Testament. After spending seventy years in captivity for disobedience, Israel was dispersed among the nations. For four hundred years, no prophetic voice came to confirm that the kingdom promises of God existed for His people. But, with the coming of Christ into the world, a new era was launched. God's holy nation, the church, would be empowered by the Holy Spirit to make Christ known to the ends of the earth. With the death and resurrection of Christ, salvation from sin and access to a holy and righteous God was made possible for all peoples. The Holy Spirit now indwelt and empowered the people of God. His church was commissioned to complete what Israel had failed to do—tell of His salvation to the nations and proclaim His glory to all peoples.

The impact was as great as the contrast made when Jesus identified Himself as "the light of the world" (John 8:12) in the midst of a spiritually dark world, a darkness that continues to prevail today. Christ quoted Isaiah to declare that His coming signaled that the kingdom of God had come: "The people who live in darkness have seen a great light, and for those living in the shadowland of death, light has dawned" (Matt. 4:16). The incarnational presence of Jesus in human flesh clearly extended God's kingdom purpose beyond the narrow scope of His chosen people, Israel, as the angels proclaimed at His birth, "a Savior, who is Messiah the Lord" and declared, "[this is] good news of great joy that will be for all the people" (Luke 2:10–11). This truth was confirmed by Simeon who beheld Jesus in His infancy in the temple and declared, "For my eyes have seen Your salvation. You have prepared it in the presence of all peoples—a light for revelation to the Gentiles and glory to Your people Israel" (Luke 2:30–32). Israel's glory was being the channel through which salvation would come, which puts all that Old Testament history in perspective. But the salvation that was provided would be revealed to the Gentiles, the nations of the world.

This enabled Paul to declare in Romans 10:13, "For everyone who calls on the name of the Lord will be saved." Salvation was no longer the special domain of the chosen Jewish nation; it was now available to anyone and everyone throughout the earth. Paul quoted what had happened as God's promises culminated in the coming of Christ; He would now be glorified through non-Jewish nations and peoples previously not identified with His chosen people coming to faith. This was fulfillment of Hosea's prophecy. "I will call 'Not-My-People,' 'My-People,' and she who is 'Unloved,' 'Beloved.' And it will be in the place where they were told, you are not My people, there they will be called sons of the living God" (Rom. 9:25–26). In Matthew 13, Jesus told a series of kingdom parables to illustrate how the kingdom of God would grow to massive proportions permeating the whole world and incorporating all nations. The fulfillment of God's kingdom promises at the end of the age was revealed in Revelation, but Jesus affirmed its global scope in revealing that "the good news must first be proclaimed to all nations" (Mark 13:10).

We have already noted that Jesus explained to His disciples in Luke 24:46–47 that His death and resurrection were consistent with prophecy and the plan of God for forgiveness of sin to be proclaimed to all nations. Ironically, Caiaphas, the high priest, unintentionally stated this truth as the Sanhedrin was plotting the death of Jesus. John quotes Caiaphas as saying, "You're not considering that it is to your advantage that one man should die for the people rather than the whole nation perish." John goes on to explain, "He did not say this on his own, but being high priest that year he prophesied that Jesus was going to die for the nation, and not for the nation only, but also to unite the scattered children of God" (John 11:50–52). Obviously, the death of one man, Jesus Christ, was the eternally, divinely planned alternative to Israel and those who would ultimately become the children of God perishing in their sins.

God's purpose is to honor Himself by redeeming the nations through His divine actions and the witness of the apostles. The fact that "devout men from every nation under heaven" (Acts 2:5) were gathered in Jerusalem and heard Peter's sermon on the Day of Pentecost was no coincidence. He made it clear that forgiveness of sins and the promise of the Holy Spirit was available to all whom God would call, including "all who were far off" from the nation of Israel (Acts 2:39). The book of Acts describes how God used persecution to disperse believing Jews who took the gospel to Gentile communities throughout the world. It is a record of the apostles fulfilling the Great Commission mandate. Apart from intentional initiatives of the early church, the Spirit of God moved in revival among the Samaritans, drew Cornelius into the kingdom, and gave evidence to a reluctant Hebrew-centered church that the gospel was for all peoples. When the issue of Gentile believers came before the Jerusalem Council, the prophecy of Jeremiah was interpreted as applying to what God was apparently doing among the nations: "So that those who are left of mankind may seek the Lord—even all the Gentiles who are called by My name, says the Lord who does these things, which have been known from long ago" (Acts 15:17–18).

The church should take careful note of the phrase "even all the Gentiles," since by a large majority we are the Gentiles referred to in the verse. Too often we become caught up in a mythological feeling that we hold a unique place in God's history. The reality is, we are both wrong and right. We are wrong in that God has not chosen us because we are any better than the rest of humanity. Without Christ, we are not of great value. But we are right in that God has uniquely created, called, and qualified all Christians for the task before them. God's presence guarantees that outcome.

The assurance of God's glory among the nations, or Gentiles— peoples of the world who were not ethnic Jews—was unequivocally stated by Paul in quoting several Old Testament references. "And so that Gentiles may glorify God for His mercy. As it is written: 'Therefore I will praise You among the Gentiles, and I will sing psalms to Your name.' Again it says: 'Rejoice, you Gentiles, with His people!' And again: 'Praise the Lord, all you Gentiles; all the peoples should praise Him!' And again, Isaiah says: 'The root of Jesse will appear, the One who rises to rule the Gentiles; in Him the Gentiles will hope'" (Rom. 15:9–12). We must not miss the implications of these prophecies that Paul noted and ratified. The objective was not just an obligation to cross-cultural missions or to state the reality that non-Jews were welcome into the kingdom of God. The purpose in providing redemption for the nations is that all peoples and nations would glorify and praise God.

The passion of the church and every follower of Christ should be that all peoples have an opportunity to hear, understand, and respond to the gospel.

Paul expressed the conviction that he had been called to "preach the gospel to the regions beyond you" (2 Cor. 10:16). In his testimony before King Agrippa, he quoted Jesus, who called him on the road to Damascus, "For I have appeared to you for this purpose, to appoint you as a servant and a witness. . . . I will rescue you from the people and from the Gentiles, to whom I now send you . . . that they may receive forgiveness of sins and a share among those who are sanctified by faith in Me" (Acts 26:16–18). The compelling passion of his life was "to evangelize where Christ has not been named, in order that I will not be building on someone else's foundation, but, as it is written: 'Those who had no report of Him will see, and those who have not heard will understand'" (Rom. 15:20-21).

The passion of the church and every follower of Christ should be the same—that those who have not heard the gospel would have the opportunity to hear, understand, and respond in faith so God might be glorified in their salvation. Paul connects this objective all the way back to God's covenant with Abraham in Galatians 3:8–9, "Now the Scripture foresaw that God would justify the Gentiles by faith and foretold the good news to Abraham, saying, 'All the nations will be blessed in you.' So those who have faith are blessed with Abraham, who had faith."

The Scripture affirms that "God . . . wants everyone to be saved and to come to the knowledge of the truth" (1 Tim. 2:3–4). The early church had a confessional statement regarding Jesus Christ: "He was manifested in the flesh, justified in the Spirit, seen by angels, preached among the Gentiles, believed on in the world, taken up in glory" (1 Tim. 3:16). As central to our faith is the coming of God in the flesh and dying for our sins, so is His being preached among the nations that they might believe on Him throughout the world.

God Is Being Deprived of the Praise and Glory Due Him from the Nations

When I (Jerry) was selected to serve as president of the Southern Baptist International Mission Board after twenty-three years of missionary service, I was confronted with many challenges, including the adjustment of living in America once again. Administrative responsibilities for a global mission agency put me on a steep learning curve of comprehensive demands, not the least of which was technological challenges. I had not even owned a computer but suddenly had to function in an office environment in which all our systems and communication were computerized. My assistant was bemused to find she had to show me how to turn on my computer and then explain how to key in a document and save it. Every time I presumed to master a function, the program would be eventually upgraded, the same keystrokes no longer worked, and I invariably found myself starting over in that learning mode.

However, as I began to master some of the basic functions, I was intrigued to discover automatic spell-check in our word-processing program. If I misspelled a word, it was highlighted on the screen. No longer did I have to know how to spell! All I had to do was click the mouse, and it would give me the correct spelling. I would not have gotten so many red marks on my papers in school if I had had access to such a tool in those days. The only problem with this embedded service was that all my vocabulary wasn't logged into that spell-check program. There were words such as *Kazakhstan* and *Azerbaijan* that I didn't know how to spell and the computer didn't either! I was surprised that one common word was not in our spell-check dictionary—the word *unreached*. We often talk about unreached people, unreached families, and unreached nations. The computer presumed it was a misspelled word, so when I clicked the mouse, the program suggested the intended correct spelling was "unrelated."

Now I don't think there was a theological basis for our word-processing program, but it is exactly correct in this regard. Who is it that is unreached? It is those who are unrelated to our heavenly Father; that is what it means spiritually to be unreached. However, the greatest tragedy is not just their lostness, or even the fact that many have never heard the gospel and have no opportunity to know God. The greatest tragedy of multitudes of individuals, peoples, and nations who are unreached—unrelated to God—is the fact that He alone who is worthy of all honor, glory, and praise is being deprived of the praise and worship of those He created, loves, and died to save.

> The greatest tragedy of lostness is that God is being deprived of the honor, glory, and praise among those He loves and died to save.

But Paul says this about those who do know Him: "He chose us in Him, before the foundation of the world, to be holy and blameless in His sight. In love He predestined us to be adopted through Jesus Christ for Himself, according to His favor and will, to the praise of His glorious grace that He favored us with in the Beloved" (Eph. 1:4–6). All that God has done in manifesting His grace toward us in our sin, enabling us to hear and respond to the gospel, calling us to faith in Jesus Christ, and being adopted into His family is to the praise of His glory. But that grace is not just for a special class of spiritually minded people or those with the proper religious heritage. Ultimately, it is for all nations.

Revelation 5:9 tells us that Jesus is worthy of praise and worship, "Because [He was] slaughtered and [He] redeemed people for God by [His] blood from every tribe and language and people and nation." In the coming kingdom we are told, "The nations will walk in its light, and the kings of the earth will bring their glory into it" (Rev. 21:24).

But how long must the nations wait before the light dawns and dispels the pervasive darkness of the world? How many multitudes will perish without knowing a Savior died for them and without hope of eternal redemption until the good news reaches every people, tribe, and nation? We are assured of God's glory among all peoples, but why is it taking so long for the people of God to fulfill His mission? Why was Israel continually diverted from their task to proclaim His salvation and declare His glory to the ends of the earth? Why, after two thousand years in which the church—the people of God—received the power of God's Holy Spirit to be His witnesses—do thousands of people groups remain unreached and there are more lost people than ever before in history?

We are told, "Be sober! Be on the alert! Your adversary the Devil is prowling around like a roaring lion, looking for anyone he can devour. Resist him, firm in the faith" (1 Pet. 5:8–9). Our enemy is not a house pet who likes to nip at our heels. He is not even satisfied with trying to trip us up with temptation and occasional trivial sins. He seeks our total destruction. It is evident historically that he has devoured nations and peoples of the world. He will do whatever he can to thwart God's people from fulfilling God's mission.

In the seventh century a pious hermit in the Middle East presumed to receive a special revelation from God and teach his disciples to follow the tenets of the Qur'an. The expansion of Islam quickly took on an aggressive, militaristic nature that subjugated surrounding tribal groups and expanded across Northern Africa and into Europe. Convinced that followers of Allah represented spiritual truth in contrast with Christianity, more than 1.3 billion people throughout the world have been devoured by the teachings of Islam and barricaded from knowing Jesus Christ. We are told about these future descendants of Ishmael, "His hand will be against everyone, and everyone's hand will be against him; he will live at odds with all his brothers" (Gen. 16:12).

Generations before Christ came to live upon the earth and die for the sins of the world, a pantheistic Hindu philosophy became firmly entrenched in the societies of South Asia until today almost one billion people still adhere to the deception it represents. The teachings of Gautama Buddha have been embraced by hundreds of thousands of people in Asian cultures and continue to bring multitudes into bondage to a futile search for enlightenment in a modern New Age movement that has moved around the globe. More than a billion people in animistic cultures are struggling to deal with demons and spiritual powers over which they have no control in superstition and hopelessness because the enemy has isolated them culturally and geographically from hearing the truth of God's Word.

Satan has free reign in the hearts and cultures that have rejected or never heard of the hope that can be found in Jesus Christ. He uses godless rulers, government authorities, legal restrictions, and social pressures to maintain his dominion and deprive God of being glorified among the peoples of the world. "We know that we are of God, and the whole world is under the sway of the evil one" (1 John 5:19). If his strategies prove to be vulnerable, his backup plan is to work among God's people to create indifference and lethargy. Instead of pressing the battle with conscientious urgency, Satan has readily convinced Christians that missions is optional or is the responsibility of only an elite few who have a special mystical call to serve as missionaries. Regardless, it appears the strategies of our enemy have been immensely successful as we see the realities of a lost world and the formidable barriers to proclaiming the gospel today.

Jesus said, "I have come that they may have life and have it in abundance" (John 10:10). We know that applies to those who have come to faith in acknowledging Him as Savior and Lord. But we must not subtly be led to embrace an egocentric faith that is just for us. God's purpose is that the whole world would find and experience that abundant life in Christ which would be to the praise of His glory! Jesus preceded that statement by alerting us to the thief who "comes only to steal and to kill and to destroy" (John 10:10). Not only does Satan try to keep the individual from coming to faith in Christ; he tempts the Christian to forfeit the abundant life. He works to rob our understanding of the peace and joy we have been given, destroy our assurance of blessings, and cause us to doubt Christ's power in us through inflicting carnal behavior and filling our minds with doubts and anxiety. Satan does all of this for one purpose—to deny God of the praise and glory from our lives. Likewise the thief is intent on robbing God of His glory among the nations by destroying our witness and barricading the cultures against the light of the world.

> *Satan has free reign in the hearts and cultures that have rejected or never heard of the hope that can be found in Christ.*

Is it because God's promises throughout Scripture of being exalted among the nations is just an implication for end-times rather than His practical directive in our world today? Are we to believe that God's sovereignty is limited, unable to overcome the extensive domain of evil and worldliness that stands against His kingdom? Are we to assume that the power of the gospel is not sufficient to penetrate Muslim, Hindu, and Buddhist cultural worldviews holding masses in bondage to sin and to draw them to the truth? Could it be that the people of God today, like Israel, have become ingrown, concerned more about their own blessings and welfare and become indifferent to the mission to which God called them into His kingdom?

The reality is that there is an enemy of the kingdom of God who is intent on depriving God of His praise and glory among the nations. He works subtly in darkness and anonymity to defeat the individual Christian, distort the mission of the church, and divert God's people from their calling to declare His salvation and proclaim His glory among the nations. God's Word alerts us to this enemy and admonishes us to be alert to his devious schemes; we are told to stand firm against his deception, resist temptation, and claim the victory that has already been assured. It is a victory rooted in God's character, won for us by Christ's resurrection, and manifested by the Spirit's indwelling presence in the church. God's praise and glory is our supreme priority, and proclaiming and displaying it our greatest privilege.

I often wonder to what extent Israel comprehended the scope of God's purpose and their responsibility to make Him known among the nations. How big was their world? They were certainly familiar with the various tribes in the Middle East such as the Edomites, Canaanites, Amalekites, and Philistines, but God instructed the Israelites to destroy them lest they compromise their allegiance to God and their unique witness of the one true God be eroded. Abraham had come from Ur of Chaldees, and Old Testament history is filled with an obvious awareness of the Egyptians, Assyrians, and Babylonians. But how much were they aware of the extensive world that would later become the Greek and Roman empires. That ancient world of people groups and languages dispersed from the Tower of Babel did not include the extensive list of more than eleven thousand socioethnic linguistic groups we know of today that need to know Jesus Christ.

You don't see so much of an overt evangelistic witness of Israel in making God's way known among the nations as much as simply the witness of their unique lifestyle of righteousness and as a people through whom God demonstrated His mighty power. God demonstrated his compassion for the Assyrians by sending Jonah to Nineveh, but the power of Israel's testimony was how they lived among the nations and was more of a passive witness that was to draw the peoples to the worship of the true and living God. The temple was to be open to foreigners in their midst.

The tragedy of periodic apostasy and failure by Israel was far beyond punishment and forfeiture of God's blessings. Israel's failure destroyed their witness to the world. What would be the implications of that today? When the holiness of God and the love for one another is not evident in His people, the church, does that not erode our witness among the peoples around us who are searching for spiritual truth and reality? Failure to show faithfulness is failure to display God's goodness and glory.

King Hezekiah had the proper perspective as he prayed for deliverance from Sennacherib and the Assyrians, "Now, Lord our God, save us from his hand so that all the kingdoms of the earth may know that You are the Lord—You alone" (Isa. 37:20). Isaiah made it clear that God's demonstration of power on the behalf of His people was related to His glory among the nations. "The Lord has displayed His holy arm in the sight of all the nations; all the ends of the earth will see the salvation of our God" (Isa. 52:10). Of course, this is in the context of a prophecy related to the Messiah and the coming kingdom of God. However, the story should put in perspective how and why God is working in current affairs, not only in the history of Israel, but in our lives today. The impetus for our mission task is to understand that everything we are—everything that happens to us and everything that we do—is to align us with the kingdom purpose for God to be exalted among the nations.

The apostles and that first generation of Christians understood the scope of their Lord's mandate to disciple all nations beyond the limited provincialism of ancient Israel. What represented the "ends of the earth" to them? The birth of the Syrian church reflected the witness of some of the apostles. There is historical evidence that Thomas made it all the way to India. But it was a new generation of evangelists, beginning with Paul and Barnabas, and the vision of a multiethnic church at Antioch that God used to grasp the scope of His mission. God called subsequent believers to bring the gospel out of a narrow, Jewish context. The expanding church in Acts saw the gospel as applicable to all cultures and endeavored to spread the message of "the way," as it began to be called, to all nations.

Paul responded to the Macedonian vision and swept across the civilized provinces of Europe planting churches. He envisioned going to Rome and on beyond to Spain, reflecting a view of the world broadened by Roman roads and maritime commerce. But it is doubtful they knew anything about an oriental culture that was already flourishing in what is now China or the barbaric tribes of Northern Europe. Yet they pressed forward to penetrate the world they knew with the life-saving message of God's love. Today we are without excuse in regard to a lack of awareness of the nations and peoples that need Jesus. Modern sociological research gives us an intimate knowledge of every language and culture and where they live. But too many Christians are content in their own salvation and allow an ethnocentric provincialism to dismiss the imperative of God's mission to the nations.

Paul was convinced that God wanted him to go to Thessalonica to minister and share the gospel, but he confessed, "So we wanted to come to you—even I, Paul, time and again—but Satan hindered us" (1 Thess. 2:18). There are sins of commission—what we do that is wrong and should not do—but there are also sins of omission. These are those things we should do but fail to carry out. Satan often opposes the will of God being done by simply dissuading us from doing what we ought to do. We are going to see that this tactic may be his most effective strategy to delay God's kingdom reaching the nations and His being glorified to the ends of the earth—simply hindering us from being obedient to what God has called us to do as His people.

Going Deeper

1. Reflect on and journal about what is receiving worship in your life other than Jesus. What receives the greatest intentional focus of your time, energy, and resources? Ask God to give you a discerning spirit. Then ask two other trusted friends to speak into your life about this issue.

2. Do you know about any unreached people groups? Pick a group and study them. If appropriate, involve your family or a group of friends. Then begin praying for that group to be drawn to Jesus Christ and that He would raise up missionaries to reach them with the gospel. (Find information about people groups at www.imb.org and www.joshuaproject.com.)

3. What is Satan's greatest weapon in your life? Pride? Fear? Indifference? Ask God to reveal Satan's strongholds in your life and then ask Him to break them so you will be more active in His mission.

4. How might God want to adjust your perspective about worship? How will a renewed sense of worship change your activity in the mission of God?

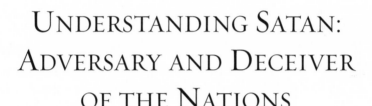

CHAPTER 3

UNDERSTANDING SATAN: ADVERSARY AND DECEIVER OF THE NATIONS

Satan is described in Scripture as a thief, ruler of the world, god of this world, beast, prince of the power of the air, spirit of disobedience, and evil one, but he exists as an adversary of God and His purposes. The word *devil* comes from the Greek *diabolos,* which means to oppose. *Devil* is one of the twenty-two different names used to describe Satan in the Bible and is used thirty-five times in the New Testament. The devil is opposed to the extension of God's kingdom on the earth and is actively seeking to deprive God of being glorified among the nations through the proclamation of the gospel as well as in one's life personally. No doubt his mission is clear: to keep lost people lost.

Among the sequence of events that characterize the end-times and the return of Christ is the fact that Satan will be thrown into the abyss, "so that he would no longer deceive the nations" (Rev. 20:3). Meanwhile he appears to have free reign in the world today, continuing to deceive the nations.

In the temptation experience of Jesus, Luke's Gospel tells us, "So he took Him up and showed Him all the kingdoms of the world in a moment of time. The Devil said to Him, 'I will give you their splendor and all this authority, because it has been given over to me, and I can give it to anyone I want. If You then, will worship me, all will be Yours'" (Luke 4:5–7). Of course Jesus did not succumb to this temptation, but neither did He contradict the right of Satan to make that claim. He came to proclaim the kingdom of God and claim the kingdoms of the world for God's dominion and glory. Satan appealed to this purpose, claiming authority to grant the very thing Jesus desired. It would be so easy—no suffering, no cross—just acknowledge and yield to Satan's perceived authority.

Of course to do so and yield to this temptation would have forfeited the act of obedience to God in dying on the cross that would defeat Satan and render him powerless. Where and how did Satan acquire dominion over the kingdoms of the world? It was God's intention for man to have dominion over the earth. In Genesis 1:26 we read, "Then God said, 'Let Us make man in Our image, according to Our likeness. They will rule the fish of the sea, the birds of the sky, the animals, all the earth.'" But in disobedience and listening to Satan's lies and influence, Adam and Eve relinquished their dominion over the earth. That disobedience has continued to be manifested in the sin nature that is passed on to humanity. We can blame Adam and Eve for messing things up, but the problem is: we have continued to do what they did by choosing to live for false riches, personal gain, and the godless principles of this world.

First John 5:19 says, "We are of God, and the whole world is under the sway of the evil one." God has claimed for Himself a people to serve Him. We are His possession and called to proclaim "the praises of the One who called you out of darkness into His marvelous light" (1 Pet. 2:9). But where Christ is not known—where the gospel has not penetrated and transformed society to acknowledge the lordship of God—the nations, cultures, and peoples of the world are still in darkness under the dominion of Satan.

I (Jerry) often tell about going to Indonesia as a new missionary in 1970. I had felt God's call many years earlier and, following years of preparation and anticipation, went to the largest Muslim country in the world with the solid conviction that this was in obedience to God's leadership. I had no question as to the gospel being the power of God unto salvation to draw people to Jesus Christ. My international travels and study convinced me that proclamation of the good news was all it took to create a response. Peoples living in despair over the depravity and hopelessness of sin would readily embrace a message offering deliverance from the consequences of sin and providing eternal life. I was confident I would arrive in Indonesia to join other missionaries, and, as in the pages of Acts, multitudes would come to faith and be saved each day!

However, instead of massive response, I encountered indifference and antagonism, in spite of open opportunities for witness. I realized that to expect a Muslim in Indonesia to respond to the gospel was not unlike asking a blind man to read a newspaper. The Bible provides an explanation: "Regarding them: the god of this age has blinded the minds of the unbelievers so they cannot see the light of the gospel of the glory of Christ, who is the image of God" (2 Cor. 4:4). There is nothing deficient about the power of the gospel message. The Holy Spirit still actively convicts of sin, truth, and righteousness. But we need to recognize that we have an enemy, the god of this age, who has the ability to blind the eyes of the unbelieving to the truth of the gospel. He works his deception with apparent impunity to lead the nations astray from knowing God.

Even where the gospel can be freely shared, the enemy is actively distorting the message and filtering it through contrary traditions and worldviews to keep the seed from taking root in the human heart. The parable of the sower (Luke 8) tells us the reality of the world we are responsible for evangelizing. The analogy of the diverse kinds of soil represents various responses to the gospel. Some will welcome the good news, but it will not really profit them because they continue to be consumed with the cares of the world. The message does not take root in the lives of others because of barriers to understanding and belief as represented by the rocky soil. Occasionally one's witness will encounter fertile soil in which it is received, grows, and multiplies. But some of the seed falls on the hardened pathway as reflected in many cultures. Jesus explained that, rather than taking root, the seed remains exposed on the surface of the ground where the birds come, take it away, and devour it.

> *Even where the gospel can be freely shared, the enemy is distorting the message to keep it from being received.*

In explaining this parable, Jesus says the birds are the devil—"Then the Devil comes and takes away the word from their hearts, so that they may not believe and be saved" (Luke 8:12). Remember, Satan is identified as a deceiver and liar. When Paul expressed concern that the believers in Corinth were being led astray from purity of doctrine and the simplicity of faith in Christ, he concluded, "And no wonder! For Satan himself is disguised as an angel of light. So it is no great thing if his servants also disguise themselves as servants of righteousness" (2 Cor. 11:14–15).

He is deluding others to think their way to God, though false, is the way of truth and righteousness. He distorts the truth of God's Word, just as he sought to do in the temptations of Jesus. He takes the pluralism of Hinduism and Buddhism to deceive them into believing there are many roads to God, and whatever path one chooses to follow is valid. He uses traditional distorted teachings within Islam to convince them Christianity advocates three gods—twisting the concept of a Trinitarian God to persuade them it represents a blasphemous doctrine. His lies find ready reception in allegations that the Bible has been corrupted, an imposter rather than Jesus died on the cross, and Christianity represents the immoral lifestyles seen on television and movies from America.

Among cultural Catholics, he allows them to give intellectual assent to the role of Jesus as Savior, but Satan erodes the possibility of it becoming a God-glorifying faith of a born-again life. Knowledge of Jesus is superseded by adoration of the Virgin Mary; adding the sacraments and church tradition to the atoning work of Jesus, multitudes around the world are encouraged to embrace a salvation of works that is ineffectual and robs God of the glory that comes from exclusive allegiance to Jesus Christ as the provision of salvation.

In characterizing those who would succumb to Satan's deceit, even religious leaders, Jesus says, "You are of your father the Devil, and you want to carry out your father's desires. He was a murderer from the beginning and has not stood in the truth, because there is no truth in him. When he tells a lie, he speaks from his own nature, because he is a liar and the father of liars" (John 8:44). He is deceiving the nations to believe what is false. Global evangelism does not take place in a demilitarized zone but on the battleground of spiritual warfare. Satan, in vengeance and jealousy for that which belongs to God, is deceiving the nations and holding them in bondage to a lie. That's why Paul described our task of winning the Gentiles and claiming the nations for God's possession as one "to open their eyes that they may turn from darkness to light and from the power of Satan to God" (Acts 26:18).

> *Global evangelism does not take place in a demilitarized zone, but on the battleground of spiritual warfare.*

In our American culture, we are witnessing the consequences of not recognizing supernatural opposition. It results in indifference to the gospel and a lackluster response to facing powerful, supernatural resistance. Furthermore, the mind-set of Christian leadership has attributed lostness to the fact that people have not found the right church yet. The wayward hope is placed in offering people better churches and better lives while Satan and the demons of hell wrestle for their souls. We are in danger of reducing the battle for souls to offering a supermarket approach for religious consumerism.

John Piper, in his book *Let the Nations Be Glad!*, defines the problem and the solution:

> Life is war. That's not all it is. But it is always that. Our weakness in prayer is owning largely to our neglect of this truth. Prayer is primarily a wartime walkie-talkie for the mission of the church as it advances against the powers of darkness and unbelief. . . . Prayer gives us the significance of front-line forces, and gives God the glory of a limitless Provider. The one who gives the power gets the glory. Thus prayer safe-guards the supremacy of God in missions while linking us with the endless grace for every need.[1]

Satan is identified as a fallen angel. Created to serve and worship God with the vast array of heavenly hosts, he was jealous for God's glory. Isaiah 14:12–14 is considered by most biblical commentators to be an analogy of what led to his downfall. "Shining morning star, how you have fallen from the heavens! You destroyer of nations, you have been cut down to the ground. You said to yourself: 'I will ascend to the heavens; I will set my throne above the stars of God. I will sit on the mount of the gods' assembly, in the remotest parts of the North. I will ascend above the highest clouds; I will make myself like the Most High.'" The result of his rebellion was being ejected from heaven, and the warfare began. Job 1:7 alerts us to the fact that the world is the principality of Satan's domain. "The Lord asked Satan, 'Where have you come from?' 'From roaming through the earth,' Satan answered Him, 'and walking around on it.'"

God knew the consequences that would follow when Satan was cast out of heaven. He knew the temptation Satan would bring to man, the crown of His creation. He foresaw the evil and conflict that would be fomented in the world and the effort that would be made for Satan to claim upon the earth what he could not gain in heaven. But God's love was so amazing He went ahead with creation in spite of the battle that would ensue.

Even before the foundation of the world, redemption was planned and victory assured—not just ultimately or theoretically but as a daily reality to those who are in Christ. "The Son of God was revealed for this purpose: to destroy the Devil's works" (1 John 3:8). Satan is a defeated foe. He has already been conquered on the cross when the shed blood of Christ overcame the power of sin and death. One day he will be cast into outer darkness, and all his wickedness and deceit will be finished forever. So

> *Satan is seeking to claim upon the earth what he could not gain in heaven, but redemption was planned and victory assured before the foundation of the world.*

what is the explanation of Satan's power and influence being so pervasive in our world and in our lives? Why do the nations continue to be susceptible to his lies and deception, thwarting God's purpose to be exalted among them? Basically, it is vengefulness. Since Satan cannot win, he hopes to embarrass God through our personal failures and carnal living. To him, we are just pawns in the battle for the spiritual realm. This is a war between Satan and God in which we, and the peoples of the world, are but instruments in the conflict to bring glory to God or to deprive God of the praise and glory He is due by yielding to Satan's devious strategies.

Satan's Purpose Is to Deprive God of the Praise and Glory Due Him

When Satan tempts a Christian to sin, it is to deprive God of praise and His glory in that person's life. When he leads us to embrace the carnal and self-serving values of the world, he is merely thumbing his nose at God. When we indulge in lustful gratification rather than walking in holiness and obedience to God, it gives Satan the glory rather than our Lord.

Many Christians continue to struggle with the tension between the flesh and the Spirit when, in fact, God has given them the victory. However, we are taught that the battle is constant and victory elusive; therefore, we embrace defeat in the effort to live for Christ. As an angel, a created being, Satan is merely a messenger. He speaks to our minds, persuading us to interpret truth and reality by our feelings and experience rather than the truth of God's Word. The Scripture tells us, "For we know that our old self was crucified with Him in order that sin's dominion over the body may be abolished, so that we may no longer be enslaved to sin, since a person who has died [with Christ] is freed from sin's claims" (Rom. 6:6–7). But instead of accepting by faith and living in this victory to the glory of God, Satan persuades us that the old sin nature still has dominance.

Throughout Scripture we are told that faith is the victory: "Because whatever has been born of God conquers the world. This is the victory that has conquered the world: our faith" (1 John 5:4). "Your adversary the Devil is prowling around like a roaring lion, looking for anyone he can devour. Resist him, firm in the faith" (1 Pet. 5:8–9). "In every situation take the shield of faith, and with it you will be able to extinguish the flaming arrows of the evil one" (Eph. 6:16). Because believing God and accepting the truth of what He has said as reality is the victory, one of Satan's favorite tools is doubt. Just as he implanted doubt in the mind of Eve when he said, "Did God really say . . . ?" (Gen. 3:1), he continues to plant doubts in our minds to reject the truth of God's Word and the victory over sin we have been given in Christ.

The result is living for self instead of a cross-centered, Spirit-filled life. Abandoning His promises of peace, joy, power, holiness, and blessing, we strike out on our own and forfeit the power available for our witness that would bring glory to God. Satan robs us of peace and leaves us with anxiety and worry; he destroys our joy, leaving us struggling with despair and depression. We often attribute personal discomfort or pain to satanic intent. But our downfall and failure is not all about us! Satan has a much greater purpose in orchestrating our defeat. He deprives God of the glory He desires and has provided in our life in order that the world will not see a living example of the gospel.

Satan's strategy is to replace glory to God with what brings glory to us. Even our modern attempts to give all glory to God sometimes miss the point. Coming to Christ in the 1980s, I (Ed) was a huge fan of the arena rock era of music and consequently of the same genre of Christian music. The decade of the 1980s was a time when many Christian musicians came to great prominence and financial security—for a short while. But it was also a time when many of the values of Western culture seeped into the Christian music industry. Though they began in 1969, the Dove Awards became a prominent feature of our subculture in the '80s. They are essentially the Christian version of the Grammy awards, given out by the Gospel Music Association.

> *Satan's strategy is to replace glory to God with what brings glory to us!*

Is anything inherently wrong with recognizing artistry among believers? No. We also applaud excellence in music and excellence in artistry. However, it seems a tenuous balance to give out awards to Christian artists for *their* efforts in writing and singing music about the One who deserves all the worship and praise. Even one well-known Christian song was lauded as a work of great art when it proclaimed that God thought of mankind "above all" as He died for sins.

Intentionally or unintentionally, such lyrics feed the myth that what Jesus did on the cross was "all about me." In fact, the content of many modern Christian songs holds this juxtaposition throughout their lyrics: I will glorify God because God is glorifying me in His death. Yet the opposite is true. The defeat of every kingdom and every power was what drove Jesus to the cross. The purpose of His death was His glory and desire to be lifted up. You may think this is theological semantics. But the danger is making the story of Jesus so small and personal it can fit on a necklace worn around one's neck.

When Satan can reduce the work of Christ to "all about me," then the next religious idea can be considered just as important as the gospel because it is a matter of personal preference. Today's culture seems to make all religious ideas morally equivalent to one another and cast them simply as personal choices. In such a dynamic, the claims of Christ have no place because they are exclusive. In a religious culture that touts religion's highest form as free choice regardless of the apparent contradictions, Christianity is easily rejected. We must in turn show that the claims of Jesus are meant not to manipulate mankind but to offer freedom to participate in God's glory for our good. We must help the lost understand that a choice against Jesus has consequences in this life as well as in the next life.

The God-sized, world shaking, eternal implications of the work of Jesus is seen clearly in Philippians:

> Make your own attitude that of Christ Jesus, who,
> existing in the form of God, did not consider equality
> with God as something to be used for His own
> advantage. Instead He emptied Himself by assuming
> the form of a slave, taking on the likeness of men.
> And when He had come as a man in His external
> form, He humbled Himself by becoming obedient to
> the point of death—even to death on a cross. For this
> reason God also highly exalted Him and gave Him the
> name that is above every name, so that at the name
> of Jesus every knee should bow—of those who are in
> heaven and on earth and under the earth—and every

tongue should confess that Jesus Christ is Lord, to the glory of God the Father. (Phil. 2:5–11)

Big deal, right? Is this story good news for me? Yes, of course the gospel is good news for all who follow Jesus. But is the gospel about me, "above all"? Satan would love for me to think so. The gospel is about the warm, fuzzy thoughts Jesus has for me and just how special He thinks I am. He loves me, no doubt, but He loves the nations as much. He loves my neighbors. He loves people who are not like me. He loves the marginalized and hidden people groups of the world. His glory is the goal to His embrace of the lost. When the gospel is all about me, it is easy for Satan to create indifference toward the nations and a lost world, which is what was really on the mind of Jesus on the cross.

On the cross the heart of Jesus is seen before the beginning of the end for Satan. Jesus prayed the big picture and the big purpose in John 17: "Jesus spoke these things, looked up to heaven, and said: 'Father, the hour has come. Glorify Your Son so that the Son may glorify You, for You gave Him authority over all flesh; so He may give eternal life to all You have given Him. This is eternal life: that they may know You, the only true God, and the One You have sent—Jesus Christ'" (John 17:1–3). Notice the big words: *glorify, authority, eternal life, true God, Jesus Christ*. . . . These big words represent big ideas. Why is this important? Again, the argument goes back to there being only one way to God—through Christ—and God being glorified. Satan does not have to insult our Savior directly or discredit Him in order to keep lost people lost. All he needs to do is make Jesus one of many "viable" choices in the crowded market of designer religions.

As Satan attempts to keep lost people lost, keep in mind that a counterfeit gospel can be a version of the Christian gospel. How clever would it be to present a partially true, more politically correct version of Christianity? Along with a more acceptable form of Christianity comes a higher level of social consciousness that cares for the environment and the poor. Conversion to Christ then becomes conversion to an ideology instead of true spiritual rebirth accompanied by repentance and faith in Jesus Christ. A "Jesus" that believes what I believe about politics is also false and dangerous. A politicized Jesus is not the Christ but a pawn in the bid for power.

Our era of history is like all others; there is extreme political polarization in our culture. People are passionate about their politics. Emerging media outlets (Facebook, YouTube, blogs, and Twitter) promote a plethora of solutions to the world's problems. Political views we hold deeply may be passed down from our own families and can often be supported by anecdotal evidence. Evidence like "Jesus would vote for this candidate" or "God does not like this view" needs to be carefully considered. God has been cited as a political backer of everything from gun control to veganism and smoking marijuana. Jesus, no question, has a moral will for the operation of culture from our treatment of the poor to an ethic regarding preborn human life. But our political views should not be the criteria for what make us feel "Christian." Should our faith inform our politics? Of course it should, but I fear that the opposite is more often true. When our politics informs our faith, Satan wins. Moral or political rightness should not substitute for radical followship of Jesus Christ as Lord. The values and practices of those who embrace "Jesus is Lord" will look less political and more culturally redemptive.

Power sought—whether as an office in secular politics or an award in Christian culture—shifts the place of glory. Removing it from God, we have curiously proclaimed, "It's all for the Lord." Yet, in every practical sense, Satan wins the battle when the focus of our personal efforts is on earthly reputation. We have accepted Satan's veiled version of glory and weakened ourselves as soldiers.

Weakened dosages of an injected virus have been proven effective against experiencing a full-blown version of the virus. We call it a vaccine or inoculation. I (Ed) found that when pastoring in the South, we have to look out for those who are inoculated against the gospel. Satan enjoys leading people to be nominally religious but apathetic against the gospel. Many Americans have been inoculated by the gospel by being shown or told about a weakened version of the real thing but not the true thing. In some subcultures in North America, being "Christian" is a cultural moniker represented by dress, morality, and ritual. On the surface, certain versions of Christianity do not appear false, yet they are eternally lethal if not recognized and overcome. Satan would love for people to think their "tofu Christianity" is one of many significant things in their lives but never important enough to be everything.

The information of the gospel goes out with various degrees of results. Satan interferes with gospel seed the moment the seed goes forth. Satan's options are still open, but He must move quickly and decisively. I (Ed) have experienced the incredible joy of spending time in places where the gospel seed is unfamiliar to the people. Places like China and Cuba, to name a few, experienced a new level of true conversions to Christ because the gospel seed was new. In Russia, the gospel went forth quickly after the fall of the Berlin Wall in 1989. Regardless of new or old ground, Satan is present to build counterfeit gospels and religions that replace a real relationship with Jesus.

Satan attempts to keep lost people lost by making Christians apathetic and interfering with receptivity of the seed.

What happens to the seed of God? Let us look further at the explanation of Jesus in the familiar parable mentioned earlier in Matthew 13 of a sower and seed. To me it's remarkable how this farmer, perhaps a picture both of God and us, spreads the seed with great abandon. The seed is on the side of the road. The seed is in rocky places. You have to wonder if the sower is that good of a farmer. I don't know much about farming, but I'm pretty sure you don't throw seed in rocky places. You don't throw seed on the side of the road. You put it in rows, right? So what happens to the seed? The result of sowing is dependent on the condition of the soil. This is the focus of the story. The seed is the same, the sower is the same, but the soil is not. Our work is to scatter the seed no matter the environmental conditions.

Matthew 13 described four kinds of soil. As we revisit this familiar story, think of the potential of the seed and the battle over the result. The seed carries the potential of an incredible harvest. Christians on mission with God will be sowing here, there, and everywhere according to Acts 1:8. The sower is optimistic, or otherwise there would be no reason to sow. Getting the seed out of the bag and on to the ground is part of the battle. Satan does all he can to stop Christians from sowing. He wants the gospel to get no farther than the parking lot of the church. That is his first line of defense. Once courageous Christians sow, Satan presents another line of defense to keep lost people lost. He creates barriers in the soil. These barriers are personal, cultural, social, and religious obstacles that affect the receptivity of the soil.

The first soil is referred to as unprepared ground: "As he was sowing, some seeds fell along the path, and the birds came and ate them up" (Matt. 13:4). Jesus used a common picture in the minds of the original hearers. A sower would walk in a field throwing seed. The hard ground or "wayside" was hardened by foot traffic and the hot sun. The seed had no potential for taking root or producing mature plants on the wayside. Jesus later gave the interpretation of this image, "[Whoever] . . . hears the word about the kingdom and doesn't understand it, the evil one comes and snatches away what was sown in his heart. This is the one sown along the path" (Matt. 13:19). The seed can't get any soil because the ground is unprepared. Often we sow on hard lives. People can be superstitious and fearful to leave religious roots or years of false beliefs. Other people believe the Christian message insults their intellect. Years of bad habits and immorality will often harden the ground in the life of a person far from God. They may believe the lie that they cannot change bad habits or overcome bad choices.

No matter the reason for rootlessness, Satan is pleased to scoop up the seed before the ground is even aware of its presence.

This is why so many of us have come to faith in Christ in the midst of a crisis in our lives. Have you ever noticed that people come to Christ when the ground of their lives has been broken up by some tragedy? When the rhythm of life changes dramatically through circumstances beyond our control, we listen more attentively. Otherwise we're busy with family, with work, and with personal interests; we don't have time to listen. "The birds come and sweep it away" when we live blissfully in our ignorance to the kingdom. But when life hurts, God breaks up the ground. Then the seed can take root in your life in a way that it couldn't before. God can use an economic downturn, disaster, or personal crisis to break up the hard, unresponsive ground. We are going to see how God is using the chaos and crisis in our world today—war, ethnic violence, political disruption, natural disasters—to turn the hearts of people to a search for hope and assurance that can be found only in Jesus Christ. But make no mistake about it, Satan will use those same occurrences to harden the heart and steal the seed.

> *God is using chaos and crisis in our world to turn the hearts of people to a search for hope and assurance that can be found only in Jesus Christ.*

The second soil is rocky ground: "Others fell on rocky ground, where there wasn't much soil, and they sprang up quickly since the soil wasn't deep" (Matt. 13:5). Later Jesus explained, "And the one sown on rocky ground—this is the one who hears the word and immediately receives it with joy. Yet he has no root in himself, but is short-lived. When pressure or persecution comes because of the word, immediately he stumbles" (Matt. 13:20–21). In Palestine the picture was not ground with rock mixed in but a thin layer of soil on top of a plate of limestone rock. What little potential existing soon disappears. Things looked great during the early stages of sowing, but the conditions had an inherent flaw. The crop failed because of a shallow embrace of the truth. Ridicule or wrong motives for embracing Christ result from a shallow soil experience. During the early era of international missions, some converts were described as "rice Christians." "Rice Christians" embraced Christ because of the added benefit of a needed bowl of rice. Shallow faith does not sustain life during seasons of intense heat. Satan devours those who follow Christ for the wrong reasons.

A guy named Larry Flynt is a famous magazine publisher. *Hustler* magazine and his stores are part of his adult (porn) entertainment empire. In 1977 a *60 Minutes* producer introduced him to someone named Ruth Carter Stapleton, an evangelist and sister of President Jimmy Carter. Soon afterward Larry Flynt announced his conversion to Christianity. Being discipled by Stapleton, he went around, spoke at churches, changed the content of his magazine for an issue or two, and said, "I'm a Christian now." Then the reality of life set in, and today he claims to be a devout atheist. Why? Because the seed came, and maybe it got a little root, but it couldn't last because the pressures of life, the immorality of the industry, and the call to continue the worldliness was too much.

The third soil is called "thorny ground." "Others fell among thorns, and the thorns came up and choked them" (Matt. 13:7). Later in the passage the thorny ground is described, "Now the one sown among the thorns—this is one who hears the word, but the worries of this age and the seduction of wealth choke the word, and it becomes unfruitful" (Matt. 13:22). The strength and rapid growth of weeds literally chokes the good plants in their infancy. Some people initially embrace the truth, but they get too caught up into the other things in life before growth happens. Faith gets choked out by the weeds.

Our enemy is never happy when the seed takes root. But he finds refuge in the believer whose faith is choked by the distractions of the world. The weeds of materialism, lust, or pride overpower the tender shoot; and it remains a solitary plant. God's intention was for the new sprout to become fruitful, but the enemy tricked the young plant into existing alone, without reproducing itself. It is easy to point out this trait in others, "Just look at that Larry Flynt." But we should examine our own lives to see where the world's distractions and the enemy's temptations have transformed our desires from kingdom reproduction to worldly enticement.

Finally we have soil that produces a desirable result—the good ground. When we study the four types of soil, we see a reality. Most soil does not produce good crops. Satan is at work in the soil sowing the seeds of misunderstanding, materialism, and religious darkness. But the sower is intentional and optimistic. Don't lose your courage to sow because of the lack of responsive soil. Satan would love for you to give up. Remember, the problem is not with the sower or the seed. The problem is the soil. And the condition of the soil is out of our control.

Jesus does save the best soil for last: "Still others fell on good ground, and produced a crop: some 100, some 60, and some 30 times what was sown. Anyone who has ears should listen!" (Matt. 13:8–9). "But the one sown on the good ground—this is one who hears and understands the word" (Matt. 13:23). There's a difference between hearing and understanding. Jesus keeps saying, "He who has ears to hear . . ."(v. 9 NKJV). Be encouraged by the fruitfulness of good soil! For all of the difficult and unproductive sowing you do, you will one day come across the good soil that will produce fruit beyond your own work. The potential of good soil is greater than just one good harvest.

The good ground represents Christians who fully embrace Christ and His mission throughout creation. The only question in their lives is where and how they will live out their calling. The message is much bigger than the short-term help a relationship with Jesus provides. The new Christian should be interested in more than their patch of land but consumed with changing the world. Christian Swartz described the supernatural process of multiplication displayed by the Christian of good soil:

> Just as the true fruit of an apple tree is not an
> apple, but another tree; the true fruit of a small
> group is not a new Christian, but another group; the
> true fruit of a church is not a new group, but a new
> church; the true fruit of a leader is not a follower, but
> a new leader; the true fruit of an evangelist is not a
> convert, but new evangelists. Whenever this principle
> is understood and applied, the results are dramatic.[2]

No wonder Satan is so anxious and responsive to the seed. The fact that seed is being sown indicates that Satan's first line of defense has failed. Now his barriers are in the lives of people. If he is unable to intercept the seed or sabotage the soil, multiplication and life change are possible. Movements of God are experienced through the rapid multiplication of new churches and new Christians in a region.

We Must Be Vigilant to Claim the Victory

We have been given victory over all the schemes and strategies of Satan. With the death of Christ on the cross, the power of sin was conquered not just theoretically but as a daily practical reality for those who choose to walk in the Spirit that indwells every believer. "The Son of God was revealed for this purpose: to destroy the Devil's works" (1 John 3:8). Paul explains what happened in the atoning sacrifice of Christ in which He took upon His sinless body the sins of the world: "He erased the certificate of debt, with its obligations, that was against us and opposed to us, and has taken it out of the way by nailing it to the cross. He disarmed the rulers and authorities and disgraced them publicly; He triumphed over them by Him" (Col. 2:14–15).

Satan and his minions of darkness—his principalities and rulers of this world—have been defeated. A Christian is a partaker in the divine nature of Christ. When we are "in Christ," a continual carnal lifestyle is antithetical to our true nature. But it is Satan's only hope of stemming the tide of God's work on the earth. The enemy's deception and lies rob God of His glory in our life. But because of the victory procured by Christ, the ultimate triumph belongs to God, and He will be exalted to the ends of the earth.

However, one should not underestimate the determination and devious capabilities of our enemy to keep others from the kingdom of God. As we consider our mission and the fact God has chosen us as His people to reach the nations, we would be naive to think that endeavor would not encounter barriers and severe opposition. It is important to understand the nature of our enemy.

One of the most familiar passages regarding spiritual warfare is the exhortation to put on the armor of God in Ephesians 6:10–18. Our purpose is not, at this point, to elaborate on claiming the personal victory or the implications of being armed with all the implements God has made available to us. We need to understand what the Word of God reveals about how our enemy operates. We are told, "Finally, be strengthened by the Lord and by His vast strength. Put on the full armor of God so that you can stand against the tactics of the Devil. For our battle is not against flesh and blood, but against the rulers, against the authorities, against the world powers of this darkness, against the spiritual forces of evil in the heavens. This is why you must take up the full armor of God, so that [we] may be able to resist in the evil day, and having prepared everything, to take your stand" (Eph. 6:10–13).

Each piece of armor is tied to a principle of the Christian life. God specifically calls us to defend ourselves in these arenas of life because they are the places where Satan attacks. Because he is the father of lies, he attacks truth. The adversary seeks to bring division so we need to defend unity. Most of all, Satan seeks condemnation for us so we need salvation. In the whole of life, we must be aware of our enemy's strategy so we can be prepared and take our stand against him.

To assume a pattern, grid, or matrix to Paul's description of our spiritual armor in Ephesians 6 might be taking too many liberties with the text. However, to dismiss it simply as allegory is to treat the subject too lightly. We suggest that a study of spiritual warfare throughout the Scripture is needful for the church to understand the war we wage. Our purpose in writing this book is not only to encourage the church in our mission to which God has called us but also to result in His glory among all peoples, and to alert us to the subtle and devious ways Satan is attempting to deprive God of that glory. In relation to the description of our spiritual armor, a discipleship process might mirror something like the chart on the next page.

Christ has defeated these rulers, authorities, and spiritual forces of evil; but Satan, as we will see in the following chapters, has no limit to the devious schemes in his efforts to defeat the individual Christian and defer the kingdom of God being extended to the nations. Paul said in his second letter to the church at Corinth, "So that we may not be taken advantage of by Satan; for we are not ignorant of his intentions [schemes]" (2 Cor. 2:11). The church at Corinth was aware of Satan's tactics as they had been subjected to dissension and conflict, immorality on the part of members, perversion of doctrine, etc. To be ignorant of the nature of our enemy and his methods is to be taken advantage of and defeated.

We need to understand while Satan operates in the world and there may be physical manifestations of his attacks, he is not a visible enemy. He may demonize and so control the minds and actions of evil rulers and people in society that they become the personification of Satan's nature and actions. But he operates in the spiritual realm or the "heavenlies," as some translations of Scripture refer to it. As the "prince of the power of the air," (Eph. 2:2 KJV) he is not omnipresent but is operative in everyone where Christ is not given dominion.

Jesus told a parable in Luke 11 in which an unclean spirit had been cast out of a man. The "house" had been swept clean and put in order, but because it was still empty, the spirit returned and brought along seven other spirits more evil than itself; "As a result, that man's last condition is worse than the first" (Luke 11:26). Satan still reigns over the kingdoms of the world because they have not been surrendered to the presence of Christ. Satan's strategies seem to have proven to be effective for more than two thousand years so that today most of the peoples of the world do not know or glorify Christ.

Discipleship Process Based on the Full Armor of God (Ephesians 6:10–18)

Armor	Key	Delivery Ideas
Belt	Truth	Preaching, Doctrine, Teaching
Breastplate	Righteousness	Mentoring, Coaching, Groups
Shoes	Gospel of Peace	Sectors, Ministries, Relationships
Shield	Faith	Stories, Celebrations, Hearing
Helmet	Word of God	Reading, Meditating, Memorization
Sword	Prayer	Groups, Stories, Journaling

Discipleship Process Design Questions
- Brainstorm potential answers with staff or leadership teams
- Implement specific action plans over the year
- Implement a specific intercessory prayer strategy for deeper disciples
- Assess results

Truth: How will we help people grow deeper in truth this year? What would a priority list of truths from God's Word look like for the year? What criteria would you use to create a list?

Righteousness: How can I help people understand their position in Christ? How will they be encouraged to make right choices consistent with their position?

Gospel of Peace: What in our system helps people experience the peace of God? How will we equip people to experience and explain the Gospel of Peace?

Faith: What does a person need to grow deeper in faith? How can we intentionally create an environment that nurtures faith?

Salvation: How can you help people review their journey to faith in Christ? What are some ways you can help people assess if they really have experienced genuine salvation? What can you do to keep an invitation to receive Christ in front of every man, woman, and child who comes in contact with your church (people)?

Word of God: What are some new ways to keep disciples connected to the Word of God? How can you encourage personal spiritual disciplines?

Prayer: What are some ways we can increase the amount and intensity of prayer? How can we encourage people to pray more as families and individuals?

Satan manipulates and controls the rulers of this world to serve his devious purposes. He is responsible for the unseen forces of darkness as represented by world powers. He is behind every evil thing that is contrary to holiness and the character of Christ. But we cannot stand firm against such an unseen enemy that works in anonymity and darkness unless he is exposed and his tactics brought to light. The victory will not come through our efforts and ability but only as we take our stand in Christ who is victorious and in the power of His vast strength.

> *We cannot stand firm against such an unseen devious enemy that works in darkness unless he is exposed and his tactics brought to light.*

We have been called into a spiritual battle. Not unlike the challenge of the children of Israel to go into the land of Canaan and possess the land, we are commissioned to take the rulership of Christ to every tribe and nation. But missions must never degenerate to a patronizing, colonizing endeavor of Christians to subjugate a pagan world. We are a spiritual people charged with a spiritual engagement to displace the dominions of darkness with the light of the glory of God. Paul told Christians in Rome, "The God of peace will soon crush Satan under your feet" (Rom. 16:20). It is a battle that will be won! But victory will not come if we fail to understand the nature of the enemy and discern the challenges we face in overcoming him.

We often think of the final judgment when all people will stand before the throne of God to give an account of their lives, but this will be a time when all the nations of the earth will be gathered for an accounting. "When the Son of Man comes in His glory, and all the angels with Him, then He will sit on the throne of His glory. All the nations will be gathered before Him, and He will separate them one from another, just as a shepherd separates the sheep from the goats" (Matt. 25:31–32). Those who will enter into God's eternal glory are those who belong to Jesus Christ and serve Him in this world. But those Satan kept from the kingdom of God will be cast away into eternal punishment. Who will claim the victory among the nations? There is evidence Satan's strategy of the ages is no longer working, and God is moving in providence and power to claim the kingdoms of the world as the kingdoms of our Lord.

Going Deeper

1. What religious worldviews are dominant in your community?

2. What are the unique ways Satan is "keeping lost people lost"?

3. What issues in your life are depriving God of His glory? How can you address them now?

4. What issues in your local church are depriving God of His glory? How can you join with church leaders to address them now?

5. What "soil" best describes your life over the last year? Why?

6. How might Satan have exercised influence over your life to keep you from using the spiritual armor provided by God?

CHAPTER 4

SATAN'S STRATEGY: KEEP NATIONS CLOSED TO THE GOSPEL

It was my (Jerry) first trip to the Central Asian Republics of the former Soviet Union early in my tenure as president of the International Mission Board. Having served for twenty-three years in South and Southeast Asia, my overseas experience was provincial, and I envisioned, as quickly as possible, visiting all the places our personnel serve around the world. In spite of extensive travel, I still haven't fulfilled that ambitious goal as it is a moving target that continues to expand.

I received my itinerary for an overseas trip and found it included Kazakhstan, Uzbekistan, and Azerbaijan. Not only did I not have a clue where I was going and where these places were located, I had never heard of these countries, now a part of the Commonwealth of Independent States of the former Soviet Union. It was a time of instability and social turmoil as these and other republics were experiencing political freedom but still ruled by socialistic leaders who simply adapted the authoritarian communist system to local governments. I traveled to city after city lacking any evidence of aesthetic value. The dismal gray appearance of endless blocks of cookie-cutter apartment buildings reflected the melancholy society and impersonal ethos of people who had known nothing but oppression.

A handful of passionate, innovative missionaries had seized this time of upheaval and changing government policies to go into the area on creative access platforms as teachers, business consultants, and humanitarian workers. They found an environment that continued to be restrictive to a Christian witness but people who were open and receptive to the message of hope they came to communicate. Building friendships characterized by love, a servant heart, and caring relationships, these pioneer missionaries began to nurture a newfound faith in those who had for many years been deprived of an opportunity to hear of God's love and the salvation He had provided. Christian workers went through frigid winters in unheated apartments and stood in lines for hours to buy a loaf of bread when the shelves of provision stores were empty. Their presence was met with suspicion and the stress of constant surveillance by the police. But the incarnational witness of those who risked planting their lives in these new fields bore fruit. One convert testified, "I don't remember what the missionaries told me, but I will never forget how they loved me; I had never known anyone like that before."

Seeing this part of the world for the first time was intriguing and not without anxiety regarding safety and security. We traveled with a degree of paranoia after being briefed to avoid using Christian terminology in conversation and instructed on how to behave at frequent checkpoints. One night we were gathered in a recondite location with our personnel for a retreat and time of fellowship. As we were engaged in an extended time of prayer one evening, I recall my personal meditation being disrupted by the vocalized prayer of a colleague. Without equivocation he prayed, "I praise God for the seventy years the Soviet Union dominated these people groups," referring to those throughout Central Asia. I thought, *Why would anyone praise God for that communist, atheistic government dominating these people for generations, prohibiting religious freedom and depriving them from knowing Jesus Christ?*

Later, as we concluded our fellowship, I found this person and asked him for an explanation of his prayer. He said, "Jerry, it is not the sparsely populated Middle East amidst the Muslim shrines that is the heart of Islamic influence, but for hundreds of years the great universities and mosques here in Central Asia propagated the Muslim faith throughout Asia. However, in a mere seventy years of domination by the Soviet Union, that atheistic influence has emasculated the Muslim stronghold of this region, leaving the people spiritually destitute and open to the gospel as we move toward the end of the twentieth century!"

I stood there speechless in response to this revelation and new insight. I thought, *What was seventy years of Babylonian captivity from the perspective of God's providence and plan for His people Israel?* While seventy years seemed like a long time to the generations in bondage, isolated from their homeland and living with fading memories of the glories of Jerusalem, it was but a brief moment in God's sense of history and all that was necessary to fulfill His purpose. So what was a "mere" seventy years—as my friend referred to it—of communist domination in the twentieth century in God's providence and plan to break down religious strongholds and soften the hearts of people to be responsive to the gospel.

What we see happening as we move further into the twenty-first century is a sovereign God moving through global events to open doors once closed to the gospel. In 1999, when Hong Kong was to revert back to China after ninety-nine years of being controlled and governed as a British territory, someone asked one of our missionaries there how the change of political sovereignty would affect Christian work. He put the issue into spiritual reality with his reply: "The sovereignty of Hong Kong is not changing when this colony is restored to China because God is sovereign over the nations and has never relinquished His throne." The psalmist declares, "The LORD has established His throne in heaven, and His kingdom [sovereignty] rules over all" (Ps. 103:19).

It doesn't matter who presumes to be in charge of nations and states or how restrictive government structures are; God is the ultimate authority, and His purpose will be fulfilled in His timing. That is hard for us to grasp from a human perspective when so many places officially prohibit expressions of Christian witness. Researchers tell us that in the last ten years an average of three countries per year close their doors to a missionary presence. Satan is using the adversarial inclination of communist and totalitarian governments or those dominated by Islamic or Hindu worldviews to prohibit an open Christian witness. Paul's accusation of the sorcerer, Elymas, on Cyprus, is descriptive of these nations historically. He described him as "Son of the Devil, full of all deceit and all fraud, enemy of all righteousness" (Acts 13:10). But in the next chapter he puts the opposition and resistance of the nations in the perspective of God's providence: "We are proclaiming . . . the living God, who made the heaven, the earth, the sea, and everything in them. In past generations He allowed all the nations to go their own way, although He did not leave Himself without a witness" (Acts 14:15–17).

> *As we move further into the twenty-first century, a sovereign God is moving through global events to open doors once closed to the gospel.*

God Is Moving through Global Events

We need to recognize and affirm our confidence in the *providence* of God. That word comes from two Latin words, *video* meaning "to see," and the prefix *pro* meaning "beforehand." God is able to see beforehand all that happens in our lives and in the world, and He is able to establish a plan of how it can be used for His purpose and His glory. We are assured, "All the nations You have made will come and bow down before You, Lord, and will honor

Your name" (Ps. 86:9). The prophet Haggai declared that day when God would shake the heavens and earth, overthrow earthly powers, and destroy the kingdoms of the world. "I will shake all the nations. . . . I will overturn royal thrones and destroy the power of the Gentile kingdoms" (Hag. 2:7, 22). God is fulfilling that word of prophecy today as He is shaking the nations and overthrowing powers of governments that have long stood in the way of His kingdom.

Jesus declared the ultimate outcome of God's mission as He defined the responsibility of His followers to make disciples of all nations. Mark would describe the task as no less than to "go into all the world and preach the gospel to the whole creation" (Mark 16:15). Luke would express this mandate of our Lord in terms of faithfully witnessing "to the ends of the earth" (Acts 1:8). And Jesus said, "This good news of the kingdom will be proclaimed in all the world as a testimony to all nations. And then the end will come" (Matt. 24:14). I (Jerry) believe these declarations incited Satan to intensify the warfare against the kingdom of God as never before. He recognized the authority of the Son of God and the inevitable fulfillment of His words. He understood the implication of the end-times when he and all his demonic host would be cast into outer darkness and the lake of fire. Jesus was prophesying that final victory when He would return and Satan would no longer deceive the nations; all his wickedness and evil would come to an end.

When I played high school football, I recall nothing infuriated our team and stirred our resolve as a challenging and condescending statement by someone on the opposing team. On one occasion we were having a mediocre season at best and were facing an undefeated team in our next game. The coach of the opposing team was quoted in an interview as saying that this would be an easy victory in which they would probably win by three touchdowns. Our coach put those comments on a poster over the door of our dressing room. All week as we went out to practice, we were confronted with the arrogant words of our opponents. Our players would slap the poster as they exited to practice each day; we were fired up to apply ourselves with maximum effort in every drill by that challenge. We were unified, aggressive, and motivated to play above our normal skills, infuriated by the presumption of victory by our opponent.

I can picture such a reaction from Satan to Jesus' confident affirmation of victory for His coming kingdom and the fact that the gospel would be proclaimed in the whole world as a testimony to all nations. But Jesus stated a contingency that the end-times and final judgment would not come until a Christian witness had touched all nations. That resulted in Satan resolving to do everything in His power to inhibit such a worldwide witness from becoming a reality. The confident declaration of our Lord continues to incite Satan to do all he can to keep nations closed to a Christian witness, to delay the inevitable final judgment and the potential of people from every nation and people being represented around the throne of God.

> *The confident declaration of our Lord that the gospel will be preached in the whole world incites Satan to keep nations closed to a Christian witness.*

For several centuries the Mongol Empire stretched across what is now Central Asia and the hinterlands of Russia. Arising out of the barbaric aggression of Attila the Hun, the empire reached into Southwest Asia and much of China. By the second millennium of Christian history, the Syrian church had spread eastward, and there is an abundance of archeological evidence of the Nestorian sect throughout China. Tamerlane, often known as Timur the Great, was the Mongol emperor that arose in the fourteenth century. He was the nephew of the great warrior Kublai Khan and one of the most cruel and despotic leaders in the history of the empire. He determined to eliminate a Christian presence in his kingdom and proceeded to massacre communities of believers, destroy churches, and burn Bibles and Christian literature. By his death in 1405, he had successfully fulfilled His mission to obliterate any vestige of the Christian faith. The region was already being influenced by Arab traders and Muslim feudal lords spreading the Islamic faith.

The tomb of Tamerlane, an impressive blue mosque like structure, is located in Samarkand, an historic city in Southern Uzebekistan. One of our early missionaries, who arrived in the city for language study during the period of political disruption and change in the early 1990s, was familiar with the history of the region and the impact of this ruler in decimating a Christian presence almost six hundred years earlier. While touring the city, he walked up to the tomb and announced in a lilting tone, "We're back!" And a Christian witness is back, indeed!

God has used hundreds of years of spiritual darkness to create a hunger in the hearts of people for what only Jesus can provide. In His providence He allowed an atheistic ideology in the twentieth century to erode the resistance of a Muslim stronghold for seventy years. He then brought an open door through political freedoms to extend His kingdom in what, for too long, had been Satan's dominion. For seventy years Satan thought that his strategy was succeeding as he kept the Soviet Union and Eastern Europe sealed behind the iron curtain of communism.

I (Jerry) grew up as a boy hearing frequent prayers lifted in church for those behind the iron curtain, a barrier for Christian witness for generations. But now global events have flung open the door of opportunity beyond what anyone would have imagined. In 1989 the Berlin Wall fell, and a sequence of events caused the monolithic Soviet Union to disintegrate. *Glasnost* brought a new era of openness and thousands of missionaries, and Christian volunteers swept into Eastern Europe, joining forces with a remnant of persecuted Russian believers to proclaim the good news of the kingdom.

Satan, the great deceiver, thought his strategy was working as he used Karl Marx, Lenin, Stalin, and others to propagate a godless society. They, and subsequent Soviet rulers, subjugated the nations of Eastern Europe and barricaded peoples from freely hearing the hope of the gospel. An older generation today can never forget stories of brutality that slipped out of the former Soviet Union during the cruel Stalin regime in which millions of writers, teachers, artists, and religious leaders were swept away by what Alexander Solzhenitsyn described as the Soviet sewage disposal system. Those who were not shot outright disappeared into the vast Gulag camp network in Siberia. Long before the terror reached its height in the 1930s, Stalin deliberately engineered a terror famine in the Ukraine that starved up to seven million human beings in order to impose collective farming and crush a proud people. Whole nationalities were deported from their homelands, forcibly resettled, and driven into the frozen wilderness.

But God in His providence and timing was simply waiting for the opportune moment to assert His sovereignty when hearts would be prepared to turn to Him. It should remind us that in troubled times God still rules the nations despite the men who try to break them. He doesn't cause the suffering inflicted by despots, but He brings good out of it for His purposes. As we recall the intrigue of those who smuggled Bibles into Eastern Europe and heard tales of believers assembling at night in the forest to baptize new believers, we need to realize a spiritual vacuum was being created into which the fresh wind of the gospel would eventually blow.

In the fall of 2009, we were celebrating the twentieth anniversary of the fall of the Berlin Wall. Many will recall watching the evening news, spellbound as jubilant Berliners danced upon the wall the night of November 9, 1989. East Berliners were flowing through Brandenburg Gate uninhibited. A news reporter asked the exuberant crowd, "Who is responsible for this new day of freedom?" They began to shout, "Gorby! Gorby!" in honor of the Soviet premier, Mikhail Gorbachev. Yes, God used political pressures and global leaders to precipitate such events, but they didn't have a clue to the divine power behind these events.

An American evangelist had described the austere scene in the years before when this wall was constructed to hold an entire nation captive. The Berlin Wall dominated the landscape; buildings behind it were dark with their windows bricked up and sealed. Spotlights lit up every square inch of open ground with guard towers placed strategically along the perimeter. Yet, now, this evangelist tells about singing "Amazing Grace" with Russian believers inside the walls of the Kremlin, preaching in community centers in provincial cities and witnessing to Russian Army officers in the Moscow subway!

Recently a tiny group of aging Russians gathered in front of the redbrick edifice of the Lenin Museum in Moscow to celebrate the glory of communism and to bemoan the end of the Soviet Empire. As they shouted, "Death to capitalism," and marched around Red Square, few seemed to pay attention to them. Meanwhile crowds of families, tourists, wedding parties, and stylishly dressed women with cell phones and shopping bags continued about their business. Not far away in a public park, Christian worshippers gathered on the banks of a canal to watch as two new believers were immersed openly in the chilly water. Afterward, the small congregation sang and took part in the Lord's Supper.

Mikhail Chekalin is a leader among an association of Baptist churches in Moscow. He is the grandson of a Baptist pastor shot for his faith under Stalin's reign of terror. He relishes the new freedoms that have come. As he reflects on an estimated eight thousand evangelical believers in the city, he says, "It is wide open. We can do evangelism without being reprimanded. We can witness openly, preach in the streets, and start churches without problems. People are searching for Christ, and God has inspired us with a new opportunity to reach them."

Albania had been the most atheistic country in the world, prohibiting any form of religious expression, including token exhibits of Orthodox Christianity or the historical Islamic practices common to its culture. Immediately after the collapse of the Soviet Union, missionary teams were sweeping into Albanian villages showing the *Jesus* film and bringing a message of hope to the spiritually starved people. Romanian churches had stood firm in their faith, enduring horrendous persecution throughout the Soviet era. But once the pendulum swung, evangelists and pastors poured across the border sharing the gospel in Moldova, Belarus, Yugoslavia, and the Ukraine.

I (Jerry) recall sharing at a mission conference when our organization had just sent our first missionary into Albania. A lady approached me after the service; emotionally and tearfully she asked me repeatedly, "Do we really have a missionary in Albania? Do we really have a missionary in Albania?" I assured her that we did.

Then she related how God had disturbed her deeply as she read about the atheistic and oppressive policies of the Albanian government several years earlier. She said that she had asked a ladies group at her church to join her in praying for Albania. Then she added, "For seven years we have been praying for Albania; I can't believe our prayers are being answered." There is no question in my mind that God moved in response to those prayers to open Albania to the gospel. He tells us to pray for the nations, not because He is incapable of intervening and changing societies but because He has chosen His people to be a part and involved as an instrument of His mission through witness and prayer. He said, "Ask of Me, and I will make the nations Your inheritance and the ends of the earth Your possession" (Ps. 2:8).

A missionary strategy coordinator in the Ukraine reported that believers started twelve hundred churches in the eight-year period immediately after the fall of communism. That is 150 per year! Well over ten thousand baptisms were reported each year, as those deprived of hope discovered a new life in Jesus Christ. Now Baptists in the Ukraine have become the forefront of a movement sending missionaries to Kazakhstan and other Central Asian republics.

Globalization and Technology

Although there are massive population segments that have yet to be touched with the gospel and significant numbers of unreached people groups, there is no nation that has not been penetrated with a Christian witness. The artificial boundaries of geographic, political entities cannot be fortified against emerging technology producing diverse and accessible tools of communication.

Bill Bright, the founder and past president of Campus Crusade for Christ, was an amazing visionary who challenged and mobilized Christians in innovative approaches of saturation evangelism, not only on college campuses but in cities and population segments throughout the world. More than thirty years ago he led in the production of the *Jesus* film. With a script based on the actual text of the Gospel of Luke, the film portrayed the life of Christ in a dramatic and universally cultural presentation. Campus Crusade used advanced technology to translate and produce the film in multiple languages. Isolated tribal groups in Africa would jump and dance for joy upon seeing the film, shouting, "Jesus speaks our language!" People who had never been exposed to the Bible and the message of the gospel would be deeply moved by the graphic portrayal of the crucifixion and the injustice of Jesus' suffering, then applaud with jubilation when He arose from the grave. Videos and DVDs were mass produced, and clandestine distribution enabled them to be viewed in countries closed to a missionary presence.

Working with the Billy Graham Evangelistic Association, Bright and his Campus Crusade staff produced a satellite broadcast that reached every nation. Internet accessibility has exploded throughout the world so that the most isolated people in restricted totalitarian countries are being exposed to Western ideas and expanded worldviews, including a Christian witness. Satan can poison the minds of men and influence power-hunger, self-serving rulers, but his strategies to keep countries closed to the good news of the kingdom seems to be vulnerable to modern technology.

Globalization has opened previously isolated peoples in closed nations to new ideas and concepts beyond their protected provincial worldviews. Travel and immigration have exposed the world to Western cultures and with it a Christian message. It would be difficult to find any people group not represented by a remnant community in the United States. Those who hear and respond to the gospel—and whose lives are changed by discovering a personal, redemptive relationship with Jesus Christ—invariably transmit this good news back to the network of family and friends in their place of cultural origin. In spite of government restrictions, legal barriers, and the lack of a missionary presence, God's Word is reaching the nations in a "flat world."

Mission historians considered the regime of Mao Tse Tung and the communist takeover of China following World War II as one of the most tragic setbacks to Christian missions of all time. Many missionaries were interred in prison camps; and some, such as Bill Wallace, were martyred. By 1950 all had been deported, and one of the most prominent mission fields in the world was closed. However, many of these missionary personnel were redeployed and opened new fields of work. Missionary witness was established in countries such as Indonesia, Thailand, Malaysia, and Singapore while other displaced China missionaries strengthened the work in Taiwan and the Philippines.

As the New Testament church grew in Jerusalem, God allowed persecution to intensify, and the believers were forced to leave the comfort and security of the birthplace of the church. It is easy, and perhaps natural, for Christians to be drawn into a fortress mentality enjoying fellowship with fellow believers, but God's intent is that our witness be spread abroad. Our Lord will go to any extent as sovereign over the nations to fulfill His purpose of being exalted throughout the earth.

"On that day a severe persecution broke out against the church in Jerusalem, and all except the apostles were scattered throughout the land of Judea and Samaria" (Acts 8:1). An inordinate focus on China in the nineteenth century and first half of the twentieth century had resulted in neglect of the larger Great Commission task, so God has used closed doors on traditional fields to give mission agencies a renewed global vision. The terrible global conflagration of World War II gave Americans an expanded awareness of our world. The rural provincialism of those sent to battlefields in the Pacific, across Europe and Northern Africa was changed. Confronted with a world devastated by war and suffering, not only in need of rebuilding their societies but desperate for spiritual hope, Americans responded to a missionary call. In the 1950s and 1960s the number of countries being served by Southern Baptist missionaries alone actually tripled.

While that growing missionary witness expanded in Asia to Thailand, Malaysia, Indonesia, the Philippines, Japan, and Korea, China became more isolated under growing communist domination. However, after the relative brief time of a few decades, seeds of the gospel planted in the harsh spiritual climate of China continued to bear fruit. Even the repressive cruelty of the Red Guards imposing persecution in the mid-1980s could not squelch the life-transforming power innate in the hope of the gospel.

For more than a century Christians had proclaimed God's Word, initially in the coastal cities and later in interior provinces following the initiative of the China Inland Mission. As many as one million believers reflected the fruit of these labors when the missionaries left and the new Peoples Republic of China sought to force socialism and an atheistic ideology upon the people. However, years later, communication and response from those within the country to continuing radio broadcasts indicated an underground Christian movement that was gaining momentum. Today most researchers agree that the number of Christian believers in China exceeds a hundred million!

While attending a meeting of Southern Baptist personnel in East Asia, I listened intently as a researcher explained that relationships had been developed with seven of more than twenty house church networks. Although many others were rather small and provincial, these networks were multiplying throughout the nation. Westerners may see these as we would view various denominations, but it was more the retention of relationships and nurturing leadership networks than doctrinal distinctions that characterized these groups. Southern Baptists in America take pride in being the largest evangelical denomination in America, but, it was reported, not one but three of these house-church networks were each larger than the Southern Baptist Convention with more than sixteen million mem-

> *Satan can use government restrictions and atheistic worldviews, but his strongholds cannot stand against the life-transforming power of the gospel.*

bers. The government does not recognize or report these nonregistered Christian groups and, in fact, continues to harass members, threaten and arrest pastors, and use social and economic repercussions to deter Christian growth. In the meantime, China has become one of the most evangelized nations in the world! Satan can use government restrictions and atheistic worldviews, but his strongholds cannot stand against the life-transforming power of the gospel!

Suffering and Human Needs Open the Door

I (Jerry) recently had the unexpected privilege of preaching at the first open, government-sanctioned gathering of Baptists in Vietnam. Memories are still fresh in the minds of many Americans of the tragic years of military engagement in Indo-China and the subsequent communist takeover and domination of Vietnam, Cambodia, and Laos. Millions of citizens were killed by the terrorist reign of Pol Pot and the Khmer Rouge in Cambodia, including not only Christians but anyone who was educated or identified with foreign influences. However, changing circumstances, modernization, and the pressure of international relations have produced amazing openness among a society hungry for spiritual truth and assurance.

Initial Christian workers, responding to a destitute society in Cambodia and the need for social ministries and rehabilitation, were restricted as foreigners in being allowed an overt witness or identifying openly with a surviving remnant of Christian believers. But the love they demonstrated and the power of an incarnational witness in the midst of such spiritual hunger found a response. Building relations and explaining the motives for their ministry resulted in twenty-four house churches being established in the capital city of Phnom Penh within two years. After two more years, these churches had multiplied into forty congregations throughout the country. Five years later there were more than three hundred churches with thousands of baptized believers, and today their witness continues to multiply openly.

What is the explanation for such receptivity and growth in a resistant Buddhist stronghold and in the context of a restrictive socialist government? The people found that their ancient Buddhist faith had no answers or hope for the suffering and atrocities experienced in the genocide of the Pol Pot era. And, in a classic understatement, one pastor explained the response by saying, "The poor don't get much good news." When people, impoverished economically without anything to hope for in this life, hear of the hope and assurance that can be found in Jesus Christ, it readily overcomes religious and cultural barriers in which Satan has held the people in bondage for generations.

With a population of eighty-five million, Vietnam is emerging as an economic power in Southeast Asia. As they compete for world trade, they are beginning to understand that human rights and religious freedoms are expected in the global community. In spite of a strong commitment to socialistic ideology, they are taking a pragmatic approach and tolerance of human rights, allowing churches to register and meet openly after years of restriction. Free from threats and intimidation, house-church networks have been able to emerge and meet together openly. More than three hundred Baptist churches have been planted during the previous thirty years of repressive religious policies.

The reclusive kingdom of Bhutan, tucked away in the Himalayas between Nepal, China, and Northwest India represented a formidable barrier geographically as well as limited access to foreigners. In Bhutan it is necessary for one to pledge adherence to the Buddhist religion in order to buy land, get a job, or enroll children in school. Receiving permission for a cultural documentary, a film team from a Christian media group was able to spend a couple of weeks in the country. The government-assigned tour guide wanted to know why they did not go to the bars and drink in the evening after an exhausting day of travel and work as other Western tourists did. This gave an opportunity for them to explain their Christian faith and convictions. Upon hearing this testimony, they were surprised at her response as she said, "That's what my father believes." The media crew discovered that he was a part of dozens of groups of secret believers throughout the country. Lay evangelists from Nepal had persisted in crossing the mountainous barrier between the two countries at great risks in order to share the gospel in this closed country.

Satan's strategy to use totalitarian governments and ideologies to keep countries closed to the gospel is not working. Government restrictions and persecution cannot inhibit the advance of the gospel when, in God's providence and timing, He determines to advance His kingdom among the nations. In fact, there are those in the Muslim world who would say that two men used to open the hearts of Muslims to the gospel are Ayatollah Khomenei and Saddam Hussein! The Ayatollah took

> *Islamic fanaticism manifested in terrorist bombings has brought disillusionment to millions who realize this is not the path.*

control of Iran and imposed religious vigilantism on society; along with the tyranny of Saddam Hussein, the depraved nature of Islam was revealed. In the name of religion, these and others have carried out ethnic genocide and turned villages into killing fields and torture chambers. An era of Islamic fanaticism manifested through terrorist bombings and commitment to the destruction of life has brought disillusionment to millions who realize this is not the path they want to follow.

On September 11, 2001, Muslim hijackers flew planes into the Pentagon and the World Trade Center buildings in New York, killing thousands of Americans. A pattern of terrorist activities has continued to spread from the Middle East across Asia, Africa, and into European cities. Suicide bombers are deluded to think they can gain entry into paradise by the destruction of life. Missionaries throughout the Muslim heartland of Northern Africa and the Turkic-Persian world say people are asking questions that reflect a search for hope and security—questions that can only be answered by Jesus Christ.

The majority of residents in Saudi Arabia and the United Arab Emirates, a region that is the center and bedrock guardians of the Muslim faith, are not Arab Muslims but laborers flowing from the Philippines, South Asia, and the Far East. Although prohibited from open evangelistic witness and restricted in being able to gather for public worship, they are bringing their faith and Christian influence into areas deprived of the seed of the gospel for centuries. However, with the wealth of these oil-producing countries, its citizens are flying all over the world. They are sending their young people to school in America and Europe, locating families in the West where they manage investments and direct multinational companies. From countries that remain relatively closed to the gospel, God is using globalization to disperse them where they can be exposed to a Christian witness.

Several years ago while traveling throughout this Islamic stronghold, I (Jerry) received communication from one of our local contacts preparing for our visit. His cryptic message said, "When you come, bring more seeds as many gardens are being planted." My initial reaction was to think what kinds of seeds was he requesting. I didn't realize he was engaged in an agricultural ministry! Then I realized he was asking for Bibles as we had received reports of numerous house groups being started by local people hungry for God's Word.

Upon our arrival, a foreign worker told about a policeman coming to his house, which was unnerving because they knew he and his family were under constant surveillance. The policeman assured him there was no problem and then explained why he had come. He related that he was the duty officer at the local police precinct at night, and one of his responsibilities was to check the inventory. In one of the storerooms he found stacks of Bibles that had been confiscated. He went on to explain that he wondered why that book was so dangerous that His government would not let the people read it. Since he was the only one at the station in the early hours of the morning, out of curiosity he acknowledged he began to read one of those Bibles. Then he got to the purpose for his visit. He asked, "Can you tell me who this Jesus is I am reading about?"

At the ancient cultural crossroads of Europe and Asia, Turkey was the heart of the Ottoman Empire, the crown of Islam's golden age of conquest for more than six centuries. At its zenith its territory stretched from the gates of Vienna to the southern tip of Arabia. While its population today of seventy-two million people remain overwhelmingly Muslim, the government and military have become solidly secular, increasingly democratic, and Western oriented. The country is a member of NATO and has been seeking entry into the European Union for years. While Christians still number only a few thousand, that is significant progress from the few handfuls of secret believers and expatriates a few years ago. With 60 percent of its population under thirty years old, the people of Turkey are more interested in modern trends and making a good living than in preserving the ways of traditional Islam.

A few years ago I was traveling in the Middle East at the time Mel Gibson's film *The Passion of the Christ* had been released. While visiting Amman, Jordan, and the cities of Beirut and Damascus, I was amazed to see *The Passion of the Christ* being advertised and promoted on billboards and posters and being shown in public theaters. This is the heart of the Muslim world, and missionaries would be arrested for daring to show the *Jesus* film publicly. But officials got the impression that this film was anti-Semitic; so with their animosity toward the Jews, they readily allowed it to be viewed. The movie set box-office records. My friends told about sitting in crowded theaters and hearing burka-clad Muslim women weeping as they saw portrayed for the first time what Jesus had done to save them from their sins. A report from Kuwait indicated that no one was going to the other movies in a cinemaplex so they canceled them and put *The Passion of the Christ* on all ten screens. The DVDs of the movie were being pirated and distributed in Cairo, Baghdad, and Saudi Arabia. That was never in our strategic planning for mission work in the area. It is a testimony of the sovereignty and providence of God who would have all men come to the knowledge of the truth and be saved!

Even natural disasters are being used to plant the gospel in countries and areas traditionally closed and hostile to a Christian presence. Many will recall in December 2005 the most destructive natural disaster in modern times when an earthquake-spawned tsunami devastated the coastlines of eight Asian nations. The tidal wave was generated off the Indonesian island of Sumatra and killed up to 230 thousand people. Many of these were in the province of Aceh, a fanatical Islamic region of the country, relatively autonomous and restricted to foreigners. Historical efforts to penetrate this area with a Christian witness had proven futile.

In the aftermath of the tsunami, it wasn't Muslim communities from abroad that responded to provide relief and development but Christians organizations and churches. They did not sweep into the area in a desire to capitalize on this tragedy, take advantage of traumatized people, and proselytize them to the Christian faith.

No, compelled by the love of Christ, they reached out to comfort and minister to those in need. However, such selfless sacrifice stirred the hearts of people. They wanted to know why they would come, freely dispense millions of dollars in relief supplies, and help them rebuild their homes and their lives. It opened the door to explain the love of God and the way to have a personal relationship with Him.

Destructive earthquakes in places like Pakistan, Iran, and Turkey, floods in China and Myanmar, a famine in North Korea, typhoons and tidal waves killing hundreds of thousands in Bangladesh and India have all resulted in destruction and a massive loss of life. In times of such need, philosophical worldviews and government restrictions that have kept people isolated from the rest of the world suddenly don't seem so important. Barriers are lifted, and doors are opened for God's people to be His instrument to declare His glory among the nations.

Isaiah described the strength and power of the Lord: "The Lord GOD comes with strength, and His power establishes His rule. . . . Who has measured the waters in the hollow of his hand or marked off the heavens. . . . Look, the nations are like a drop in a bucket; they are considered as a speck of dust on the scales" (Isa. 40:10, 12, 15).

In God's rebuke of Job, He reminds him of His creative power and sovereignty over nature and elements of the universe in these statements in chapters 36–38: "Where were you when I established the earth? Who fixed its dimensions? Who enclosed the seas? Who cuts a channel for the flooding rain or clears the way for lightning . . . or to satisfy the parched wasteland?" "God thunders marvelously with His voice; He does great things that we cannot comprehend. For He says to the snow, 'Fall to the earth,' and torrential rains, . . . serve as His signature to all mankind, so that all men may know His work" (Job 37:5–7). God declares, "Everything under heaven belongs to Me" (Job 41:11), and manifests His sovereignty in the natural realm that all men might know Him.

We are told, "The Lord does not delay His promise, . . . but is patient with you, not wanting any to perish, but all to come to repentance" (2 Pet. 3:9). He is using warfare, ethnic violence, political disruption, economic uncertainty, and natural disasters to open closed doors. Religious opposition and government restrictions cannot keep countries closed to a Christian witness when in His divine providence and power the fullness of time has come for "righteousness and praise to spring up before all the nations" (Isa. 61:11). Satan's strategy to keep nations fortified against God's message of redemption has been successful for centuries but is no longer working!

Going Deeper

1. Take some time to research nations and people groups that were at one time closed to the gospel. What factors led to open doors and those people coming to Christ?

2. Explore the issue of adoption.

3. What impact have global and national relief efforts had in spreading the gospel? Research places like www.imb.org, www.namb.org, Samaritan's Purse, and other religious organizations that offer physical relief in times of community crisis.

4. Find several countries that are currently closed to missionaries and begin a prayer group to intercede for those people. Pray that the gospel will find a path into the country.

CHAPTER 5

SATAN'S STRATEGY: KEEP PEOPLE GROUPS HIDDEN FROM OUR AWARENESS

It was not hearing a missionary speak in church or an emotional response to a call for commitment at a youth camp but in a junior high geography class that I (Jerry) felt God's call to missions. We were studying the peoples and countries of Asia, China in particular. I was overwhelmed by the incomprehensible largeness of population figures in the hundreds of millions. We learned something of their Confucian culture, the Buddhist religion, and the fact that the country had come under the grip of atheistic, communist philosophy.

The spiritual reality occurred to me that here were millions of people living a lifetime, dying, and going to hell, not because they had rejected Jesus Christ but because they had never heard of Him as the way, the truth, and the life. Being a church kid familiar with the missionary enterprise, I thought, *Why don't more missionaries go to tell these people the gospel so they would have an opportunity to be saved?* It was as if God reflected that thought back into my own heart to realize there was the potential in my life of going and telling people of Jesus who would not otherwise have an opportunity to hear.

I could never escape that impression, and God continued to confirm that this was, indeed, His will and calling for my life. When it came time, after college and seminary training, for my wife and me to be appointed as missionaries, we were confronted with the decision of choosing the country to which we would be assigned. I had traveled to the Philippines, Hong Kong, and Japan on a student summer missions assignment; there were personnel needs in each of those places and no lack of people needing to hear the gospel. We were impressed initially that we were to go to India where Southern Baptists were just beginning mission work; however, because that was limited to medical work, we were unable to get visa approval to live and work in the country. Praying for God's direction, we were led to accept an assignment in Indonesia where missionaries were seeing a phenomenal harvest after an aborted communist coup. In spite of this being the country with the largest Muslim population in the world, multitudes were responding to the proclamation of the gospel, and additional church planters were needed.

The specific location of our assignment had not been determined. We were to spend a year in language study, make some survey trips and, in consultation with mission leaders, determine where we would live. Most of our missionary colleagues were stationed on the island of Java among the greatest concentration of the population. The primary criteria for our assignment was to go where people were responding, and that was among the Javanese in the Central and Eastern part of the island. Though Indonesia was a relatively new country with a common national language, we were aware of a vast diversity of ethnic groups and local languages. Most of them were known as being fanatical in their Muslim faith, so we were to avoid wasting time in those areas. Besides, it would be somewhat risky for a Christian missionary to live among some of them as well as possibly incurring the wrath of the government.

The strategy was to find people who were responsive and pour our efforts into planting churches among them. Upon moving to our assignment in East Java, we discovered the dominant people group there were Madurese. These people had migrated from the nearby island of Madura and are still one of the largest unreached people groups in the world. Not only were they fanatical in their practice of Islam; they were known to be a violent people who carried machetes and were antagonistic toward Christians. In the years of ensuing work, whenever I encountered a Madurese community, I would quickly move on in my search for the more responsive Javanese. I recall one of my colleagues challenging our leadership to consider placing personnel among the Minangkabau on the island of Sumatra. The request to engage this strong Muslim people group was rebuffed as being a waste of personnel and resources.

We later became aware that more than nine hundred distinct ethnic and tribal groups occupied the six thousand island archipelago that made up Indonesia, most of them with their own language and distinct territory. A few had been evangelized during the four hundred years of Dutch colonial control. The Ambonese and Minahasa had been Christianized in the Molucca chain of islands, and German missionaries had eventually evangelized the Batak on Sumatra, after the first two evangelists had been eaten by cannibals. The island of Flores had long been a Catholic enclave. The Balinese retained a syncretized version of their ancient Hindu practices, and innumerable isolated tribal groups on Kalimantan (Borneo) and Irian Jaya still lived in their primitive animistic cultures. But most of the peoples had, for centuries, embraced the teachings of Arab and Malay traders as followers of Mohammed, devoted to Allah.

In spite of a rich missionary history and impressive results, large numbers of the peoples of Indonesia have yet to hear the gospel today. Though many are aware of the Christian religion in this pluralistic nation, one would not find a follower of Christ among them. Ache, on the northern tip of Sumatra, is identified as the front porch of Mecca, so fanatical are its people and closed to outside influence. The Banjar, Bugis, Makassarese, Osing, Komering, Pasemah, Sasak, and Sundanese barely begin the listing of unreached people groups in a country considered open and responsive by mission strategists.

Meanwhile, Indonesia would have been one of the countries on mission maps colored in as being evangelized due to the presence of missionary personnel proclaiming the gospel. The historical mission objective had been to plant a Christian witness in as many countries as possible. There had been more than a millennium of benign neglect of the Great Commission from the Christianization of the Roman Empire in the early fourth century until the age of European explorers and colonization. Catholic Orders followed the Spanish Conquistadors to establish mission outposts in the New World, but William Carey's departure to India in 1793 launched the modern missionary movement and revitalized an awareness of Christians' responsibility to disciple the nations, and nations as we know them became the target.

Southern Baptists focused their initial efforts on China, later sending missionaries to Nigeria and Italy; Mexico and Brazil soon followed until, after a hundred years of mission efforts, twenty-seven countries were being targeted. The number of countries being served grew gradually but later exploded with a new global awareness following World War II. Until recent years, advance in global evangelization was measured in the number of countries in which missionaries served and churches were being planted. Southern Baptists eventually counted 134 countries on their mission maps, excluding those which were "Christian," missionary-sending countries and those which were closed to a missionary presence. Little thought was given to the vast numbers of ethnic-linguistic people groups that are yet to be untouched by the gospel.

The Discovery of a People-Group Focus

Missiologist Donald McGavran, with the School of World Missions at Fuller Theological Seminary in Pasadena, California, began to draw attention to the nature of the Great Commission in the context of sociological groups of ethnic peoples. In his landmark book, *Bridges of God* (1955), he highlighted the fact that evangelistic movements in India followed ethnicity. The gospel spread, often to the fringes of people of similar language and caste but did not bridge into other peoples, even though they might be intertwined geographically in the same area. Ethnicity is what makes a distinction of "we" and "they." If you are a part of a homogeneous people who have the same language, culture, and ethnic origin, you would relate as "we" in contrast to others who have a different language and culture. Ethnicity often determines unspoken norms of marriage and communal relationship; it is also a factor in discrimination and strained relationships with other races and cultures. People groups tend to reside in common geographic areas, but even if they are widespread, their ethnicity represents stronger ties than relationships with other near neighbors. Even in large cities, which become a matrix of multiple people groups, those with similar backgrounds and kinship tend to live in ghettos and communities with their own kind of people.

Not surprising, the gospel tends to follow lines of these relationships. In fact, the gospel may find a receptivity and permeate an entire people and not even touch another ethnic or language group living and interacting in the same vicinity. Though tens of thousands of people in India were coming to faith in Christ, McGavran pointed out that it was exclusively among the Telugu. This is what has happened on other historic mission fields like Nigeria as the gospel spread among the Yoruba and in Indonesia as it spread among the Javanese. Mission strategists have simplified the definition in reference to our task of global evangelism by saying, "People groups are those of common ethnic

> *People groups are those of common ethnic identity and relationships through which the gospel can spread without encountering a barrier.*

identity and relationships through which the gospel can spread without encountering a barrier." If a Christian witness must bridge to another language or cross from "us" to "them," it normally distinguishes separate people groups.

The late Dr. Ralph Winter made a presentation at the Lausanne Conference in 1974 highlighting what he called "hidden peoples." The conference, sponsored by the Billy Graham Evangelistic Association, brought together evangelical denominations and mission leaders from all over the world to discuss collaboration in advancing toward the fulfillment of the Great Commission. Winter brought to the attention of those in attendance that, in spite of tremendous advance in global evangelization in the latter half of the twentieth century, most of the peoples of the world remained untouched and neglected in our mission efforts and strategies. One of his primary premises was to point out how we had misinterpreted the concept of "nations" in the Great Commission mandate to refer to the political states or countries on our maps.

Actually, the reality of nation-states with geographic borders, ruled by a common government, is a rather modern development in world history. In the colonial era of the last few centuries, countries were delineated on the map, many with artificial and arbitrary borders. When the King James Version of the Bible was translated in 1611, "nations" was the appropriate and accurate word to mean ethno-linguistic people groups. That understanding has been carried over in reference to Native American tribal groups. These are still referred to as the Apache Nation, the Choctaw or Cherokee Nation, or Sioux or Navajo Nation.

The instruction of Jesus to His followers in Matthew 28:19 was to make disciples—to win to faith, bring into the kingdom, and teach to become followers of Christ—the *panta ta ethne*—all the "ethnos" or peoples of distinct ethnic languages and cultures in the entire world. It is the same terminology used by Jesus in Matthew 24:14 when He alluded to the future reality of the gospel being proclaimed to all nations, literally *"panta ta ethne"* (all peoples). And it is the same terminology used to portray the ultimate fulfillment when "a vast multitude from every nation, tribe, people, and language, which no one could number" (Rev. 7:9) would be represented around the throne worshipping the Lamb of God.

A Biblical Understanding of Our Mission

Tribe, *people*, and *nation* are terms carried over from the Old Testament referring to extended families, clans, and entire *ethnos*. The call of Abraham and God's covenant in Genesis 12:3 included the promise: "all the peoples on earth will be blessed through you." In several places in the Old Testament, Israel, as God's mission people, was to "declare God's glory among the nations." The psalmist captured this universal purpose of God which was to be reaffirmed by Jesus in the Great Commission: "All the ends of the earth will remember and turn to the LORD. All the families of the nations will bow down before You, for kingship belongs to the LORD; He rules over the nations" (Ps. 22:27–28). "All the nations You have made will come and bow down before You, Lord, and will honor Your name" (Ps. 86:9).

The Hebrew word for "nations" used in these instances and other places in the Old Testament is *goyem*. It is translated by the Greek Septuagint as *ethnos;* in fact, the covenant promise to Abraham is translated *panta ta ethne* just as it is in the Great Commission. The word *Gentiles* also is sometimes translated "nations" but actually refers to all peoples or *ethnos* who are not of the Jewish people. The expression *panta ta ethne* is used more than a hundred times in the Old Testament, clearly revealing God's mission to be worshipped, exalted, and glorified by all peoples in all the earth. This carries special significance in the compelling mission of Paul and others in the New Testament to take the gospel to the Gentiles.

Jesus put His own death and resurrection in proper perspective relative to the Great Commission in His explanation to His disciples in Luke 24:46–47: "This is what is written [referring to the Old Testament]: the Messiah would suffer and rise from the dead

> *The word "nations" from the Abrahamic covenant to the Great Commission refers not to collective individuals or countries but to the vast diversity of ethno-linguistic people groups throughout the world.*

the third day, and repentance for forgiveness of sins would be proclaimed in His name to all the nations, beginning at Jerusalem." His atoning work on the cross was not just for the benefit of those, such as us, who have the privilege of hearing and believing; it was to give us a message of salvation to proclaim to all peoples.

Interestingly, a similar link of Jesus with God's expressed mission was in Mark 11:17 when He quoted Isaiah 56:7 to say, "My house will be called a house of prayer for all nations."

I (Jerry) confess I have used that passage as an exhortation for churches to pray for the nations and for mission efforts to reach all peoples. However, the house of God was to represent the place His people would meet with Him to worship and commune with Him. That place was intended to be for all peoples.

All of these words, by their nature and meaning, do not refer to people in terms of collective individuals but as groupings of ethnic and linguistic peoples. This is important as we look at one of Satan's deceptions that has led many to interpret our mission as winning as many individuals as possible while neglecting God's intended purpose of declaring the gospel to all peoples.

Only recently has it been recognized in terms of missiological implications that the world is a waffle, not a pancake. If you pour syrup on a pancake, it will likely flow all over the smooth round surface, but not so with a waffle. A waffle has a multitude of small squares separated by ridges. If you want syrup on your waffle, you have to be deliberate to pour syrup into each square. The world is not made up of homogenous people who are all alike and speak the same language. The world is a vast matrix of more than eleven thousand distinct languages and cultures, separated by ethnic identity. If each one is to hear the gospel, mission efforts must be deliberate to pour the syrup of the gospel into each one in a culturally appropriate way and in a language people can understand.

We used to think sending a missionary to Yugoslavia was evangelizing the country of Yugoslavia. But with the fall of Communist control in Eastern Europe and the splintering of the Soviet Union, we discovered there really wasn't a Yugoslavia. That country, like many others, was an artificial alignment of political borders. It had been made up of Serbs, Bosnians, Slovenian, Macedonian, Croats, and Kosovars, and it was evident all those peoples—some Catholic, some Orthodox, and others Muslim—didn't like one another. There was ancestral enmity between them that went back for centuries. Evangelizing one of them did not facilitate the gospel spreading to other peoples with a different language and culture and antagonistic attitudes toward one another. Bosnians had no respect for Serbs and would not listen to them. Kosovars would have been unresponsive to efforts of Croats to influence them to consider the Christian faith.

Mission leaders look to Nigeria as a successful example of historical mission efforts. In 1999 I (Jerry) attended a celebration of the one-hundredth anniversary of Baptist mission work in that country. Several thousand Baptists from all over the country gathered in a stadium in Abeokuta for the occasion. Included in that gathering was president Obasanjo, himself a Baptist who had been educated in mission schools. Over the years Christian hospitals and schools had made a remarkable impact on winning people to the Lord and nurturing church growth. After a hundred years Baptists were claiming more than a million members in seven thousand churches in that country—primarily among the Yoruba and Hausa people. Researchers could still identify more than two hundred tribal groups in Nigeria in which there were no churches and no Christian witness.

The Great Commission was not intended to result in disciples being made in Senegal, West Africa, but for the Lebou, the Sereer, the Wolof, Fulbe, Mandika, and others to be brought to faith, baptized, and taught to be followers of Christ. God did not intend for us just to win Pakistanis to the Lord but to persist in the task until the Baluchi, Sindhi, Punjabi, Hazara, and Pushtu had become discipled and a part of the kingdom of God. It was 1997 before the International Mission Board began to focus on people groups. We did not even know how many distinct people groups were being engaged with the gospel through our presence and evangelistic efforts in about 130 countries. Research later revealed that we had, after 150 years of global mission efforts, engaged only 338 people groups among the more than eleven thousand researchers identified throughout the world!

Satan's Distortion of Our Mission Task

Did Satan have anything to do with keeping the nature of our Great Commission task obscure? Nineteenth-century missionaries made bold and sacrificial efforts to plant the gospel on African soil, across Asia, and throughout Latin America. Churches were established that became the foundation for future indigenous growth. Only later was there an organized effort to push beyond the primary coastal cities into the foreboding interior of colonial territories; hence, the formation of organizations such as the China Inland Mission, Sudan Interior Mission, and African Inland Mission. Still the intention was to evangelize ever larger swatches of territory with little regard for the distinctions of the people who populated these countries.

McGavran had described those who failed to see church growth in terms of homogeneous groups as being in a fog. Winter clarified the concept of "hidden peoples" as those that were hidden from our awareness in our passionate pursuit to be obedient to the Great Commission. After almost two thousand years of Christian history, we were so far from discipling the peoples of the world because we had focused strategies on geopolitical entities identified as countries on our maps. He wrote an article "Seeing the Task Graphically" in 1975 in which he blamed the problem on people blindness. It is not that all the ethnicities, races, languages, and people groups could not be readily seen but that we had chosen not to see them as integral to a strategy for fulfilling the Great Commission.

"A malady so widespread that it deserves a special name . . . let us call it people blindness, that is, blindness to the existence of separate peoples within countries . . . which prevents us from noticing the sub-groups within a country which are significant to the development of an effective evangelistic strategy. Until we recover from this kind of blindness we may confuse the legitimate desire for church or national unity with the illegitimate goal of uniformity" (Winter, 1975).

Did this just happen, or did the deceiver of the nations distort the thinking and perception of well-intended mission strategists? Could it be possible that the one who has the capacity to blind the hearts of the unbelieving lest they be saved could also blind our eyes to the nature of the task. Our enemy has a lot at stake in inhibiting the gospel being preached among all peoples, as his adversary, the Lord Jesus Christ, has declared that when that happens the end will come. Satan is doing all within his power to keep the good news from being proclaimed in all the world among the *panta ta ethne.* Obscuring the nature of our task in reaching all peoples has been one of his most effective strategies.

> *Has the deceiver of the nations distorted our thinking and blinded our eyes to the nature of the mission task?*

A major aspect of Satan's strategy is to convince us that the task of missions is to win as many souls to Christ as possible. Certainly God is not willing for any to perish but desires that all men come to repentance and the knowledge of the truth (cf. 1 Tim. 2:4). God has called us to the task of evangelism—proclaiming the gospel through any and every means; we are to be His witnesses to the ends of the earth. He is pleased and rejoices over every soul who repents and receives the salvation He provided on the cross. But populating heaven with as many believers as possible and snatching them from an eternity of torment in hell is not fulfilling God's mission of reaching the nations.

Several generations of missionaries in the last century fell victim to the lie that evangelism and missions were one and the same. One does not do missions without doing evangelism as the basic purpose of missions is to engage and win the lost. But one can actively engage in evangelism without doing missions since the focus of missions is to reach all peoples. How many multitudes among unreached people groups have died without Christ over the years because of neglect? They are lost for eternity not because they rejected the gospel or had no spiritual need that would lead them to embrace the gospel; they are lost because no one ever bothered to reach them with the good news that Jesus died for them, and salvation can be procured through faith in Him alone.

Missions and evangelism are not the same tasks. However, a true heartbeat for evangelism (all people) will result in an insatiable passion for missions (all people groups). I (Ed) fear what often drives churches to a single focus on evangelism is an unawareness of God's greater mission that reaches beyond our local community. When our heart is for all people to know Him, then we will understand the need to multiply evangelists in every people group rather than just witnesses in our locality. Step one to multiply evangelists is to win evangelists to faith in Jesus Christ. When we look at the overwhelming number of peoples (www.peoplegroups. org) worldwide, we should not say, "Let's go to the nations and win *souls* for Jesus." What we should say is, "Let's go to the nations and win *evangelists* for Jesus." The vision of Jesus for true engagement of the harvest is seen in Matthew, "Therefore, pray to the Lord of the harvest to send out workers into His harvest" (Matt. 9:38).

Notice Jesus' heart for souls is seen in His exhortation to pray for laborers, not souls. How could one possibly have a true passion for souls and not be driven by the desire for more laborers? The drive of the evangelist and missionary is knowing people are coming to faith in Christ, not the need to be present for each event when someone comes to Christ. Rather, knowing others have been called to the work is cause for celebration.

My (Ed) friend Neil Cole sheds light on the critical mind-set shift concerning missions and evangelism. Neil is a speaker, writer, and church planter from California (www.cmaresources.org). Neil said, "We have made a terrible mistake by separating the convert from the worker. They are not two, but one. . . . Each new convert is a new worker, immediately."[1] The shift in mind-set that says we are going to win evangelists to Christ frees us to a reckless abandonment to the people groups of the world.

Many faithful godly, evangelistically minded servants of God just do not grasp the scope of God's mission to which He has called us. I (Jerry) get letters critical of a mission strategy to engage unreached people groups with the gospel instead of places of open response. Some think it is a waste of resources for a missionary to go to an unresponsive Muslim country or where government restrictions limit open proclamation. They are apparently willing to relegate these people groups to hell without any effort to penetrate their spiritually deprived hearts with the hope that can be found in Christ. In fact, let news spread of an explosive harvest somewhere in the world, and pastors and evangelists will swarm to the area to get in on the action. There is pride in being able to report vast numbers responding to our witness. And let me remind you where pride comes from; it's not from God.

We could concentrate the more than five thousand missionaries serving with the International Mission Board into seven open and responsive foreign countries and could probably report twice as many baptisms of new believers coming to Christ as in our current annual reports. Mexico, Brazil, Nigeria, Kenya, India, the Philippines, and Korea have traditionally been places of harvest with many people being saved. But what would happen regarding the eternal destiny of more than ten thousand people groups in other countries in the world? Such a strategy would not only be a distortion of our mission but absolute negligence of the Great Commission, which is to win and disciple all peoples.

Jesus did not send us to declare the gospel only where people are responsive or where our witness is welcome. He did not expect us to be on mission to disciple peoples only where there is no danger or risk involved. He was unequivocal in His mandate to disciple the nations (peoples)—all of them! Romans 10:13 reminds us, "For everyone who calls on the name of the Lord will be saved." But this passage goes on to confront us with a sequence of important questions: "But how can they call on Him in whom they have not believed? And how can they believe without hearing about Him? And how can they hear without a preacher? And how can they preach unless they are sent" (Rom. 10:14–15)?

> *Jesus did not send us to declare the gospel only where people are responsive . . . or where no risk or danger is involved but to all peoples.*

God loves all people. Jesus died for them all. His heart yearns for all people to know and worship Him. He assures us that one day He will be exalted among all people. The focus of our mission task can be no less than that end—God being glorified among all people. If we are not to be misled by the archenemy of global evangelization, we must view the world as God does.

Another strategy Satan uses to keep people groups hidden, neglected, and unreached is our self-centered fleshly nature to create an ethnocentric approach to missions. Subsequent chapters will reveal how Christians around the world, particularly in America, have become provincial, focusing resources, energies, and concern on their own growth and welfare of their own members to the exclusion of other peoples. This was primarily the cause of Israel's downfall. It wasn't just because of their apostasy and backsliding, occasionally falling into the worship of Baal and other pagan religious practices that brought on God's punishment. They were rejected and punished, and they forfeited God's favor because of their disobedience and failure to fulfill His mission.

God reminded them through the prophet Isaiah, "It is not enough for you to be My servant raising up the tribes of Jacob and restoring the protected ones of Israel. I will also make you a light for the nations, to be My salvation to the ends of the earth" (Isa. 49:6). He had called them to be a mission people, not just to revel in their ethnocentric blessings. Churches have tended to focus on their own programs; the priority is growth among their own kind of people rather than recognizing it is God's intention for them to be a light to other peoples, races, and cultures.

This is reflected in a pattern of abandoning areas of one's city when it begins to be inhabited by migrant residents. Anglo-American churches relocate in the suburbs among their own kind of people when African-Americans, Hispanics, and Asians begin to populate their communities. Rather than welcoming this social change as an opportunity to fulfill God's mission, we discriminate against others by holding the good news tightly within our own fellowship. Instead, we should seek opportunities to exploit this development to share the gospel among those not like us. We no longer have to go overseas to reach all peoples; God is bringing them to America and into our communities, but we choose to be blind to the opportunities God has placed on our doorstep!

Do you realize that this was Jonah's problem in his disobedience and seeking to flee from God's will? It wasn't because he was afraid or just rebellious; he hated the people of Nineveh. He did not want God to save them. When he finally relented and declared God's message of judgment and they repented and turned to God, Jonah was angry. "But Jonah was greatly displeased and became furious. He prayed to the LORD: 'Please, LORD, isn't this what I said while I was still in my own country? That's why I fled toward

Tarshish in the first place. I knew that You are a merciful and compassionate God, slow to become angry, rich in faithful love, and One who relents from sending disaster'" (Jon. 4:1–2). Jonah was pleased to enjoy God's favor, but in discrimination he did not want the people of Nineveh to experience His compassion and love. Some Christians today actually do not think we should try to evangelize Muslims; they are so hated that many think they are deserving of hell. But aren't we all? Are we readily going to accept the grace of God in forgiveness of our sins and deny others that privilege due to our attitudes of racism and discrimination? Like Jonah, we neglect God's mission because of discrimination and ethnic pride.

> *Like Jonah, we neglect God's mission because of ethnic pride and discrimination toward others who are different.*

We are told in Acts 2 that there were "devout men from every nation under heaven" (Acts 2:5) gathered in Jerusalem on the day of Pentecost. There's that word again—every *nation*—not country but every ethnos or people group. There were Parthians, Medes, Elamites, Cretans, and Arabs, as well as peoples from Phrygia, Pamphylia, etc. These were not nationalities as determined by their country of citizenship but ethnic people groups. Their languages were distinctive. But what happened that notable day? Each of them heard the gospel in their own language because of the amazing work of the Holy Spirit, and this was God's desire.

Why should they be amazed at this occurrence? Had not Jesus just told them fifty days earlier they were to go and make disciples of all peoples? God was communicating through this event, "This is what I was talking about! I have brought them to you, so you could see what the Great Commission is all about. All peoples are to hear and understand the gospel in their own language." It was as if God were saying, "I have told you what to do. I have demonstrated the power of My Spirit to enable you to do it. Now get with it—be My witnesses to the ends of the earth."

We have done a disservice to the Great Commission in categorizing our mission task in stages of concentric circles. Since Jesus noted the witness of His disciples was to begin in Jerusalem, then spread throughout Judea and into Samaria, we have presumed that we are to follow the same progression of giving priority to our "Jerusalem" where we live. Then we are to extend our witness into the province beyond our community, or throughout our state, then eventually reach a larger geographic area of North America. Like the contrast between Jews and Samaritans, we are even to share the gospel cross-culturally. Eventually we are to take the gospel to the ends of the earth.

Satan used the Word of God to tempt Jesus to embrace a shortcut to fulfilling His messianic task. In the same way Satan has twisted this challenging, encouraging, empowering instruction of our Lord to get us to justify the distorted priority of just reaching people where we live and ignoring the responsibility of being witnesses to the ends of the earth among all peoples. Had Jesus yielded to Satan's deception, He would have forfeited God's plan for world redemption. Satan deceives us into thinking we are faithfully fulfilling the mission of God when in reality we are neglecting it!

In Acts 1:8, Jesus was outlining for the disciples the historical progression of the gospel about which we read in Acts. They did permeate Jerusalem and Judea with their witness. It spread through a lay revival in Samaria and the witness of Peter to Cornelius; now it remains to reach the ends of the earth. But we are to seek the gospel's impact in all places at all times by all possible means.

We need to remove any geographic conceptualization of the Great Commission. Many read Matthew 28:18 as a mandate for foreign missions since it is focused on the objective of the nations. We do evangelism at home and missions abroad. But we need to overlay Acts 1:8 on Matthew 28:19–20 as to "make disciples of all nations" means wherever they are. The ends of the earth are just as much the peoples of America as peoples in remote areas of Africa or Asia. Just as the disciples did not have to leave Jerusalem to reach the peoples from the ends of the earth, we need to open our eyes to the ends of the earth that are living in our own cities and communities. We have made the Great Commission to have a geographic focus that was never intended. To see the mission of God in terms of going to my own people first and maybe others after them is to run the risk of committing Jonah's ethnocentric sin and to fall into the same mistake that Israel made over and over again. And yes, the "ends of the earth" include our own people group identity—any who are not Jews and Samaritans.

Failure to replace "nation" or "nations" in our English translations of the Bible has led us to see the Great Commission as reaching foreign countries, a task for which most local churches are not prepared or practically equipped to accomplish. So this misunderstanding has distorted our thinking and continues to lead successive generations of Christians to misunderstand the task.

> *The ends of the earth are just as much the peoples of America as peoples in remote areas of Africa or Asia.*

The trend has been evident within every generation of Christians of churches becoming ethnocentric and geographically oriented by believing and demonstrating that priority in time, money, prayers, and programs should be given to their own people. The result is that little time and money are left to focus on the vast diversity of people groups in the church's vicinity and beyond. In our failure and lack of diligence to take the gospel to every tribe, language, and people group, we are assuming they will find some way to hear and respond on their own, but it is not our responsibility since that is not where we live. It is unrealistic to think that unsaved people will cross cultural and language barriers to follow a way of life embraced by those who are foreign and different from their own cultural traditions.

When the IMB began to organize mission strategies around a people group focus, understanding that people will respond and the gospel will more readily spread among homogeneous communities, this got an angry reaction from many around the world. Opponents of this position pointed out that the gospel was to break down these barriers and Christians were to be drawn together in unity by the Holy Spirit. That is certainly true when one comes to Christ and the Holy Spirit creates that fellowship of unity with other believers, regardless of race and ethnicity. However, it is unrealistic to think that a lost person would cross such barriers before being transformed by the redemptive power of Christ to make them a new creature.

Some African Baptist leaders pointed out how they were working hard to break down the tribalism that was rampant on the continent and has caused so much hatred, warfare, and suffering throughout history. Who can forget the horrible genocide of the Tutu and Hutsi in Rwanda as they slaughtered each other in bloody ethnic violence less than twenty years ago? They saw us as creating divisions and splintering the unity toward which they were striving. In those conversations in Nigeria, we pointed out that all of the leaders of the Baptist convention with whom we were conferring were Yoruba, and most of those in Kenya were Kikuyu. Many tribes in their countries had never been told the gospel and had no opportunity for the Holy Spirit to draw them into the unity of the body of Christ that those who were Christians enjoyed with their fellow tribesmen. The worst expression of tribalism is for one people group to receive the gospel and not share it with others!

Korean-American churches in the United States have shown strong growth. Koreans who come to America, like those in their homeland, are evangelistic and fervent in their worship and faith. Suppose these Korean immigrants were the first to bring Christianity to America, but the only possibility of anyone in the United States hearing the gospel would be to go to a Korean church and hear it in the Korean language? Not many others would ever become Christians! Or what if the gospel had not come to America with our European ancestors but with African slaves? How many white Americans would have gone into an African-American church in order to get saved? That is what we are expecting to happen among people groups around the world when we are not faithful to share the gospel among each distinct people group on the planet. Someone has said that expecting a person to cross social, cultural, racial, and linguistic barriers in order to get the gospel is like waiting for a fish to crawl out of the water in order to get to the bait on the shore.

Encouraging Progress in a Massive Task

Defining the task in terms of identifying and reaching all peoples has been somewhat elusive in a practical sense due to a significant discrepancy that exists among various databases. New isolated people groups are constantly being discovered, while language variations and communal distinctions separate those thought to have a common ethnicity. One of the largest people groups in the world without their own nation is the Kurds with twenty-four million people. While some researchers treat them as one distinct people group, others separate Iraqi Kurds, Iranian Kurds, and Turkish Kurds since those political boundaries discourage commerce and require different channels of access to the gospel.

Another issue is the fact that almost half the eleven thousand to twelve thousand ethno-linguistic people groups in the world are identified as "Christian" in that a majority claim adherence to the Christian faith. However, this, too, is misleading and is one of Satan's most effective deceptions. Most of these peoples would be "cultural Christians" in Catholic countries or citizens of countries where the Eastern Orthodox, Russian Orthodox, or some other Christian tradition is dominant. Having been born into these traditions, multitudes of hidden peoples remain lost and with no salvific knowledge of the gospel. While ancient practices passed down through the centuries define their culture and set them apart from others who follow the ways of Islam or secular materialism, they remain outside the kingdom of God. Although they know the name of Jesus and something of the Bible, they have no exposure to the gospel; they are in plain sight but hidden and lost.

An additional challenge beyond identifying all the people groups in the world is that of getting the Word of God to them in their own language that they might readily understand it. Whether hearing it orally or reading the Bible, God's revelation and knowledge of the gospel need to be known by every language group. The first database of peoples occurs in Genesis 10 in the listing of the sons of Noah and the various nations—tribes, clans, and people groups that descended from each one. They are listed by families, location, and languages. There was further dispersion after the futile attempt of the people to build the Tower of Babel. God said, "Let Us go down there and confuse their language so they will not understand one another's speech" (Gen. 11:7). "The LORD confused the language of the whole earth, and from there the LORD scattered them over the face of the whole earth" (11:9).

Don't miss the implications of this event. God alone is deserving of all glory and praise. In pride the people were striving to make a name for themselves; but God's actions were for His future and ultimate glory. It was one thing for His own chosen people to praise Him in their language, but the greater glory would be when people of every language and nation blend their voices in praise to the Father. When we sing "O, For a Thousand Tongues to Sing" in our worship service, it is not about a record attendance in church on Sunday morning but thousands of languages praising together the One who is worthy to receive glory and praise!

Scripture translation and a vision of getting the Word of God to all peoples have been only recent developments. Cameron Townsend was frustrated in the effort to communicate the gospel to the indigenous peoples of Guatemala who could not read or understand the Spanish language. He began Wycliffe Bible Translators seventy years ago. Bible societies and other organizations focused on the task of Scripture translation, and today approximately 93 percent of the world's people have at least a portion of the Scripture in their own language. However, that means only about a thousand languages have a full Bible, and about twelve hundred others the New Testament. There are more than sixty-seven hundred known languages throughout the world, but at least two thousand additional languages already have a portion of Scripture. Cooperative efforts are accelerating progress, and the vision of Wycliffe is to have a translation of the Bible in all remaining languages of the world in process by 2025.

Any aspirations of Satan to keep people groups hidden and deprived of the life-changing message of God's Word are failing. Even among illiterate people groups and oral cultures, coordinated Bible storying and oral strategies are reaching these peoples. More than 90 percent of the world's population are estimated to have radio broadcasts and other media tools available in their own language. These developments in the latter half of the twentieth century have supplanted all that Satan has done to claim the people groups of the world in his dominion of darkness.

Just as light dispels the darkness, knowledge of the Word of God is bringing light to hearts held in bondage for generations to the power of sin. When one turns on a light switch in a darkened room, there is no struggle to see whether light or dark will prevail. Darkness is the absence of light, so when the light of the gospel shines into previously hidden and neglected people groups, the kingdoms of the world become the Kingdom of our Lord! We used to think that unreached people groups were unreached because they were unresponsive and resistant to the gospel; to the contrary, they are unreached primarily because they have never heard!

The understanding of the Great Commission in terms of ethno-linguistic peoples due to the influence of McGavran, Winter, and others resulted in a refocusing of mission strategies and renewed resolve to reach all peoples. Computerization and access to anthropological and sociological data became tools to measure progress and identify the remaining task. Unsaved individuals had long been identified by the church as unreached, just as mission agencies had identified countries closed to a Christian witness as unreached. Now it became possible to identify people groups that were unreached and find deliberate means to get the gospel to them.

> *Unreached people groups are not unreached because they are resistant to the gospel but because they have never heard!*

Strategies emerged of targeting an expatriate population segment—those peoples who lived outside the geographic area of their ethnic origins. "Tent makers" began to discover channels of creative access as teachers, business consultants, and humanitarian workers to gain entry into countries restricted to the gospel. The creative concept of a "nonresidential missionary" was incorporated into the strategy to reach all peoples. Even though one could not live among the people, they could be a prayer advocate for them, develop radio broadcasts and media resources, and find ways to transport Bibles and other evangelistic materials into their communities.

A coordinated movement, led by Luis Bush and others, sought to rally churches, denominations, and mission agencies from all over the world to complete the Great Commission by the end of the twentieth century. Under the banner, "AD2000 and Beyond," the goal was to see an indigenous church planted among every people group that would be a nucleus of Christian witness eventually to spread the gospel within each homogenous culture and language. That was a formidable challenge as there were still thousands of unreached people groups untouched by the gospel making up the last frontier of an evangelized world.

A distinction began to be made between those who were unreached and those yet to be engaged. An unreached people group (UPG) may have been the target of a missionary witness and even have some churches among them; yet there is still no spiritually vital indigenous witness spreading among most of the people, and less than 2 percent of them have access to the gospel. In contrast, an unengaged, unreached people group (UUPG) is one in which there are no churches, no known Christian believers, no Bible or Christian resources in the language, and no missionary or agency making an effort to engage them with the gospel.

The AD2000 and Beyond movement held a Global Consultation on World Evangelization in Seoul, South Korea, in 1995 to share research information and challenge evangelical Christians to intensify efforts to complete the task. More than four thousand participants from 186 countries gathered for the singular purpose of reaching and discipling all peoples with a view toward completing the Great Commission. At that conference researchers reported they had identified 2,161 unengaged people groups, each with a population of more than a million people who had never even heard the name of Jesus. Those in attendance began to adopt these people groups and accept responsibility for strategies to reach them. In a subsequent conference two years later in Pretoria, South Africa, all but 746 of these unengaged people groups had been adopted.

As the number of these major groups began to gain access to the gospel—there remain only 47 UUPG with more than a million people—the goal shifted to engage all people groups with at least one hundred thousand people. The number of those who have yet to hear the gospel is now less than four hundred! Of course, there are many additional unreached people groups with smaller numbers of people, identified as micropeoples. But as the gospel is planted among major, gateway peoples, the nature of the gospel is to overflow and spread to smaller, "near neighbor" tribes and peoples who have an affinity with the larger cultural, geographic, and economic context in which they live.

People groups are no longer hidden; systematic progress is being made to provide all peoples access to the gospel. Patrick Johnson, director of research with WEC International has served the missions community with valuable insights and information into the complexity of God's mission as we moved toward the twenty-first century and the third millennium of Christian history. He has published periodic updates in his well-known book, *Operation World*. It has been used around the world as a tool for expanding mission strategies and a resource for churches to pray for the unreached. He wrote a captivating book in 1998 entitled *The Church Is Bigger than You Think*. In tracing the progress and advancement of the gospel among all peoples, the book incites a vision of the possible completion of the Great Commission in our generation.[2]

Twenty years ago it would have been considered a dream for there to be churches among the Uzbeks, Tajiks, Kazakhs, Karalkapak, Azeris, and other people groups of Central Asia, yet there, as Paul observed in Colossians 1:6 that the gospel is bearing fruit and multiplying. As the barriers to the former Soviet Union fell, there was not just an explosive response among Russians, but minority peoples such as the Udmurts and others in the far reaches of Siberia began to hear the gospel for the first time. The movement in China is not just bringing growth among the majority Han Chinese but is touching the Yi, the Tung, the Zhuang, the Uigiurs, and others with the gospel for the first time.

> *People groups are no longer hidden; systematic progress is being made to provide all peoples access to the gospel.*

Missionaries found a ready response among the peoples of East Africa as concentrated strategies resulted in churches being planted in Kenya, Tanzania, and Uganda over the last half century. One group, however, that had never been penetrated with the gospel was the independent, warrior-like Maasai. Not only were these people closed to a Christian witness; they were intimidating to outsiders. Several years ago an itinerant missionary stopped by a Maasai village for rest and to obtain information about the area. As he conversed with the people, he found them receptive and interested in his message. Having established a relationship, he returned to the village and continued to nurture an understanding of his witness resulting in the clan leaders deciding to follow Christ. When the missionary returned, he found that they had told other Maasai clans what they had done. The movement continued to grow until now more than one hundred thousand Maasai have been baptized in Kenya and across the border in Tanzania, and they are becoming evangelists to neighboring tribal groups.

A similar movement has spread among the Berber people of Algeria. Located in the heart of a radical Islamic belt across Northern Africa, this Muslim people group discovered that their people had been Christians more than a thousand years earlier. In fact, Augustine had been a Berber. Some of their traditions and practices could be traced back to their Christian roots. As they gained access to the Bible, were exposed to the *Jesus* film and other resources, it gradually became acceptable for them to revert to Christianity. Churches are spreading across the Berber Valley, and a Christian witness is being spread among the diverse Berber peoples in Morocco and Tunisia as well as in Algeria.

On a recent trip to Nepal, I (Jerry) was meeting with a large group of mission workers in this beautiful but impoverished mountain kingdom in the Himalayas. Until recently Nepal had been the only country in the world in which Hinduism was the state religion. It had been illegal for citizens to follow any other religion. When I coordinated work in the region twenty years ago, I can remember mobilizing prayer for thirteen pastors who had been imprisoned. There had been three struggling churches in the capital city of Katmandu. On this particular trip I had the privilege of having fellowship and conducting training with fifty-three pastors now openly leading churches in the city.

Previously we had asked itinerant missionaries coming into the country to work with the Tamung and Rai peoples in remote valleys of the Himalayas. Some of their influential leaders had heard the gospel on treks into India. Contacts there had arranged for us to follow-up with discipleship and training. On this return trip almost twenty years later, I asked our workers which of them were working with the Tamung and Rai. When they replied that no one was assigned to work with them, I felt a little indignant that this current generation would be neglecting work in which we had invested so much effort years before. Asking them for an explanation, they replied matter-of-factly that the Tamung and Rai had been evangelized, and, in fact, many of them were relocating into other valleys in order to evangelize neighboring people groups!

Throughout the years one of the most resistant people groups in Nepal was the Newar. These were the elite, original Nepalese who considered themselves the leaders and guardians of their Hindu heritage. They lived in distinct, readily identifiable neighborhoods of homes with ornately carved doors and windows. I began to hear testimonies of how several Newar had become believers; Scripture in their language had just been translated and distributed. Someone had taken the unique music style of the Newar and had given it Christian words. Whenever the people heard the music, they would come out of their homes and apartments to gather where Christians were singing, and a movement to Christ began to sweep through this elite, resistant people group.

It was suggested that we go into the Newar community between 6:00 and 7:00 p.m. in the evening when house groups would gather for worship. As we walked through the narrow alleyways, we could hear Christian music coming from a home. As we walked on and the music faded, we would begin to hear another group singing as we approached. Throughout the neighborhood Christians were gathering to fellowship and pray and sing praises to God.

This is happening all over the world. Systematically people groups are being engaged with a Christian witness. In 1999 International Mission Board personnel engaged 192 new people groups with the gospel. Each year since then more than one hundred people groups are engaged by mission strategies and are hearing of Jesus, many for the first time. This is multiplied by the work of other mission agencies and Great Commission Christians; national churches around the world are catching the vision and taking the gospel to people groups beyond their own as never before.

Our global research department publishes information on the status of global evangelization and has developed maps portraying the locations of those peoples who have yet to be engaged with the gospel. These are represented by a matrix of red dots relative to the size and population of each particular people groups. Those that are unreached are represented by orange dots, and those still unreached but where evangelism is taking place are yellow. People groups that are evangelized are green. The matrix of dots appear to be swatches of color across the map.

I (Jerry) recently was introduced to an electronic version of this map. When the cursor was clicked on any specific dot, Google Earth would open on the screen, showing the actual area and location where the people group represented by that dot lives. People groups are no longer hidden. We know where they are. We understand the barriers that have kept them from the gospel, and strategies are emerging to reach them all with the gospel. Churches everywhere are adopting unreached people groups, interceding on their behalf, and praying for the Lord of the harvest to call out laborers to engage them with the gospel. It is just a matter of time until all peoples, tribes, and languages, like the Newar in Nepal, become a part of that heavenly choir singing praises to God and giving Him glory.

God yearns to be exalted among all the peoples of the earth. He is tracking the progression and fulfillment of His mission. The psalmist gives us a vision of Zion, the kingdom of God. He mentions the nations and tribes and identifies where each member of the kingdom was born: "I will mention those who know Me: Rahab, Babylon, Philistia, Tyre, and Cush—each one was born there. . . . This one and that one were born in her. . . . When He registers the peoples, the Lord will record, 'This one was born there'" (Ps. 87:4–6). God is registering the peoples as they come into His kingdom because He desires that none will be absent when they gather around the throne to worship the Lamb who was slain and "redeemed people for God . . . from every tribe and language and people and nation" (Rev. 5:9).

Satan cannot keep it from happening! His strategy to keep people groups hidden from our awareness so that they will never have access to the good news of Jesus, so successful for almost two thousand years, is no longer working!

Going Deeper

1. How has this chapter challenged your thinking about tasks of evangelism and missions?

2. Brainstorm the possibilities of how you will approach evangelism differently in your community as a result of what you've learned.

3. List some of the ways you hope to begin reaching out to other nations (people groups) with the gospel.

4. How can you begin involving and leading others to reach other nations with the gospel?

5. Explore www.peoplegroups.org. You will discover people group resources for you, your family, and your church. Ask God how you can go deeper in praying and engaging people groups of the world (including North America) with the gospel.

CHAPTER 6

SATAN'S STRATEGY:
PERSECUTION OF BELIEVERS
AND THE CHURCH

In recent years reports had been coming from a South Asian country that Muslims among several communities were becoming followers of Christ. When the numbers being reported exceeded five hundred thousand MBBs (Muslim Background Believers) who had been baptized, even mission leaders in the region became skeptical regarding such a massive response. After all, how reliable are statistics coming from remote villages and uneducated people, most of whom would have no grasp of such a movement beyond their own limited area.

IMB personnel organized a research project and trained local Christians who spoke the language of these people to go into the villages and talk to leaders in an effort to discern realistically what was happening. They found entire villages and extended clans had become Christ followers. They met with house church leaders and found these multiplying groups were indeed functioning as authentic New Testament churches in gathering for worship, practicing the ordinances, and witnessing and ministering in their communities. They traced the reproduction of these simple gatherings of believers and the process of discipling new converts. As the research was compiled, however, they could not find evidence corroborating half a million baptisms. The statistics reflected only about four hundred thousand Muslims who had actually expressed their commitment to follow Christ through public baptism! But the numbers were continuing to grow as their witness was spreading among three people groups.

This movement began with a young man we will identify as Abdullah. As with all the young men in his Muslim community, he was being trained in the village Madrassah to read the Qu'ran and quote the tenets of his faith. As an unusually gifted and perceptive youth, Abdullah would ask questions regarding perceived inconsistencies in what he was being taught. The response was to be chided, reprimanded, and even beaten by his Mullah (instructor). Finally, to the embarrassment of his family, he was thrown out of school.

One day while walking forlornly along the road leading into the nearby town, a missionary stopped and offered to let him join him in the cycle pedicab in which he was riding. Responding to this offer of friendship, Abdullah poured out his heart about all that had happened to shame him and his family and expressed his confusion regarding what he was being taught. The missionary gave him a tract and explained that Jesus Christ was the truth he was seeking. Subsequent visits and conversations led to his receiving a Bible that he read diligently and eventually became a Christian.

Excited about what he had discovered, he indiscreetly shared the joy he had found in his salvation from sin through faith in Christ, something that was lacking in the legalistic Muslim ritual he had been taught. He was unprepared for the radical response and anger he encountered. His father beat him and threatened to kill him. His brothers dragged him into the yard where they continued to kick and beat him, and even his mother spit on him for disgracing the family. He found refuge in a shed behind the house of his best friend. In isolation and hiding, he spent his days reading the Bible, absorbing its teaching, and discerning how to use it as a counter to Muslim teachings.

His friend responded to his witness, became a believer, and the two young men baptized each other in obedience to what they understood God's Word instructed them to do as believers. Though they constantly encountered persecution, they also found a hearing. A man of peace would provide acceptance into a community and often provide an opportunity for dialogue in the local mosque. They would lead people to see the futility in their religious traditions and beliefs as a way to God; they would bridge the discussions to show why Nabi Isa (Jesus), a revered prophet, was the hope of eternal life.

Those who dared to become believers were often ostracized and persecuted, but the movement continued to grow. Muslim authorities came into the area trying to find who was responsible for the apostasy, as they perceived it, spreading among the people. One believer, subjected to interrogation in an effort to get him to tell who was responsible for his conversion, refused. His fingers were cut off one at a time, but he still refused to expose the names of the zealous evangelists who had introduced him to Jesus, and he bled to death.

Abdullah's friend became the primary discipler and trainer of house church leaders. One night responding to a knock, he opened his door and was stabbed to death. So far, nine of the leaders have been martyred, but the movement continues to grow. Even in the bleakest of circumstances, the power of the gospel draws people to Jesus Christ. When someone's religious worldview is empty ritual and following the cultural traditions of society, the hope of salvation provided by the God of love is irresistible. A life transformed by Jesus is a powerful witness that cannot be restrained. When people see that the Christian faith is not just a religious choice worth living for, but a conviction worth dying for, suffering and death become a powerful witness of the truth.

Among another South Asian people group, thousands of Hindus were professing faith in Christ and being saved. Radical

Hindu mobs would come into the villages, drag Christians out of their homes, and threaten to burn their houses if they would not recant and bow before a Hindu idol. Many of them were being killed, yet the movement could not be deterred. New believers were taught at the time of baptism to say to their captors or tormentors if their life was ever threatened, "You do not take my life from me, but I gladly give it and die that you, too, may someday know my Lord Jesus Christ."

The Power of a Testimony of Suffering

It is apparent that Satan does not understand the power of suffering as a testimony that powerfully authenticates a Christian witness. It goes back to his being deluded by the cross. Conspiring to influence Judas to betray Christ and working through the envious hearts of Jewish religious leaders to have Him crucified, Satan thought that he had won. Instead, the suffering and death of Christ empowered the kingdom and assured Satan's ultimate defeat. The Bible makes it clear that persecution will accompany proclamation of the gospel in a world hostile to a Christian witness and will be used of God to advance His kingdom.

"'I assure you,' Jesus said, 'there is no one who has left house, brothers or sisters, mother or father, children or fields because of Me and the gospel, who will not receive 100 times more, now at this time—houses, brothers and sisters, mothers and children, and fields, with persecutions—and eternal life in the age to come'" (Mark 10:29–30). Jesus prepared His disciples and followers for this certain response to their witness because their witness stood in such contrast to the sinful ways of the world. "If you were of the world, the world would love you as its own. However, because you are not of the world, but I have chosen you out of it, the world hates you. . . . If they persecuted Me, they will also persecute you. . . . But they will do all these things to you on account of My name, because they don't know the One who sent Me" (John 15:19–21).

Just as the sufferings of Christ resulted in God being glorified through redemption being provided for a lost world, God is glorified through the faithfulness of those who suffer persecution for their faith. But also His divine providence uses it as a powerful testimony to advance His kingdom. Paul observed the reality of this paradox in his ministry at Ephesus. Receptivity to the gospel and an open harvest will inevitably be accompanied by adversaries and opposition: "Because a wide door for effective ministry has opened for me—yet many oppose me" (1 Cor. 16:9).

> The Bible makes it clear that persecution will accompany the proclamation of the gospel in a world hostile to a Christian witness.

Jesus told His followers they should not be surprised at opposition and the fact that they would be rejected, reviled, hated, and persecuted for standing up in identification with Him. Peter reminds us that we cannot hope to stand firm in our faith as a follower of Christ without it entailing suffering. "Therefore, since Christ suffered in the flesh, arm yourselves also with the same resolve . . . in order to live the remaining time in the flesh, no longer for human desires, but for God's will" (1 Pet. 4:1–2). Peter had just put this in perspective earlier: "For you were called to this, because Christ also suffered for you, leaving you an example, so that you should follow in His steps" (1 Pet. 2:21). Believers who are persecuted have a choice—to live for their own safety, comfort, and protection in denying the faith, which would be sin, or to deny themselves for the sake of Christ with the consequences of suffering.

We need to dispel the prominent myth that the safest place to be is in the center of God's will. Certainly, obedience to God's will is the only place to be for a Christian, but that does not assure us of comfort, safety, and security. God has not guaranteed the believer exemption from suffering and opposition. He does promise to bless us, empower us, and protect us, but His primary concern is not our safety and avoidance of suffering and inconvenience but His glory in our lives. The Bible clearly teaches that God is glorified through our faithfulness and obedience even in times of suffering for our faith.

Just as believers in the hostile environment of Muslim societies or communist, totalitarian countries have learned harassment and persecution goes with the territory, New Testament believers accepted that as a reality. Once again Peter put this in perspective: "Dear friends, when the fiery ordeal arises among you to test you, don't be surprised by it, as if something unusual were happening to you. Instead, as you share in the sufferings of the Messiah rejoice, so that you may also rejoice with great joy at the revelation of His glory. If you are ridiculed for the name of Christ, you are blessed, because the Spirit of glory and of God rests on you" (1 Pet. 4:12–14).

Too many Christians have embraced the myth of safety in the center of God's will. That just doesn't match up with reality spiritually, historically, or scripturally. Were Stephen and James, two of the earliest martyrs in the book of Acts, not in the center of God's will? When Paul and his companions were imprisoned, or subjected to stoning and beating, was it because they were disobedient to what God was leading them to do? Of course, not! God is not primarily concerned about our comfort, safety, and prosperity. He desires to be glorified in our lives, and that often comes through faithfulness in the midst of persecution and suffering. And it often results in a powerful witness for Christ that would not otherwise occur.

Christian history is replete with examples of Christian martyrs, those who died violently and prematurely because of their faithful witness. These are notably recorded by John Foxe in his book *Foxe's Book of Martyrs*.[1] Some include in their identification of martyrs the massive numbers of Christians who have been killed in communal, ethnic violence. They died because they were Christians, but far fewer have been killed because of persistence in an overt witness for the faith that could have been avoided. The Bible identifies them as having been worthy of participating in the fellowship of Christ's sufferings.

Susan Bergman, in her book *Martyrs,* makes the distinction: "Martyrdom occurs when a person is required to deny Christ and live, or confess Him and die. Under such duress the martyr freely chooses death over life—death that seals a life's belief—in order to act as a witness to the truth of Christ's claims and to his or her own faith."[2]

Multitudes, who never suffer to the point of shedding their blood in death, make the same decision and are subjected to torture and unmentionable cruelties. There is no question that Satan is behind the wickedness and cruelty of authorities who arrest believers and subject them to such atrocities. But he doesn't realize how much God is glorified by their witness of bearing pain and suffering and even death. Nor does he realize that the power of their testimony is used to advance the kingdom.

So Satan approaches it two ways. Not only does he perpetrate persecution on believers (it may simply be through ridicule and being subjected to condescending attitudes in our Western society), but he convinces Christians that their highest priority is to avoid suffering and danger. Our safety and security is more important than the world knowing Christ, so we avoid going to dangerous places where we might get arrested or even killed, and God is deprived of His praise and glory among people who do not have the opportunity to know Jesus.

God's primary purpose is to be glorified in our lives and exalted among the nations. Risking danger and suffering is sometimes necessary for that to happen. Certainly it will not happen without a willingness to suffer for the sake of God's glory among the nations. When Paul's friends tried to deter him from going to Jerusalem where he was certain to encounter the wrath of the Judaizers and possibly be arrested, he replied, "What are you doing, weeping and breaking my heart? For I am ready not only to be bound, but also to die in Jerusalem for the name of the Lord Jesus" (Acts 21:13).

Paul admonished Timothy, "So don't be ashamed of the testimony about our Lord, or of me His prisoner. Instead, share in suffering for the gospel, relying on the power of God" (2 Tim. 1:8). He goes on to observe, "In fact, all those who want to live a godly life in Christ Jesus will be persecuted" (2 Tim. 3:12). Persecution may take different forms in the West than in places overseas, but could it not be an indicator of our anemic faith and witness that we encounter no repercussions in seeking to live for Christ in a lost world? Perhaps we ought to ask ourselves, "Where is all that being slandered and reviled for the sake of the gospel we are suppose to be enduring?"

We forfeit God's blessings as well as an opportunity to glorify Him when we seek to avoid opposition or offending anyone by our witness in a way that would bring repercussions. In the Beatitudes Jesus reminded us, "Blessed are those who are persecuted for righteousness, because the kingdom of heaven is theirs" (Matt. 5:10). He went on to elaborate on this concept: "But I tell you, love your enemies and pray for those who persecute you, so that you may be sons of your Father in heaven. For He causes His sun to rise on the evil and the good, and sends rain on the righteous and the unrighteous" (vv. 44–45).

Persecution Is Advancing God's Kingdom

The earliest persecutors of the church were the Jewish leaders whose religious control and way of life were threatened by bold followers of Jesus. Yet their efforts could not curtail the rapid spread of the gospel. Even the chief persecutor, Paul, who was seeking out followers of "the way" and casting them in prison could not resist the truth when confronted with the call of Christ. This was followed for more than three centuries by cruel persecution of believers by the Roman state, but believers met secretly, and God's kingdom continued to advance throughout the empire.

For more than a millennium, and even into the nineteenth century, the Catholic Church became the principle persecutor of

"heretical" sects of Christians. This continued on into the twentieth century, especially in Latin America, but today more gather
for worship in evangelical and Pentecostal churches throughout
South America than those who gather in Catholic cathedrals. However, the twentieth century saw a dramatic upsurge in worldwide
persecution beginning with the Soviet communist empire and the
communist regime in China. Those believing in God and seeking
to follow Christ are intolerable to those propagating an atheistic
ideology upon the world.

Persecution of Christians peaked in Japan and areas of the
Pacific Rim where Japanese armies extended dominion from 1941
to 1945. Severe persecution has been perpetrated throughout the
Muslim world by the Orthodox Church in Eastern Europe and in
the few remaining communist and totalitarian countries such as
North Korea, Cuba, and China. A U.S. State Department report in
1997 identified sixty countries where "Christians face the reality
of massacre, rape, torture, mutilation, family division, harassment,
imprisonment, slavery, discrimination in education and employment, and even death, simply for what they believe."[3]

Persecution, at its core, is essentially a form of spiritual warfare that is completely evil in its origin and power. The apostle
Paul notes that the ultimate source of persecution of God's people
is Satan: "For our battle is not against flesh and blood, but against
the rulers, against the authorities, against the world powers of this
darkness, against the spiritual forces of evil in the heavens" (Eph.
6:12). When Joseph's brother's expected him to take vengeance
against them for their cruelty toward him, he put it in the proper
perspective of God's plan and providence. "You planned evil against
me; God planned it for good to bring about the present result—the
survival of many people" (Gen. 50:20).

What Satan and others—political and religious pawns in his
hands—mean for evil, God is using for His purpose, that many people might be saved and He would be glorified among the nations.
The suffering of believers is unfortunate and may represent temporary setbacks, but it is a necessary force in the cosmic battle

against the kingdom of darkness in order for Christ's kingdom to come on earth! Paul assured us of this victory: "Who can separate us from the love of Christ? Can affliction or anguish or persecution or famine or nakedness or danger or sword? . . . No, in all these things we are more than victorious through Him who loved us" (Rom. 8:35, 37).

Years ago when I (Jerry) was responsible for directing mission programs in India, I arrived at our Baptist hospital in Bangalore to find one of the village evangelists hospitalized. Gnaniah had once been a security guard but after his conversion became a zealous witness. Anytime he was not on duty, he would be out in

> *Persecution may represent a temporary setback, but it is a necessary force in the cosmic battle against the kingdom of darkness.*

the villages in the vicinity of the hospital passing out tracts and telling people about Jesus. He was so diligent and had such a passion for evangelism that, after being discipled, he was assigned to do outreach and evangelism.

He had gone to a village to follow-up a discharged patient who had shown interest in the gospel, but contact with the former patient brought repercussions from the family. He persisted in his visits in spite of threats from those in the community who considered themselves guardians of their strict adherence to their Hindu traditions and values. One day after disembarking from the bus on the highway and making his way to the village on a winding path through junglelike foliage, he was attacked by a group of young men. They beat him with clubs, pipes, and chains and left him bleeding and semiconscious in the brush. He was able to crawl back to the highway and persuade someone in a passing vehicle to take him to the hospital.

The next week I arrived and heard of this incident. Walking into his hospital room, I would not have recognized him with his head bandaged, arm in a cast, and leg in traction, but there was no mistaking his bright smile upon recognizing me. I sought to encourage him and minister to him. After hearing a detailed recounting of the attack, I asked Gnaniah if he was willing to continue his village ministry, considering the dangers and what had happened to him. I'll never forget his reply. He said, "This just shows how much they need Jesus. I can't believe I was doing anything worthy of suffering for my Lord." He was echoing the response of the apostles in Acts after they had been arrested and threatened and ordered not to teach and preach in the name of Jesus: "For we are unable to stop speaking about what we have seen and heard" (Acts 4:20). Later, after being arrested, the apostles "went out . . . rejoicing that they were counted worthy to be dishonored on behalf of the name" (Acts 5:41).

The sequel to Gnaniah's story is that, after recovering from his injuries, he returned to the village where he had been attacked. The community was incredulous that he would return. They were also impressed that he had something so important to share with them that he was willing to ignore the danger and personal harm. They listened to his testimony and invited him to return. The whole village would gather to hear him tell the story of Jesus. The result—a church was formed.

It was several years later after I had moved on from my India assignment, but I was back in Bangalore on a tour of India and had an opportunity for fellowship with the national pastors and evangelists with whom I had worked. Gnaniah introduced me to a tall, handsome young man and asked, "Do you remember when I was attacked at that village years ago and that a church was started there?" I affirmed my recall of the incident, and he went on, "This is one of the young men that attacked and beat me that day; he is now pastor of the church!"

There is probably no place that persecution is advancing the kingdom of God more than in China. With the takeover by the communist government sixty years ago, Christian missionaries were expelled, and local pastors have continued to be imprisoned and subjected to harsh intimidation and harassment. During the Cultural Revolution in the 1980s, campaigns by the Red Guard sought to purify adherence to communist dogma, and Christians were forced to go underground, worshipping and practicing their faith in secret. Yet the power of their testimony under persecution prevailed and drew multitudes into the community of believers in reaction to the brutality and repression of government authorities. What had been a Christian minority of about a million church members in 1950 had grown to almost 100 million fifty years later. Some researchers are estimating twenty to thirty thousand new believers a day are coming to faith in Christ throughout this nation of 1.2 billion people.

The growth is occurring in the midst of continuing persecution. The government's effort to register Christian churches has brought under their control only about twelve million adherents to the Christian faith. Those who have resisted are subjected to threats, arrest, and torture. One believer described what has been a common experience throughout many areas of the country:

> There are thirty members of our fellowship still serving long-term sentences in prison and labor reform camps. On several occasions truckloads of officers would interrupt our worship and go into our homes, tying us up with rope and throwing us into the truck to be taken away for interrogation. My interrogation lasted for three days and two nights. They would have teams of three interrogators who would come in four-hour shifts, but the suspect is not allowed to sleep. The questions are usually accompanied by physical beating with their fists and a metal stick. On one occasion when the temperature was below zero, they ripped off my clothing and blew a big fan on high speed until I began to shake so much from the cold I could not take it, and they finally stopped.

I saw them make an old man put his arms over his neck, tied them together, and then hung bricks from them creating pressure and excruciating pain. On another occasion they would tie the thumbs of two persons together and put a bar underneath and then raise it higher and higher. After several years when Christians may be finally released, they are nothing but skin and bones. When it was time to eat, a soldier would ask if you still believe in Jesus. If you said Yes, they would knock over your bowl of soup.

When the officials arrest Christians, their homes are searched, and they can take away anything— bicycles, chickens, and anything of value—so families are totally depleted of any resources.

This was confirmed in the experience of a mission partner who was training house church leaders in ecclesiology. While discussing baptism, he suggested they ask a baptismal candidate three questions to determine their authentic faith and qualifications to be baptized: "Do you believe Jesus Christ is the Son of God and died on the cross for the sins of the world? Are you trusting Jesus as your personal Savior? Are you committed to live for Jesus as Lord of your life? If they answer Yes, to each of these questions, it is appropriate for them to be baptized." The church leaders all objected, saying there is a fourth question that must be answered in the affirmative: "When the authorities come and arrest you, threaten your life and your family, and take away all your belongings, will you still follow Jesus?" Only then should they be baptized as a public follower of Jesus.

This pattern of arrests and persecution is serving only to embolden believers to stand firm in their faith. When they have already made the decision to stand firm and are even willing to lay down their life, persecution cannot deter their witness. It is like Paul's testimony about the result of his imprisonment in Rome:

"Now I want you to know, brothers, that what has happened to me has actually resulted in the advancement of the gospel, so that it has become known throughout the whole imperial guard, and to everyone else, that my imprisonment is for Christ. Most of the brothers in the Lord have gained confidence from my imprisonment and dare even more to speak the message fearlessly" (Phil. 1:12–14). The steadfast faith and perseverance of believers is contagious among other prisoners who, when eventually released, are taking the gospel back to their families and communities. And there are also accounts of police and communist authorities influenced to consider the claims of Christ due to the faithful witness of Christians in prisons and labor camps.

Persecution cannot deter the witness of those who have already made the decision to stand firm and even lay down their lives for Christ.

A growing house church in one city was coming under surveillance, and its leaders had been arrested. In order to continue to worship and study the Bible, the group would move to a different location each week. The members would never know where they were to gather, so one of the members would go to the bus terminal in the congested central market area of the city on Sunday morning. Members would come by, recognize him from their fellowship, and be told where they were to go for worship that day.

It didn't take long for the vigilant authorities to identify this street usher. He was arrested and interrogated in an effort to discover where the believers were gathered. Then someone else would step into this role. Hearing of this situation, someone observed that it must be difficult to find those willing to assume this role that would make them vulnerable to exposure and arrest.

The house church leaders replied, "Oh, no; we have a long list of members who have volunteered!"

One Chinese pastor had spent thirty-seven years in a labor camp. He was ninety years old when he was released and went to live in a rest home. He was thrilled with this situation because, as he explained it, this was one of the most valuable opportunities he ever had. All the residents of the home would die soon, so he was compelled to tell them about their need to believe in Jesus. He had been in the hospital with pneumonia, and when he was released, he was met by several policemen and arrested for illegal evangelistic activity. He was made to stand for several hours listening to propaganda. He started to giggle when he realized he was probably the only ninety-year-old allowed to suffer for our Lord. He said, "They tried to wash Jesus out of my brain, but Jesus doesn't wash away!"

In an area of Central Asia where Islamic heritage is strong, a young believer has started seventy house churches and baptized more than a thousand Muslim converts. He explained that Muslims are devout because they are crying to God and seeking Him, but they really have no idea how to find Him. He is coordinating a correspondence course that has enrolled fifteen hundred "truth seekers," but he pays a price for his faith. His family was forced out of their home by the local community because of his Christian activities, but he remains faithful and persistent in sharing Christ.

A former Taliban freedom fighter in Afghanistan came to faith in Christ when an elder brother shaved his beard, stopped going to the fundamentalist meetings and started writing poems about Jesus. He said he was bearing a heavy guilt from having killed so many people and was already disillusioned in his Islamic faith. He started reading the Bible and explained, "I was attracted to the character of Jesus and wanted to be like Him." He thought, "If anyone should be God—if there was a God—it should be Jesus. No other religion I studied had a God who loves all people."

He related how he went to some churches, but they didn't want anything to do with a Muslim inquirer, knowing they would get into trouble for proselytizing. He had to flee to a neighboring country. His family had followed him in believing on Jesus, and he was required to report to the police three times a week; the authorities would interrogate him, sought to shame him, and tried to persuade him to revert to Islam. Soon ten friends had become believers. They began to worship in secret, and within a few years the group of believers had grown to fifty. Although their church was meeting in secret, some informers reported them to the police, the meeting was broken up, and three of the leaders were arrested.

He related this experience: "We were given electric shocks, beatings, hung from our hands, and stripped naked. During this time I was kept strong by the hope I had. I was aware God had a plan for my life, and I was confident that plan would be fulfilled, so I stayed focused on Jesus and the cross." This leader continues to persevere in his conviction God is leading him to start a church movement of Muslim background believers. Muslim converts are not accepted, nor do they fit in the established churches made up of cultural Christians. He explained that the suffering to which they are subjected strengthens their faith and convictions, "We have leaders, conduct training and Bible studies, and are seeing MBB churches continuing to grow!"

Another of these leaders testified that it would be easy to seek asylum in the West but reasoned that it was his work to tell other people in his tribal group about the way of salvation. He, too, had been arrested when an informant reported him, and he was caught with twenty New Testaments. The Mujahaden commander tried to make him reveal the names of Christian believers. When he refused, they beat him, breaking both of his arms, but desisted when he reminded them that if they killed him they would not succeed in getting any information.

This believer was eventually released but has been arrested multiple times. He is practically an invalid from the beatings and injuries but has moved to a large city where he lives in a small room in a recondite location. By word of mouth people who are seeking truth hear of him, and he continues to witness and disciple a constant flow of secret believers in one of the most fanatical Muslim areas of the world.

Asked what has enabled him to remain faithful, he said:

> It would have been so easy for me to say many times that I won't have anything to do with this Christian life and live an ordinary life. But the most encouraging thing is the Word of God which says that when we receive persecution in the name of the Lord, the suffering is only temporal, and we have the security of everlasting life. That is a great comfort. Also we are told to count it all joy when we face various trials, that when someone persecutes us, they are persecuting Jesus. And Jesus said that He will bless you and help us. When people come to me, I am careful to explain that their life is going to be in danger, that they will have many difficulties and problems in following Jesus.

This faithful Muslim convert, and others being persecuted for their faith, understand and believe the exhortation of Jesus to His disciples, "You will have suffering in this world. Be courageous! I have conquered the world" (John 16:33). They accept tribulation and trials as a reality in this life, knowing they are living for a future, eternal reward. They could say with Paul, "For I consider that the sufferings of this present time are not worth comparing with the glory that is going to be revealed to us" (Rom. 8:18).

> *"The sufferings of this present time are not worth comparing with the glory that is going to be revealed."*
>
> *(Rom. 8:18)*

Anyone more than thirty years old remembers the concerns and prayers of Christians in the West for those behind the iron curtain of the communist bloc in Eastern Europe and the Soviet Union. Horror stories emerged of secret police and of pastors being arrested and sent to Siberia. We heard intriguing accounts of Bible smugglers and midnight baptisms in the woods. A believer recounts the memory of his pastor father being put in prison for six years, during which time more than ten thousand people died in the prisons from torture and starvation. He explained that there was a deliberate and well-implemented plan of the state to destroy the church. They sought to create fear and distrust as well as use intimidation.

When his father was released from prison, they were exiled to a gypsy village. The secret police came to their home and destroyed all the books and sermons his father had written. He and the other children were not allowed to graduate from school, and he was eventually fired anytime he was able to get a job. Yet he recalls his childhood memories as that of a happy family. Persecution was normal and actually enabled them to be stronger spiritually. He reported that people flocked to Christ because times were hard, and they recognized that only Christ could sustain them through times of trouble. Believers, having endured this era of tribulation and trials, were not surprised to see a mighty harvest sweep Eastern Europe when the doors opened to new freedoms twenty years ago!

An amazing testimony of a socialist country where persecution and government restrictions have not been able to inhibit church growth is in Cuba. For years pastors and anyone daring to witness openly were incarcerated. Even though regulations and some degree of freedom to practice one's religion has emerged in recent years, it is not without tremendous obstacles and personal ramifications. Every request of the government to allow a new church to be started or a new building to be built was rejected. Finally the Department of Religious Affairs told the churches, "You will never receive permission to start a new church, build new church buildings, or repair old ones; your people will just have to worship in their homes." As a result a network of house churches has emerged in every town and village. Families who would have been reluctant to go into a Protestant church building feel welcome to join in a fellowship gathering in a neighbor's home. These house churches are multiplying as they grow, making the gospel accessible to everyone at a grassroots level of society. Baptists alone are anticipating reaching one hundred thousand congregations by the end of 2010!

A prominent schoolteacher, who had excelled in her field at the national university, had been sent by the government to study in Europe and attained her doctorate in literature. Approaching sixty years of age, she was highly regarded and influential for her years of tenure. She accepted a friend's invitation to attend a house church in her neighborhood. After attending for a while, she made a profession of faith, was discipled and baptized, and became comfortable in sharing her newfound faith.

Arriving at the university for her classes a short time afterward, she was met by the dean of the school and informed that the council was waiting to meet with her. She had not heard of any such council and had no idea who the council was or what the meeting was about. When she walked into the faculty conference room, she was confronted with several high level dignitaries she recognized as being from the government, including the Ministry of Education.

The obvious leader of the council opened a folder and proceeded to review the details of her training, work experience, and personal biographical data and then asked, "Is this you?" She affirmed that it was, and the leader continued. "Is it true you have become a Christian, are attending a Baptist church, and are talking with other people about your conversion to Christianity?" Once again, she answered that it was true.

Several on the council began to rebuke her, pointing out that, as a professor at the national university, her position was representing the government and the people, and her choice to become a Christian was not a wise one. They insisted that she cease going to church, cut off all relationships with other Christians, and no longer testify of her faith as such behavior was not good for her reputation, for the government, or for the Cuban people. Her response was to say, "You need to understand that a relationship with Jesus Christ is not something that can be turned on and off like a water spigot. The choice to believe on Jesus Christ is a permanent one and cannot be turned off."

The leader of the council replied that they anticipated her answer and she would be relieved of her position at the university. She was to clean out her desk and the next week report to the local high school where she would teach literature. The high school was pleased to have such an experienced, reputable teacher. Meanwhile, she continued attending church and sharing her faith freely.

It was not long until she arrived at school to be informed by the principal that a council was waiting to meet her in the faculty lounge. Wondering what this was all about, she was not surprised to find the same officials from the council at the university. After the expected preliminaries, the council quickly got to the point. They understood that she was still going to church and sharing her faith. They said it would be acceptable if she chose to go to church and worship and then go home without publicly telling people about her conversion to Christianity. Once again she explained that her relationship with Jesus had brought great joy into her life; it was something she could not help but tell others.

When she assured the council that she would not reconsider her position of following Christ, she was once again instructed to clean out her desk; she would not be allowed to continue to teach at the high school. The following Monday she was to arrive in the market at 5:00 a.m. A dump truck that brought vegetables to the market would be cleaned out; she and other teachers assigned to a remote elementary school in the mountains could ride in the truck to their teaching duties there each morning.

Although she could ride the truck up the mountain each morning, nothing was said about getting home, so when school was dismissed at 3:00 p.m., she started the long trek home, arriving late at night. Each morning she would go to the market and ride the truck up the mountain, then after school begin the walk home. People in the village wanted to know what she had done to be assigned to such a remote village school. As people along the road saw her walking down the mountain each day, they would invite her to stop in to rest and have a cup of tea. They would all want to know what she had done that was so bad to result in her being banished to the village elementary school. Each visit was an opportunity for her to share her faith. Soon families along her route would invite her to spend the night rather than walk all the way home.

The teacher started teaching the Bible among the neighbors who would gather to hear her wherever she was staying, and after two years there was a string of churches from the mountaintop village all the way down to the city in the valley. She said, "I have never been so happy. What the government meant as harassment and a demotion has resulted in churches being started where people would never have had an opportunity to hear the gospel."

One of my (Jerry) colleagues attended a pastors' conference in Cuba and was discussing with some of the church leaders the fact that circumstances are changing. It is likely Cuba will be more open to international relations in the near future. This is likely to open up trade and international commerce; once the country begins to prosper, people will not be as receptive to the gospel and spiritual solutions to life. One of the younger leaders replied, "I have lived under a communist government all my life; I don't know what it means to be free. But I would rather not be free in order to share the freedom that can be found in Christ with my people."

God's Witness Cannot Be Silenced

Satan just doesn't get it! He doesn't understand that persecution cannot deter the advancement of God's kingdom. In fact, the circumstances in which persecution occurs drive people to search for something that will give them a greater freedom—freedom from sin that is far more valuable than living in a free society with temporal benefits. While localized persecution may silence the church and the advance of a Christian witness for awhile, it usually forces the seeds of the gospel to spread subtly underground only to emerge in a fruitful harvest among a subsequent generation as it did in China and is now doing in several Muslim countries.

On the other hand, God uses it to disperse the witness as happened in Asia when persecution intensified in China. God, who is sovereign over the nations, can turn evil into good and suffering into blessing. He used persecution among the early church in Jerusalem to force believers to be dispersed out of their comfort zone and nurturing church fellowship in order for the gospel to be taken to the nations. "On that day a severe persecution broke out against the church in Jerusalem, and all except the apostles were scattered throughout the land of Judea and Samaria. . . . So those who were scattered went on their way proclaiming the message of good news" (Acts 8:1, 4).

Christians who live in free, democratic countries in the West where persecution is not a normal occurrence often cringe in horror when they hear reports of brothers and sisters around the globe experiencing atrocities of suffering and death for their faith. Our natural inclination is to cry out in opposition against these tragedies. We want to extract these victims of persecution from the environment of persecution and thereby make the mistake of removing the power of their witness. We need to examine whether or not our responses are biblically informed. A biblical theology of persecution creates a framework for understanding God's sovereign purpose in allowing the evil dominions of darkness to inflict suffering on His children.

Believers in China, when asked how Christians in the West can pray for them, often discourage them from praying for relief from persecution. They say, "Pray that we will be faithful in suffering, but do not pray for persecution to be removed lest we become weak and lethargic like churches we hear of in the West. One can know the fullness of God's grace only in suffering and denial. One who has not suffered for his faith is as a child without training."[4]

Actually, while persecution does occur in many places through-out the world, the most dominant form is not the brutality of a police state arresting and torturing Christians but the social and family pressures against those who would follow Christ. Denial of one's culture and religious traditions subjects one to ostracism and shame in the community. To violate social norms of respect and submission to one's parents has extreme consequences within the home.

A prominent researcher studying the persecution of Christians has come to the conclusion that Satan's primary purpose in perse-cution is to deny others access to Jesus:

> Believers living in the midst of persecution suggest
> strongly that the goal of Satan is not to beat, torture
> or kill believers. The goal of Satan and his persecutors
> is to silence believers, to make them lose their voice
> and diminish their witness. They strive to silence
> witness as covertly as possible. The most successful
> persecution happens when an immediate family
> member, a boss, a spouse, or the culture in general,
> pressures the convert into remaining quiet, keeping
> faith "personal." The persecutors want to relegate
> faith to the environs of the Western world. Or they
> desire that faith be practiced only within the walls of
> a few church buildings that are closely monitored by
> the state or local religious authorities.[5]

Sometimes fear of persecution can be as effective as persecu-tion itself. Fear is one of Satan's most effective tools. If he can keep one from following Jesus, or a believer from sharing his faith because of fear of what might happen, he is just as success-ful as imposing torture and physical punishment. Generally Satan resorts to overt persecution only after covert persecution fails. If a quiet but forceful word from a friend, family, or employer stifles or eliminates a faithful witness, why would Satan draw more atten-tion to our faith by more overt persecution?

In many closed countries there is little measurable persecution as there are so few true believers. It is most prominent where the Christian faith is growing and spreading, and therefore more severe means must be taken to discourage and inhibit access to Jesus. The number one cause of persecution in the world is people coming to Jesus! If there was no response or interest in people becoming Christ followers, there would be no need to threaten and intimidate the occasional Christian. The ultimate expression of the demonic and evil among some regimes and societies is not the cruelty and injustice toward believers but the fact they are denying their people access to Jesus. That is why suffering brings glory to God as it attests to an authentic faith that actually feeds the growth of the church.

That persecution and martyrdom are predicted and necessary (though temporal) evils that are allowed in God's plan to establish His church and inaugurate His kingdom on earth. God is using the persecution perpetrated by Satan and his minions to serve His sovereign purpose to expand, purify, strengthen, and multiply His Kingdom.

In his book, *The Screwtape Letters,* C. S. Lewis helps us understand this strategy. Satan does not want, generally, to beat, torture, imprison, or kill us; he simply wants to shut us up—to diminish and stop our witness.[6]

What is seriously implied here is that each day you and I determine whether we will identify with the persecutors or with the persecuted by whether or not we give or withhold our witness.

> *The number one cause of persecution in the world is people coming to Jesus!*

Where Satan has covertly silenced the church in evangelistic proclamation, he has gained a partner. The worst persecutors on the planet are those that deny others access to Jesus. A nonwitnessing church is no worse than North Korea or Saudi Arabia who are so evil they are denying people access to Jesus Christ. But where

Satan is persecuting Christ followers overtly, he is losing the battle for God's glory in their lives and among the nations.

Hebrews 12 reminds us that we are surrounded by a great cloud of witnesses. These are not those who have gone before and are passively observing our pilgrimage through trials and suffering. They are those who bear witness of the sufferings that are an inevitable part of serving our Lord. They come from the pages of the Bible and the chronicles of Christian history, testifying to the triumph that is assured to those who are ridiculed, rejected, persecuted, and killed but are found faithful. Because of their faithfulness, the gospel has prevailed, and the kingdom of God has grown through the ages and extended to the ends of the earth.

They tell us the key to the victory for them and modern-day martyrs is suffering for their faith in China and across the world. Lay aside the sin that would so readily encumber us—the temptation to focus on oneself, comforts, and self-preservation. Endure whatever life brings by looking to Jesus and staying focused on Him. All that one may experience in persecution and torture pales in comparison to what Jesus endured on the cross. But He endured the cross and despised the shame for the sake of redeeming a lost world for God's glory.

Staying focused on Jesus is what enables those persecuted to claim the victory whether in life or through death. Satan does not realize that persecution is providing an opportunity for Jesus to be revealed! "We are persecuted but not abandoned; we are struck down but not destroyed. We always carry the death of Jesus in our body, so that the life of Jesus may be revealed in our body" (2 Cor. 4:9–10). Persecution continues to be rampant throughout the world, perhaps more widespread than ever before in history. But it cannot deter or defeat the advancement of God's kingdom. To the contrary, it is planting the seeds of the gospel and bringing glory to God as a precursor to that day when every tongue shall confess that Jesus is Lord to the glory of God the Father!

Going Deeper

1. What are ways Satan attempts to intimidate Christians from a verbal witness?

2. What are ways Satan attempts to intimidate Christians from engaging the nations with the gospel?

3. What actions can counter Satan's strategy of intimidation in your life?

4. Whom do you know that might benefit from the inspirational stories in this chapter?

5. What is your next step to deliver the stories?

Overview of Chapter 7

Satan's Internal Obstacles to the Body of Christ and Mission of God

Every Man, Woman, and Child

Every Tongue, Tribe, and Nation

SATAN'S STRATEGY: CONVINCE CHRISTIANS MISSIONS IS OPTIONAL

S atan continues to work through godless world leaders and totalitarian governments to keep countries closed to missionaries and restrict a Christian witness, but in this era of modern communication and global commerce, he is unsuccessful in barricading countries against the life-transforming message of Jesus Christ. His strategy to obscure remote people groups from our awareness has failed as sociologists and researchers have identified every ethnic language group in the world. Their location and worldviews are known and are systematically being penetrated with a gospel witness. Even persecution is feeding the growth of the church and expanding access to the Christian message. Satan does not understand the power of love that motivates a sacrificial commitment and the power of the convictions of believers willing to suffer for their faith.

Often I (Ed) will say to one of my daughters something like, "Sweetheart, will you help with the dishes?" At face value, it seems as if there is an option built into my request. In reality, I am making a gracious dictate to my little girl. The asking is actually directing. God works similarly with us. He invites us to participate in His mission. But we never find the Scriptures to list it as optional. But because He desires to operate relationally with us, God allows us to make a decision. Rest assured that Satan will seize upon this dynamic at every turn in order to convince us that missional activity is an option that can be and should be denied.

God's Word calls Satan "the god of this age" (2 Cor. 4:4). He leverages a tremendous asset when he works outside the church in the world to hinder the gospel. In the world he is on his home court. However, he is much too cunning to depend solely on closed countries, undiscovered people groups, the persecution of believers, and cultures hostile to the gospel. He employs other strategies to deter the advancement of God's kingdom inside the Christian community to hinder believers and churches from ever deploying to vast pockets of lostness around the world.

In trying to convince Christians that missions is optional, he diverts churches to focus on their own programs and to see their mission as reaching people for their own church. If he can persuade Christians that reaching the nations has no relevancy or urgency to their own life, he has raised a barrier that makes other barriers obsolete. Who, then, will be willing to leave their own comfort and security to take the gospel and declare God's salvation to the peoples of the world?

You may think this is semantics, but the body of Christ needs to hear a different descriptor than "mission volunteer." The volunteer is given high regard in our culture. Why? Volunteers do something that is not required of them. They work although they are not obligated. Volunteers contribute selflessly to a cause greater than themselves. What heroes! If the devil can convince us that engaging friends, communities, and nations with the gospel is something we really do not have to do, he wins. If he makes the smallest step of Christian service seem heroic, he creates a barrier to moving outside our comfort zones. We will serve the Lord and the church on an intuitive, feel-good level only.

Paul would have never considered himself a volunteer. His burden for men, women, and children drove him far beyond volunteering for Christ. Missions was not a voluntary act for Paul. It was compulsory. He described his commitment this way: "I am obligated both to Greeks and barbarians, both to the wise and the foolish. So I am eager to preach the good news to you also who are in Rome" (Rom. 1:14–15). The language of volunteerism would be unfamiliar with the deeply burdened missionary apostle. Paul felt obligated to do something about the lostness around him. He owed them an opportunity to hear the good news of Jesus. Also, you see that the obligation and debt he felt produced urgency and courage. In the same passage he said, "For I am not ashamed of the gospel, because it is God's power for salvation to everyone who believes, first to the Jew, and also to the Greek" (Rom. 1:16).

Prioritizing the Local—Ignoring the Nations

Throughout my (Jerry) tenure as president of a denominational mission organization, I have spoken in many churches for international missions events. It is not unusual to have lunch with the pastor after the Sunday morning worship and for the conversation to go something like this: "Dr. Rankin, we appreciate your coming and challenging our people for missions involvement. We are trying to reach our community, build up our programs, and pay off our indebtedness, and then we are going to give priority to involving our church in international missions." But the reality is they never satisfy those criteria and conditions for doing missions beyond their own location! However, we could document the churches that are leading their people to pray for unreached people groups, providing opportunities for volunteer mission trips, encouraging their people to give generously and sacrificially to missions, and all are experiencing growth and effective local outreach.

Many pastors do not understand the responsibility of the local church in God's mission. Neither do they embrace the fact that members have been called as the people of God to declare His salvation to the ends of the earth. Many are depriving their church of the very thing that would stimulate growth and a healthy, vital congregation because they see missions as secondary and something that competes with local programs for budget resources. Many pastors contend that it is necessary to give priority to facilities and local programs, designed primarily to serve and minister to members who already know Christ. Otherwise, there would not be a strong base from which missionaries are called and supported. But then, when I ask how many missionaries have been called out of the church, usually the number is negligible if there are any at all. Seldom do members sense a call to missions if a passion and heart for reaching a lost world does not permeate the DNA of a church.

When we tell incredible stories of how God is moving around the world, people in American churches often ask, "Why don't we see that happening in America? We have a strong Christian history and a prolific number of churches in every city and community. Why is there such indifference toward the gospel? Why is there spiritual coldness and lethargy? Churches no longer have an impact on society, and our country has lost its moral moorings. Why?"

Does Satan have anything to do with an obsession among churches of local over global responsibility? Is it wrong to want to minister effectively to the people that God has brought together into a local congregation? Certainly God wants us to be the body of Christ, ministering to the needs of people in our community and reaching the lost where we live. But that doesn't exempt us from the responsibility of taking the gospel to the nations. If a church does not have a plan to "make disciples *of all nations,*" then they are shirking their responsibility for the mission of God.

The apostle Paul gives us some insight into this dilemma by reflecting on the experience of Israel. In Romans 11 he says a remnant experienced the grace of God, but the rest were hardened. He quotes Deuteronomy and Isaiah: "As it is written: God gave them a spirit of stupor, eyes that cannot see and ears that cannot hear to this day" (Rom. 11:8). Then he goes on to say that salvation will come to the Gentiles. In other words, God's mission among the nations (Gentiles) will be fulfilled as He will be known and glorified by all peoples, but the tragedy is that Israel will not have a part in it.

> *Does Satan have anything to do with an obsession among churches of local over global responsibility?*

It was God's plan and intention that Israel, His chosen people, would carry out His mission to proclaim His glory among the nations that all the ends of the earth would praise and exalt His name. However, they became focused on their own, self-centered concerns, striving for their own prosperity, and became blind to the reason they existed as the people of God. Their hearts were hardened to their mission and concern for the nations; therefore, they were rejected and set aside while God moved on to fulfill His mission.

I (Jerry) have traveled throughout the world and seen masses of people who have not rejected the gospel. Instead, they have never had an opportunity to hear and respond to it. I wonder why in God's providence He allowed Christianity to move westward across Europe and subsequently to America. Why did He allow us to be born in a country where there is religious freedom, there are churches everywhere, and ample opportunity to hear and respond to the gospel? Why has He enabled us to come into a personal relationship with Jesus Christ and know our sins are forgiven, and we can be assured of eternal life when most of the world does not have that opportunity?

Is it because He loves us more than the people of China, India, or those across the Arab world? I don't think so; the Bible tells us God loves the whole world. Perhaps it is because we are more deserving than they are since we live in a moral, God-honoring society. Definitely not! We are all just sinners saved by grace, undeserving of God's mercy. So why have we been chosen to become the people of God? I don't know. Paul tried to explain this in Romans—why some, a remnant, were recipients of God's grace while others were rejected. He concludes there is no explanation: "Oh, the depth of the riches both of the wisdom and the knowledge of God! How unsearchable His judgments and untraceable His ways! . . . For from Him and through Him and to Him are all things. To Him be glory forever" (Rom. 11:33, 36). We don't know why God has chosen us to be among those who know Him. But because we are, we must take up the responsibility to make Him known among all nations so that they will glorify Him forever!

If not us, who? How will more than one billion Muslims know that Jesus is the way, the truth, and the life if we who know Him do not tell them? How will hundreds of thousands of Buddhists and Hindus discover that the way to God is not through endless reincarnations based on personal merit but through the sacrificial death of the Son of God if we don't go and speak into their lives and cultures? How will the multitudes duped by generations of brainwashing to accept the humanistic philosophies of communism know there is a God who yearns to forgive sin and reconcile them into a personal saving relationship if we don't testify to the soul-satisfying hope we have found in Him? How will the generations rejecting any idea of eternal truth in Western culture come to know the God who is right and true and desires to be known by them unless we show and share the gospel?

Christians today are identified as the spiritual sons of Abraham. God has chosen us to carry out His plan, originally intended for Israel. But like them, we are in danger of being set aside and forfeiting the calling and privilege of being His instrument to reach the nations. Like Israel, we have become self-centered and ingrown, more concerned about our own growth and ministry among God's people to the neglect of reaching a lost world!

Is Satan behind our good intentions to reach our kind of people in our community? Is it wrong to be unwilling to go overseas? Is it effective to attempt to influence other cultures and communicate the gospel in languages we do not speak or know? The Bible focuses significant attention on the contrast between the flesh and the Spirit. God yearns for us to be led by the Spirit who indwells us. Jesus said that when the Spirit comes, "He will glorify Me" (John 16:14). Obviously, Jesus is glorified when we do His will. Certainly He wants us to live for Him, reflect Christlike character, minister to the "least of these," and fulfill all of His teachings. But the compelling desire and purpose of Jesus—a purpose for which He promised the empowering of His Spirit—is that we be witnesses, even to the ends of the earth and make disciples of all nations.

Satan uses the flesh to entice us to sin through self-gratification, pleasures, and desires. God's call includes dying to self and giving ourselves in love to others. Anytime we hold on to our own plans because of what we desire instead of yielding to God's plan, it is sin. Satan is behind such self-interest. Jesus was preparing His disciples to understand the necessity of His crucifixion as they could not grasp the necessity of His death. When Peter expressed objections and a commitment to keep that from happening, Jesus responded, "Get behind Me, Satan! You are an offense to Me because you're not thinking about God's concerns, but man's" (Matt. 16:23).

> *Anytime we focus on man's concerns instead of God's, Satan has successfully diverted our good intentions.*

Anytime we focus on man's concerns instead of God's, Satan has successfully diverted our good intentions. He doesn't have to make us do evil things; all he has to do is hinder us from obedience. Jesus had just said, "On this rock I will build My church, and the forces of Hades will not overpower it" (Matt. 16:18). But what kind of church do we see today? Where are the forces of Hades overpowering our congregations? Is your church a world force for evangelism, impacting society and making a powerful impact for the kingdom of God, or is it a church devoted to serving and ministering to the needs of its own carnal Christian members? When priority is given to comfortable facilities and convenient activities benefitting the community of the redeemed rather taking the gospel to a lost world, you have located a "missions-optional" church.

In fact, even in our local communities we are abandoning our mission. God is bringing people of racial diversity from all over the world into our own cities. But churches are isolating themselves in socioeconomic havens where they can serve their families and minister to their own kind, insulated from immigrants and the multiracial diversity of people that need to know Christ. Do we not realize that so many of the Asian Indians, Middle Easterners, Orientals, and Hispanics who are moving into our communities are lost? Have we forgotten the eternal consequences they face apart from faith in Jesus Christ? God spoke through Ezekiel, "I searched for a man among them who would repair the wall and stand in the gap before Me on behalf of the land so that I might not destroy it, but I found no one" (Ezek. 22:30). The atoning death of Jesus on the cross was sufficient to save every person throughout the world. But God has chosen for His church to be His instrument—His witness—to proclaim redemption and bring salvation to the nations. If we ignore our responsibility to stand in the gap between God and a lost world due to our self-centered desires, we will stand accountable. He who is worthy of all glory is being deprived of the honor and praise of the nations, and our disobedience will bring judgment upon us as God's people.

If we neglect God's instructions to take the gospel to the ends of the earth while following our own programs, we are guilty of the condemnation of Jesus. He said, "Disregarding the command of God, you keep the tradition of men" (Mark 7:8). If we are truly committed to the lordship of Jesus Christ, the compelling focus of our life and ministry is obedience to His will. Then, making disciples of all nations represents a prominent priority in all we do as His church. Luke 6:46 does not just apply to personal behavior and individual surrender to God's will but to the Great Commission task of the church: "Why do you call Me 'Lord, Lord,' and don't do the things I say?" God forbid that the church of today would incur His judgment that fell upon Israel: "That they might be My people for My fame, praise, and glory, but they would not obey" (Jer. 13:11).

Bigger Mission or Bigger Church

Recently I (Ed) had the opportunity to visit Rome for the first time. The highlight of the trip without question was our visit to the Vatican. I remember walking to the area where Italy is on one side and the Vatican was on the other. A white line on the sidewalk separates Italy and the Vatican. Vatican City is actually a separate country. My oldest daughter, Kristen, was fascinated by the white line. She enjoyed jumping between the countries. I started doing it myself! A world unto itself, Vatican City has its own police force and military army (Swiss mercenaries—which sounds like an oxymoron). The pope is the head of state. What about a church that has grown in stature beyond its own community to become its own country!

My visit to Rome included a stop at St. Paul's Basilica. St. Paul's is the second largest church in Rome. Kristen said to me at one point, "Dad, our church is bigger than that." I am not sure her assessment was accurate. At the time I was interim pastor at a megachurch in the suburbs of Nashville, Tennessee. Most of the churches we saw were not churches as we might define them in the Bible Belt. The grand facilities that covered the beautiful countryside of Italy are monuments of a movement that has largely died away. In Italy you simply have people who visit services at these massive buildings. Most attendees are tourists. The church in Italy has lost its connection with people and communities. Something really big and once powerful lost its way theologically and missiologically.

After our visit to St. Paul's, my group and I went outside to a nearby park. I talked with them about the history of Catholicism in Rome. A point of emphasis in my discussion was how churches get distracted and lose their God-given mission. Churches in general, but big churches in particular, are easily distracted.

One of the people in our group asked an insightful question: "So, is this where the church in America is heading?" I am afraid the answer may well be yes. When we look at history, we discover a predictable cycle. Things get big, they lose focus, and then they die away. That is the normal order of things. They get big, they get distracted from their mission, and then they die.

In every organization, there are a myriad of forces at work, but two stand out to me. They can be illustrated by a yo-yo. If you swing a yo-yo around in a circle, two forces are at work (in a nontechnical sense). The first is the centrifugal force which pulls the yo-yo away and pushes it outward. This force represents the missionary nature of our work. The second force is centripetal, the force that draws things inward, the force exerted by the string. This force is necessary to care for the core, and the temptation is to make that the focus. One force spreads and the other force centralizes. For churches today, the choice is to keep pushing toward missionary work as it radiates in a larger circle or to service the needs of the tether by pulling it inward. The moment a church decides that missions is an optional activity, then the tether becomes the focus, and the radius of work by the church begins a rapid decline.

We ought not to be so naive to think that it won't happen to our churches in America. We have so many strong, healthy, large churches in the Bible Belt, right? But this is not the first time a country had a "Bible Belt." Bible Belts have lived and died just as their churches have lived and died. As a matter of fact, let's trace it historically.

Jerusalem was once the Bible Belt. Today Christians have moved out. The few that remain are under persecution. The initial migration of persecuted Christians from Jerusalem resulted in a strong community of believers in Antioch (mentioned twenty-two times in Acts). Antioch was a key location for the sending phase of the early Christian movement (Acts 11; 13; 15). Today you can't find a thriving evangelical community in Antioch. So the center of Christianity moved to Rome. Regardless of our enthusiasm about history, the reality is that a great church was built in Rome. But that great church lost its way. Then, some say, it went to Constantinople or Moscow. Great enthusiasm accompanied these church centers early in Christian history. Then, there was the Reformation in Germany, and it died away. I (Ed) was in Frankfurt, Germany, teaching evangelical pastors and missionaries there. They are trying to plant the gospel in a place that was once rich in Christian presence and influence. Germany was the birthplace of the Reformation. From Germany the Reformation took hold to influence America. We are believers in America today because from Germany the gospel moved to England and from England to the United States. America became a bastion of Christian faith. Today, however, we are watching the center of Christian faith move away to other parts of the world. The gospel is prospering like never before in South America, Africa, and Asia (particularly Korea and China). We ought not be surprised if the church in America looks a lot like the current church in Europe fifty years from now—or less.

Has a shift like this happened before in America? Actually, yes, it has. When I was a young man, I (Ed) planted a church in Buffalo, New York. It was in the end of the tail of what many call the Burnt Over District. Many years before there was a Bible Belt that stretched from Rochester, through Buffalo, across what is now I-90. The Second Great Awakening (1790–1840) took place in the region. People were converted to Christ in large numbers. "The rest of the story," as the late Paul Harvey might have said, was not so good. The place they call the Burnt Over District got its name from Charles Finney because the fire of revival came, grew large, lost its mission, and then it fell apart. What describes a region of the U.S. could well describe the entire country in the future. The church in that region embraced the mission of God and saw enormous results and numeric growth. But a new generation arose that believed missions was optional.

American culture is infatuated with big. American churches have never been bigger. In fact, *Outreach Magazine* and LifeWay Research have seen an incredible shift in the numerical size of churches. In 1970 research indicates that around thirty churches in the United States averaged two thousand or more in attendance. We categorize a church with two thousand people or more attending on weekends as a megachurch. Research has indicated the number of megachurches in America has grown to more than thirteen hundred in the last thirty-five years!

Satan has blinded our minds if we believe the mission of God will be fulfilled through building something big, filling it with programs, and admiring the crowds. Eventually, as in Rome, we will lose sight of our mission, fall apart, and fall away. How is Satan, the "liar" (John 8:44), lying to us here? He is lying when he convinces us that a big and busy church is a successful church.

> *Satan has blinded our minds if we believe the mission of God will be fulfilled through building something big, filling it with programs.*

We will readily add that God is using many large churches to reach people and touch the world. Many of them are newer churches led by men of God. Yet, as a nation other numbers reveal, we have never been less Christian. If more and larger churches are a solution to the spiritual lostness of America or the world, then they are only one solution. Our scorecard for success should never be limited to the measure of Wall Street, presuming that bigger numbers equal bigger impact. If we're big and busy, we tend to feel good about ourselves. God's scorecard measures the wideness of His glory through changed lives, transformed communities, and taking the gospel to the nations. We should work for a big, even worldwide, movement of God. But as fallible humans, remember that even the big and busy can be offtrack biblically. We can be big and busy and offtrack in our mission; I saw it in Rome.

Churches are not buildings; they are people. Rodney "Gipsy" Smith, a British revival preacher, was converted to Christ at age sixteen in 1876. He was not taken seriously at the time. He could not read or write. "Only a gypsy boy" were the words someone used to describe him the day of his conversion. "If you really want revival," Smith said, "get in a room; draw a circle on the floor with a piece of chalk, get in the circle, and cry out to God to send revival to everything in the circle." When God moves in the lives of His people, it is to move them into His kingdom activities. What does it look like when people are on mission with God?

People on Mission Live on Mission

People on mission have made an important discovery. People on mission do not go to church. People on mission are the church. Being on mission for Jesus is a way of life that frees us from the busyness of doing "Christian" activities. It is a choice to be mission-shaped and Jesus-centered disciples living for the gospel in their communities. *Mission-shaped* means God is bending me to have His heart for the world.

Church activities are a part of my life, but they are not the totality of my spiritual journey. God is shaping me with His passion for people far from Him. I engage with those church activities for a higher purpose, to glorify Jesus with my life. *Jesus-centered* means He is the focal point of my life. "For in Him we live and move and exist," as Paul described life with God in a sermon preached in Athens (Acts 17:28). Like the original twelve disciples, I do life with Jesus on a daily basis.

The devil would love for us to substitute congregational programs for a 24/7 missionary lifestyle. One common behavior of people far from God—get ready, this is profound—is they don't go to your church. Even more, the likelihood of them ever going to your church is low. An even greater reality is that people in

Oradea, Romania, or Matamoros, Mexico, who have yet to meet Jesus, will not visit your Sunday School class this Sunday either. If the reality that they are not coming really does not matter to us, then, our definition of success looks different. We become like the little boy who shot an arrow into the side of a barn and painted a bull's-eye around where the arrow landed. Our revised, freshly painted bull's-eye emerges. Our personal success for God and the success of our church are measured by how much we do on a church campus and how many people attended. Instead, our busy should be busy about the business of the King. The King is in love with every tribe, tongue, and nation. The King's heart is for every man, woman, and child in your city, wherever they are.

> *The devil would love to substitute congregational programs for a 24/7 missionary lifestyle.*

The work of God's people is not often pictured in the Bible as big. The activity of God, pictured with biblical metaphors, is often small. We love the big. God loves the significant. When we think of gains for today, He is thinking of significance in eternity. When Jesus spoke of the end of the age, He proclaimed, "This good news of the kingdom will be proclaimed in all the world as a testimony to all nations. And then the end will come" (Matt. 24:14). The final commissioning words of Jesus to His disciples included, "Go, therefore, and make disciples of all nations" (Matt. 28:19). For Jesus, there is a limitless potential for people who live on His mission.

David Platt, pastor of the Church at Brook Hills in Birmingham, Alabama, reported on a trip to Sudan where he had the opportunity to train lay pastors in a remote location in the southern part of the country. Most of these men were relatively uneducated and had never been out of the rural area where they were ministering and starting village churches. Having tea during an afternoon break time, David asked one of them about his vision for his life and ministry. The man replied, "I'm going to disciple the nations." Incredulous, David asked how he intended to do that. This humble, young Sudanese responded with an enthusiastic grin and an evasive, incongruent reply, "Why not?"

This young visionary Christian just might fit Jesus' explanation of a small object with big influence: "He told them another parable: 'The kingdom of heaven is like yeast that a woman took and mixed into 50 pounds of flour until it spread through all of it'" (Matt. 13:33). Yeast is small in substance. Yet, when mixed with something larger, yeast has incredible influence. People on mission understand the nature of influence. The nature of influence as seen in the kingdom of God, and the kingdom of heaven is different from our church mentality. For us it's not small, mixing in something big, and changing everything. Instead what we envision is to extract people from the culture, mix them together, make them really busy, and create something big. We end up with big things and little influence on the people for whom Christ died. Jesus taught us to begin with little things of great influence and change the world.

God may bless and grow our church or ministry to large proportions, but we must abandon the goal of a big and successful church. Instead, embrace that the kingdom of God appears as the smallest of seeds and a miniscule amount of leaven. Both begin small but result with tremendous impact. God does not need you and me to do large things but to trust His mission to accomplish large things.

So, if a believer is to be on mission, what's the purpose of the church? Is gathering on Sundays important? Yes, to equip you, to encourage you, and to send you out. And contrary to what some propose, we as church ought to be measured. Not for the purpose of hierarchy in a network or denomination because those are pretty low-lying goals. Rather, we take note of our impact in order to know if we are working along with the mission of God or simply servicing the temporary needs of the sheep. Traditional measurements of church growth are insignificant. Biblical score-cards include more and different measures.

Jesus could have planted and pastored a big local church. He fed five thousand people who, needless to say, were impressed by His leadership. Jesus at this point could have been king. He could have started the first megachurch in history. "When the people saw the sign He had done, they said, 'This really is the Prophet who was to come into the world!' Therefore, when Jesus knew that they were about to come and take Him by force to make Him king, He withdrew again to the mountain by Himself" (John 6:14–15). Why didn't Jesus do it? The vision of Jesus was greater than a single congregation. As much as we might consider ourselves visionaries (God forgive us for our pride), Jesus' vision will always be greater. Jesus' scorecard was greater than a church of five-thousand-plus attendees. In eternity, Jesus saw billions of people who would need to know Him. Multiplication was critical if the world was to be reached. Jesus looked to today as He prayed His high priestly prayer in John 17: "I pray not only for these, but also for those who believe in Me through their message. May they all be one, as You, Father, are in Me and I am in You. May they also be one in Us, so the world may believe You sent Me" (vv. 20–21). Jesus embraced the mission of His Father, which was for more people, but more people for God's purposes.

What will it look like then, when a local church, no matter the size, embraces the big vision of Jesus? The scorecard changes radically. Greatness is no longer measured by seating capacity. Greatness is measured by sending capacity. Being in the top one hundred fastest growing or largest churches no longer is on the scorecard. New scorecards are loftier. How many new churches did we start here and abroad? How many new ministries have begun in our community? How many people have we equipped and sent to spread His name and fame throughout the nations? How many conversations about Jesus did our people engage in last month, away from the church campus? When God's people get out, mix it up, and penetrate our communities, we change everything. Just like yeast.

Ingrown and Self-Centered to Satan's Delight

I (Ed) travel to Springfield, Missouri, more than most places. Why Springfield? A lot of churches, schools, and denominations in the area invite me there. How many of you have been to Springfield, Missouri, or nearby Branson? Branson is like Christian Broadway and Six Flags Over Jesus rolled into one! One of the most fascinating points of interest in Springfield is a Christian bowling alley called Lighthouse Lanes. I've taken pictures of Lighthouse Lanes and put them on Twitter or Facebook. I'm fascinated by this idea. "Glow bowling in a smoke-free environment," was one person's online description of Lighthouse Lanes. What makes bowling distinctively Christian? Is it holy rollers? I mean, what is it that makes a bowling alley Christian?

Being an inquisitive person, I asked people who actually bowl, why a Christian bowling alley? I thought it sounded like a fair question. One answer was, "Well, you know, so many worldly things take place in bowling alleys." I am thinking, *Really?* I've been bowling. I'm not that good, but I have been there. I've seen some smokers. And there's a bar in most bowling alleys. But is the answer really to create places like Christian bowling alleys to get away from people who need to know us?

Program-obsessed churches scare me. But even scarier are those who seek to create a modern-day fortress to protect everyone in the church from the world. We think it will protect us, but what it does is actually corrupt us because we become self-obsessed. Investing in the body of Christ is necessary to be a healthy Christian. Investing everything into the body of Christ while abandoning the mission of God for the world is a corruption of the Christian.

Churches with gymnasiums and family life centers are not unusual. Some churches have racquetball courts and bowling alleys. And I know God can use them. But maybe you could challenge your people to make a three-year commitment to join the local gym as a missionary. Make friends with people there who will never come to your church or family life center. I'll bet local health club dues will cost less money than your capital campaign. Then have a "change the world" capital campaign where the three-year financial commitments are for world missions, church planting, reaching your city, and transforming your community for Christ. What if you already have a family life center? Call your church to prayer and strategic planning on how you can use the center as a platform to glorify Christ in your community.

Buildings don't reach people; people on mission reach people. For years churches have embraced "brick and mortar" evangelism. Bricks don't witness! We believe if we can only get people on our home court (our facilities), they will surrender to Christ! At the end of the day what we've got to recognize is that buildings and programs are tools. Just like musical style, evangelism training, small groups in coffeehouses, and strategy centers in foreign lands are tools. But because we like a controllable pattern, we turn tools into rules. We begin to protect and defend the way we do things. Do you treat the tools in your garage that way? Have you ever replaced them? What happens when they cease to be effective? Do you ever upgrade them? Of course you do. Why? Your tools are there because they have a purpose—results! The moment they stop working, or a better tool is introduced, the old is gone to the thrift store or the dumpster.

> *Buildings don't reach people; people on mission reach people.*

Satan would love to convince American Christians that an effective building or program is the only thing required for completing the mission of God in our country. If you want to know the result of such a strategy, just look at the empty cathedrals in Europe. Programs offer a temptation of the "man planned, man initiated, man powered." People on mission live on mission because God has grown them beyond trusting themselves. The influence God gives is His influence in and through us. So the more we can get beyond the congregational resources, the greater the influence for Christ.

Paul explained this principle to the Corinthian Christians: "But thanks be to God, who always puts us on display in Christ, and spreads through us in every place the scent of knowing Him. For to God we are the fragrance of Christ among those who are being saved and among those who are perishing" (2 Cor. 2:14–15). When Jesus lives in believers who are filled with His Holy Spirit, they lose their natural smell (stink). Jesus in us gives us a new and beautiful odor that influences our friends, family, coworkers, and communities for Him.

Here are the essentials for people who live on mission. Get the scent of Him in your neighborhood. Be the yeast in your community. Permeate your workplace. You have the God-given potential to make a bigger difference for Jesus than the best programs or buildings that your church could ever provide.

God's purpose for His people has been made abundantly clear. While we acknowledge the responsibility for missions, it is not reflected in our activity and commitment. As God said through Isaiah about Israel, "These people approach Me with their mouths to honor Me with lip-service—yet their hearts are far from Me" (Isa. 29:13).

We belittle the nature of God and our commitment to His lordship when we fail to fulfill His mission of witness to those who do not know Him throughout the world. "'You are My witnesses'—the LORD's declaration—'and My servant whom I have chosen, so that you may know and believe Me and understand that I am He. . . . I, I am the LORD, and there is no other Savior but Me. I alone declared, saved, and proclaimed—and not some foreign god among you. So you are My witnesses'" (Isa. 43:10–12). He said in Isaiah 49:6 that it was too small a task for them just to be focused on their own people, but they were to be a light to the nations that

God's salvation might be known to the ends of the earth. That is an indictment on the people of God today who are focusing on reaching and ministering to their own kind of people locally and doing little to mobilize their people and use their resources to declare His salvation to the nations. There is no question that the adversary, who would deprive God of His glory among the nations, the enemy who uses our self-centered fleshly nature to divert us from God's purpose, is actively and subtly leading us to justify our activity-centered work while leading us astray.

People on Mission Make Missional Choices

When I traveled to Rome, I saw a lot of big churches. I also saw a lot of big empty churches. Sometimes big churches were full but empty of the gospel. What does it look like when people are on mission for God? People on mission make missional choices.

Missional is a word that has resurfaced in the Christian language these days. As with most new, cool, and trendy words, the more it is used, the less people will comprehend it. People tend to see in the word *missional* what they want to see. If they want to see the church engage in more social justice, that's "missional." If they want to be more evangelistic, that's "missional." But I still think there's power in a new or modified word that enables us to say, "We do need something different." Being missional is just a way of joining God on His mission. The shift in thinking, however, is away from a compartmentalized view of missions. People on mission understand that being on mission moves beyond doing a project. Being missional goes beyond chaperoning a group of teenagers on a trip to Ohio during the summer. Being missional goes beyond a church feeding the homeless at a local park. People on mission make missional choices as a way of life. Being outward focused and actively joining God at work in the world is what they do every day. No hype. No PowerPoint reports back to the congregation. Being missional is the outward-focused way of life of an ambassador for Christ.

> *Being missional is a way of joining God on His mission. . . .*
>
> *People on mission make missional choices as a way of life.*

I (Ed) do surveys all the time at LifeWay Research. What if we did a survey at your church to determine what you value or to determine if your church were driven by a missional mind-set? What if we asked one hundred people, "Why do you attend here?" In your opinion, what is most important to this church? Is your church all about you? We'd all say no, church isn't about me. In fact, we might say our church is "missional" or "mission minded." We hope people would answer the questions right (whatever that means). For most churches, including yours, answers will likely center on comments like: "I enjoy the preaching." "I enjoy the music." "The people are friendly." "I get my needs met here." What we don't hear enough is, "This church has a vision from God to transform our community, to make it hard to go to hell from our city, or to change the world," or, "This church challenges me to live like a missionary every day of my life." People who are on mission have discovered their greatest need is to join God at work in the world!

People on mission also choose to make intentional relationships with people outside their church. Satan would love to make Christians think these relationships are unimportant or a waste of time. To have multiple relationships in multiple sectors where you live, work, and play will be a sacrifice. Some things will need to change in order to have the time to invest in lost people.

Though we appear to be comfortable talking *about* lost people in our church environments and pulpits, people on mission make the missional choice to talk *to* lost people. For most this is a major shift. God has chosen Christians to be the relational delivery system of the gospel. Not only has He chosen us, but He trusts us to get it done. Paul described the confidence of God this way: "Instead, just as we have been approved by God to be entrusted with the gospel, so we speak, not to please men, but rather God, who examines our hearts" (1 Thess. 2:4). The word *entrusted* in this passage is normally used from us to God (John 3:16). It sounds right that we are the ones who do the "believing." But Paul was talking about God's confidence in His people. God believes in you! What a sacred responsibility! No wonder the forces of hell oppose our missional choice. God believes in us to live and deliver the message to those who are far from Him.

Paul explained to Christians at Corinth what he valued in his life as well as what he wanted them to value. "When I came to you, brothers, announcing the testimony of God to you, I did not come with brilliance of speech or wisdom. For I determined to know nothing among you except Jesus Christ and Him crucified. And I was with you in weakness, in fear, and in much trembling. My speech and my proclamation were not with persuasive words of wisdom, but with a demonstration of the Spirit and power, so that your faith might not be based on men's wisdom but on God's power" (1 Cor. 2:1–5). For most churches, if a pastoral candidate said that they did not come with brilliance of speech or wisdom but in weakness, fear, and much trembling, I think most people would not vote to install the candidate as pastor.

Some of you reading this might "feel led" to search for a place where you could "get fed." Most churches in America are preaching churches. Attendance drops when the preacher is away. This is a choice based on your preferences, not on the mission of God. People who make missional choices do not attend as a consumer. They come to church to serve in the power of God and be equipped by the power of God. They choose to value the church not based on what they want but on how they will advance the cause of the kingdom.

People on Mission Change the World

We can excuse ourselves from the bigger things of God as long as we ask smaller questions. Take this question for example: What does God want our church to do? Would you consider that the right question or the wrong question? How about this one: What does God want me to do? Would you consider that the right question or the wrong question? At first glance they sound right. Even better, they sound spiritual, committed, selfless. But there is a critical flaw with the first two questions in that they are small ideas. The right question is: What does God want? You see the first two are small questions because they necessitate answers that center inwardly. The answers must be about "me" and "my church." Let's see, what does God want from me? I have this car over here. I am good with children. I love bass fishing. I am not too good speaking in public, so let's see . . . God wants me to be happy and fulfilled in my ministry so, I am going to take my car, fill it with children, and start a kid's Christian bass-fishing club."

Nonmissional people sitting in churches on Sunday are self-centered because they are underchallenged. Church staff and key leaders complain, yet their major appeals for help on Sundays are cookies for Vacation Bible School and the need for nursery volunteers. Nothing is wrong with those appeals, but leaders in local churches must realize that the kingdom of God is bigger than Sunday mornings. Also, God has not wired everyone in your congregation to be jazzed about a trip to the grocery store to buy cookies. People on mission are driven by a bigger question: What does God want? Few churches and Christians have the courage to ask that as their primary question.

Europe was once the bastion of world Christianity. Many considered it the Bible Belt of the world. Missionaries went out from Europe proclaiming the gospel and preaching against false gods. The world was changed. And now the world is changed again. Europe is a post-Christian society. Evangelicals are small groups huddled in little churches here or there. The church—when people have heard of the church in Europe—tends to refer to the Catholic or Protestant churches as "the big Protestant cathedrals." They have become museums rather than mission stations. You see the reality that these people on mission didn't change while the world changed around them. And the danger exists for us as well.

People on mission change the world. What does that look like? John, the apostle, gives us a clue, "Because whatever has been born of God conquers the world. This is the victory that has conquered the world: our faith" (1 John 5:4). The question is: Will we conquer the world, or will the world conquer us? Now the word *conquer* can send a mixed message. I'm not talking about crusades, warlike or political. We must focus on conquering the world system that keeps humanity enslaved to sin. So, how? By living counter to cultural norms. We surprise others when we walk by faith in spite of opposition from Satan and the world's system. Confrontation will be a part of what people on mission will face for their faith. Tough choices, sacrifice, and discomfort will be part of their calling. But people on mission live above the arguments because their drive is not to prove they are right or superior.

Changing the world is not for the faint of heart. A large, program-driven ministry is a safe and comfortable alternative to missional living. But the bid to maintain our home court with sheer numbers of people and pastors on church campuses is obviously not working. The extractional impulse that results in church members gathering at the Christian bowling alley to avoid those pesky lost people is misguided. Instead, we must be those who carry the fragrance of Christ to those yet to know Him. If you prefer padded worship seating over missional living among sinners, then God's mission will not take root in your heart, and the world will not be changed by your presence in it. In fact, the world will change you, and Satan's lies will seem like the truth.

But don't miss out on this: the world is changing. It changes while we huddle together, too busy and too self-absorbed to tell them about Jesus. Or it changes when we mobilize in the power of the Spirit with the message of the Christ.

Revivals are happening all over the world. We see places where people are responding to Christ and His church in unprecedented numbers. What is the future of Christianity in America? If we don't get it now, it will sneak up on us like it did the people in Jerusalem, Antioch, Rome, and Moscow. Don't forget that people in Frankfurt and in Buffalo once had thriving churches, too. What happened? Instead of permeating and changing the world, they hid and the world changed them. So what do we do? We're to invade the world, not militaristically; we're to invade the world through the preaching and living of the gospel. As God has changed us, we're now ready to be used by Him in a mission to change others

People on mission change the world. God doesn't need our cleverness and great buildings, but He can use them. Measure your church by God's standards, not by the world's. Become a church that's known as a sending church. Send people into your community. Send people across the world. Send people to Rome, Frankfurt, and to Buffalo. Send people to neighborhoods, nursing homes, and English as a second language classes. People need to hear and see the gospel of Jesus Christ. Let's be more about the sending than about the seating; then Jesus will keep us focused on His mission, and we'll change the world for His name.

Going Deeper

1. What is God seeking to do in the world? How can you join Him?

2. In what sectors of your life away from church can you build deeper relationships with people far from God? What would that look like? What choices would you have to make to free time to invest more in people far from God?

3. Do you have a burden for the people of another country to hear and see the gospel? If not, pray and research possibilities. How can you take your burden to another level through hands-on involvement?

4. What level of priority does your church give to missions and reaching those far from God in terms of budget, programs, and time invested by members?

CHAPTER 8

SATAN'S STRATEGY: ERODE THE
AUTHORITY OF GOD'S WORD

Early in my ministry I (Jerry) was given a little book by C. S. Lewis entitled *The Screwtape Letters*. This book was a series of fictitious letters, as Dr. Lewis imagined them, written by Screwtape, one of Satan's demon agents, to his nephew, Wormwood, who had been assigned to a new Christian. The letters are advice concerning strategies and tactics by which this Christian could be rendered powerless and his life ineffective in the service of the enemy, in this case, the Lord Jesus Christ.

One of the letters advised him to influence this Christian to neglect his devotional time each day. If he did not spend time in prayer and reading the Word of God, reasoned Screwtape, he would be absolutely powerless in spite of all resolve to live for the Lord. Another letter encouraged Wormwood to use contemporary philosophies and influences to cause him to doubt the truth and authority of God's Word. This would erode any foundation for building a dedicated life of service for the kingdom of God.[1]

This book gave me some valuable insights into the reality of Satan's subtle ways of using worldly thinking and influences to undercut the victory we have been given as Christians. Of course the victory that overcomes the world is our faith, not only faith in Jesus Christ but faith to believe the truth of God's Word. If faith is the victory, then all Satan has to do is erode our faith through doubts, rationalizing away through vain interpretations the reality of God's truth. Satan's first appearance in his designs against the crown of God's creation was to confront Eve with doubt: "Did God really say?" (Gen. 3:1). Yes, God had said they were not to eat the forbidden fruit, but Satan proceeded to malign God's motives. He is a liar and deceiver, "No! You will not die. . . . In fact, God knows that when you eat it your eyes will be opened and you will be like God, knowing good and evil" (Gen. 3:4–5). He made her believe that God wanted to deprive her of something to be desired. In listening to Satan's deception, we witness one of his primary tactics: twisting what God had said. Giving in, Eve forfeited the glory for which she had been created. And Satan has been trying to rob God of His glory among His people ever since.

We are alerted to the subtle danger of this tactic by Paul in 2 Corinthians: "For although we are walking in the flesh, we do not wage war in a fleshly way, since the weapons of our warfare are not fleshly, but are powerful through God for the demolition of strongholds. We demolish arguments and every high-minded thing that is raised up against the knowledge of God, taking every thought captive to the obedience of Christ" (2 Cor. 10:3–5). Satan is a fallen angel, a messenger who speaks to our minds, seeking every means to distract us from the things of God. We are urged to bring every thought in obedience to Christ—our thinking is to be conformed to God's Word and His truth.

How important is the Word of God in confronting the forces of darkness? The last piece of the whole armor of God in Ephesians is the weapon the Spirit uses. "Take the helmet of salvation, and the sword of the Spirit, which is God's word" (Eph. 6:17). When confronting internal and external satanic obstacles to the mission of God, the Word of God is critical. The rest of the battle armor that is listed in Paul's famous warfare passage is defensive in nature.

Yet we know that to take the gospel to our friends, communities, and the nations will involve forward, offensive movement. Not offensive, like a foul odor but offensive as in the advancement of a military force. Unfortunately Christians often stink more than they march—but we digress.

The devil and our culture can intimidate us into putting God's Word in a secondary position in our efforts to reach people. Innovation, contextualization, tradition, and liturgy are held up as the primary means of ministry. Yet without the sword, the Word of God, we are left with a weakened gospel that offers only a religious life filled with compulsory good deeds. We literally are put on the spiritual defensive, forced to justify our Christian faith with no authority. Satan would prefer the world to see a false gospel that is good for self-improvement but not great enough for redemption.

Those who reject the authority of God's Word quickly lose any impetus for evangelism and missions. Once the Bible is accepted as erroneous, it becomes subjected to every whim of interpretation, and any portion or teaching becomes optional. The Word of God is foundational for any effective ministry or service that would fulfill God's mission and glorify Him in one's life. "All Scripture is inspired by God and is profitable for teaching, for rebuking, for correcting, for training in righteousness, so that the man of God may be complete, equipped for every good work" (2 Tim. 3:16–17). Peter affirms the divine origin of the message of the Bible: "No prophecy of Scripture comes from one's own interpretation, because no prophecy ever came by the will of man; instead, moved by the Holy Spirit, men spoke from God" (2 Pet. 1:20–21). The seriousness with which we are to accept and

> *It is obvious that those who reject the authority of God's Word quickly lose any impetus for evangelism and missions.*

believe the Word of God is the concluding admonition of the Bible: "I testify to everyone who hears the prophetic words of this book: If anyone adds to them, God will add to him the plagues that are written in this book. And if anyone takes away from the words of this prophetic book, God will take away his share of the tree of life" (Rev. 22:18–19).

Many unbelievers simply would say they just don't believe the Bible is true. Satan convinces them the Bible is a foolish religious book filled with mythology. Some denominations and churches have believed a version of the same lie. Cherry-picking the parts they deem acceptable, they have abandoned the utter trustworthiness of the Bible. This attitude devastates the mission of God. Christians are "witnesses" who verify not only that God's Word is worthy of consideration but that the truth of the Bible works in daily living. Once the Bible becomes an argument among believers, churches, and denominations, the devil wins again. People without Christ are left in unbelief and disbelief, longing for a witness of what is true.

Yet the Bible is not a symbolic, unifying flag to wave so everyone will cheer. The Bible is substance. The Bible is God's truth on paper. The Bible is powerful not because it is a handbook on the Christian religion but because it is the will and ways of God in print. God was teaching a young pastor named Timothy through Paul and said to him, "But as for you, continue in what you have learned and firmly believed, knowing those from whom you learned, and that from childhood you have known the sacred Scriptures, which are able to instruct you for salvation through faith in Christ Jesus" (2 Tim. 3:14–15). How important is a book that will influence and inform your eternal destiny? God's Holy Spirit takes His supernatural word and opens the heart of millions to faith in Him. The Bible is interesting but is not a special interest book. The Bible is inspired but when carefully examined can be far from inspirational. I have heard it said, "I do not read the Bible; the Bible reads me!" How can that be possible? A best seller may be worth buying. The Bible is worth living.

Simply Believing the Bible Is Not Living Its Truth

In our denomination (the Southern Baptist Convention) we spent years arguing about the inerrancy of the Bible. Those of us who defended the Bible ultimately "won" the battle but did not fix all of the issues. What does a Christian, a church, or a denomination look like who holds the Scripture in high value? They should be the most aggressive and fruitful people on the earth. This aggressiveness is not about fighting and winning. Neither is the aggressiveness about changing other cultures to look American. Christians are to hold an aggression of mission completion. The forward lean of the Christian is to glorify God and deliver the gospel so that all may know Him. The group that values the Bible should be experiencing God's blessings through unprecedented growth in new churches, healthy churches, and new converts. Unfortunately this has not been our reality.

We, as a movement of conservative evangelicals, tend to say that the Bible is true and trustworthy. As a matter of fact, I could hold up my Bible, wave it around, and everyone would say, "Amen!" I could ask, "Do you believe the Bible?" Everyone would shout, "Amen!"

But American Christians have proven what we say about the Bible on Sunday is often insincere. The measure of our Sunday confessions is made known in the facing of Monday's realities. The Bible is sufficient to make us wise for salvation. We believe the Bible is true but not necessarily adequate to live our lives. We seemingly believe the right things about the Bible except its sufficiency.

The lie we believe, however, is that the Bible is true but not true enough. The Bible is true but I can't understand it. We believe in inerrancy, but we stop short of believing in its sufficiency. If the devil can separate us from the Word of God, then we miss God's living resource. All we need to know about living, dying, growing, and changing is contained in the pages of the Bible. All we need to know to defeat the "prince of the power of the air" (Eph. 2:2 KJV) is there. No wonder the Bible makes Satan so nervous, and one of his favorite tactics is to delude us into thinking we believe its truth without living it.

I (Ed) went skiing recently for the first time in awhile. I like to call it "falling" instead of skiing, but Donna (my wife) went skiing. Our ski trip brought back memories. I had skied in the past when we lived in New York. Our normal choice for skiing was a small resort called Peek 'n Peak in Clymer, New York. I humbly confess: I am an excellent skier. I'm just not a good turner or stopper. But going straight—you cannot keep up with me!

When I got there, I thought that I was prepared for the experience. I'm not much on instructional classes. I prefer to learn on my own. The key thing for me (I thought) to ski well is to read about skiing. Once I read, I will be an expert. And so I read up on skiing before I went. I learned how to ski from a book. Donna actually took lessons and eventually became a certified ski instructor. I was in good company for many reasons.

The first challenge was the ski lift. I knew enough to pass that test until I had to dismount! I got off the lift, or fell off the lift to be more accurate. If you fall the first time you hit the snow, that's not a good sign. Next I got onto the top of the hill. Then I began my descent. For those of you who have never been skiing, slopes are designed to wander a bit. At this particular ski slope, they had orange cones along the side of the slope so you wouldn't wander into the forest.

I was an amazing skier. Faster and faster I zoomed down the slope at Peek 'n Peak. People were looking at me (I thought) saying, "Man he's good." So it was not until I'm actually heading toward the orange cones, full speed, that I figured out I could be in trouble. I was supposed to turn gracefully to the right at the first set of orange cones. I came up to the orange cones really fast. The design of a ski slope is great, with both safety and adventure in mind. The cones serve a healthy, life-giving purpose unless you don't know how to turn. So I went toward the cones, realizing I was in trouble, screaming like a four-year-old boy, "Somebody save me!" As I approached the cones placed there to guide me, I simply launched into the air. Skiing is one thing. Ski jumping was beyond my experience level. I landed right in front of a tree. I didn't actually hit the tree (thank God) but the pile of snow in front of the tree. My ego was bruised, but real disaster was avoided.

So what happened? I had gotten just enough information to make me dangerous. I knew what I needed to ski and then went out and did it on my own. I didn't pay attention to the cones or what was needed to navigate them correctly. The cones were not there to make my life difficult. The cones were there to protect me and direct me. The orange cones added value to my skiing experience. Some people treat the Bible like I treated the orange cones. They know the Bible is true. They love the idea of the Bible and are intrigued by the content. But for many the Bible is a book of the basics of the Christian faith. The Bible provides talking points for sermons. Nuances and details of Scripture are for other Christians and preachers. Great stories and passages provide beautiful readings for weddings and funerals. Even leaders, who are leading the Christian army to pierce the darkness, do not fully understand the implication of entering into battle

> *Satan's strategy is to erode confidence in God's Word or cause us to neglect it in the battle.*

while leaving the "sword of the Spirit" (Eph. 6:17) on the sidelines. Satan's strategy is to erode our confidence in God's Word or, at least, cause us to neglect it in the battle. As we distance ourselves from God's Word, all effectiveness for the mission of God is eliminated.

Satan's Lies Discredit the Authority for Mission

"All Scripture is inspired by God" (2 Tim. 3:16). So if all Scripture is inspired by God, it is inspirational, right? But sometimes I read the Bible, and it's not always inspirational. So what does *inspired* mean? Specifically, *inspired* means "God breathed." Breath comes deep from within us. Breath is personal and unique. God's breath is supernatural and life giving (Gen. 2:7). So, we handle, read, and discuss something personal and sacred from God. His Word is His will and character expressed in words.

What was the purpose of such an important book? The purpose of the Bible is for us to know God. Any book that might help me get to know the Creator of the universe is important. His plans, purposes, and expectations for me in print are worth my attention. But how does the Bible help us get to know God? The Bible "is profitable for teaching, for rebuking, for correcting, [and] for training in righteousness" (2 Tim. 3:16). The Bible is a critical part of our journey with God. We should not be surprised that Satan attempts to distract us from the Bible. One way he does this is to discredit Scripture. Satan lies to us about the Bible, to keep us from God's supernatural influence in us and through us. Below are four common satanic lies about the Bible.

One lie Satan tells us is that the information in the Bible is not a trustworthy source of information. But we know the Scripture is a worthwhile and trustworthy information source. The Bible is a perfect text for teaching. In the original language the word *teaching* also implies a high level of responsibility for the teacher to embody the message he teaches. Those who teach us the Word of God are to be models and mentors of what they are teaching. What kind of information is to be taught? All the information I need to know to find and follow God is in Scripture. God's Word is truth without any mixture of error. Every subject God addresses in Scripture is addressed with perfect accuracy. God's Word is His gift to us of truth, advice, and right beliefs. God is the ultimate life coach.

Another lie Satan tells about the Bible is that the Bible is not practical. God gives moral boundaries in Scripture. But God is not a cosmic killjoy who is out of touch with the reality of life in the twenty-first century. The same God of the universe who created sex provided instruction about right and wrong ways to experience sex. So He created something incredible that our sin nature tends to pervert and exploit. That the Creator would have advice for the creation not only makes good sense but also provides good advice.

In essence, one of the purposes of the Bible is to rebuke or scold. God's Word exposes my faults, attitudes, and rebellion. God intervenes into our lives to address our blindness to the consequences of our bad choices. Some people talk about enjoying the Bible. I do enjoy the Bible sometimes. But the Bible is compared to a mirror (James 1:23–24). For me (Ed), looking in the mirror first thing in the morning is an unpleasant experience. My first response, however, is not to avoid the mirror. Every day I get my courage up and take a look. My first response is to tell myself, "Self, it looks like we have some work to do!" There are times when I've opened the Bible and said the same thing to myself. But, thank God, I do not have to work alone. God continues to shape me into what He wants. I must have the courage and discipline to keep going back and looking. God uses His Word to rebuke me sometimes and say, "Ed, you need to change."

Another lie of Satan about the Bible is that it is irrelevant. Some consider the Bible a negative book that focuses on what God does not want us to be or do. But the Bible is so much more than a book of oughts and shoulds. Once I am in a mess, how do I get out of the mess? Is my failure fatal?

One of the most beautiful pictures of God's heart to fix broken people is seen in Jesus' conversation with the woman caught in adultery. She was guilty as charged. Even though her accusers were arrogant, self-righteous sinners, God provided no special grace because of their abuse. But Jesus knew her heart. He understood she needed help so He sent her to a place that had never failed. She needed hope, so Jesus told her to look to the future. Listen in on the conversation between Jesus and this woman immediately after her accusers/abusers had left the scene. "When Jesus stood up, He said to her, 'Woman, where are they? Has no one condemned you?' 'No one, Lord,' she answered. 'Neither do I condemn you,' said Jesus. 'Go, and from now on do not sin any more'" (John 8:10–11). Free at last! Hope. A mid-course correction endorsed and empowered by the Son of God! Sounds like God to me. To "correct" here, in the original language is the same word used when describing the resetting of a broken bone. How relevant, in a society full of broken hearts, is the life-giving Word of God?

The fourth lie of the devil is that the Bible is not a unique book. All religions have unique books they consider inspired. Bhagavad Gita (Hindu), the Qur'an (Islam), and the Book of Mormon claim to be divinely or supernaturally inspired. The books have helpful information and are a part of our religious culture. As Satan attempts to elevate religious books, he hopes to devalue God's Word. The Bible is set apart because of its claim of authorship directly from God and how it is unique in its demands and promises. I need everything God gives me through His Word. God's Word gives clear instructions on how to live life skillfully.

We call it inspired, so how does that mean we should treat the Bible? I (Ed) came to Christ as a teenager. One of my small-group teachers taught me not to put anything or any other book on top of the Bible. I "religiously" took my Bible and put it on top of all of my other books. I was afraid of what God would think if I put something on top of His Book. I was concerned that maybe God's Book would lose some of its magic if I put an empty bottle or half eaten sandwich on top. Then that same teacher later told me I should carry my Bible with me every day so my day would go better. The advice sounded like a little bit of Hindu karma mixed with conservative Christianity. God's book was like a good-luck charm or a Christian rabbit's foot. The Bible's power is not in its symbolism or style. The miracle of the Word of God is its substance. What's more important is not that it rests on a desk but that the supernatural influence of God's breath is in our hearts. Satan would rather us treat the book superstitiously than apply it to our lives. He would rather us worry about it than to read it.

In graceful contrast, God wants us to enjoy His Word. I was so busy fretting about keeping the leather cover in nice condition that I did not savor its contents. The enemy wants to distract you with life, earthbound knowledge, or just plain commonsense thinking. But why settle for anything less than the knowledge held by the Almighty One. Enjoy the Scriptures while trembling at its power, and you will find yourself victorious in battle and leading the charge to save souls.

Rationalizing God's Word Diminishes the Tragedy of Lostness

Mainline Protestant church traditions that have abandoned the authority of God's Word quickly succumb to postmodern relativism that rationalizes away the lostness of man and the consequences of sin. One quickly embraces the logic that there are many ways to God, that all religions are of equal value, and there is no need to impose our Christian beliefs on people of other faiths. Even if one holds to the belief that faith in Jesus Christ is the way of salvation, out of respect and tolerance for others our zeal for witness is diminished.

In updating the core values of the Southern Baptist International Mission Board to be relevant in a contemporary world, it was stated, "We believe Jesus Christ is the only way of salvation and all who live apart from faith in Him are lost and will spend eternity in hell." That is not a politically correct statement but is exactly what the Bible teaches regarding the way of salvation and the consequences of those who do not confess Jesus as Lord and Savior. No statement like this was found in the historical documents of the mission board; none was needed because in the past this truth was assumed. But that is no longer the case in our pluralistic society. However, if this is not true, there is no need to do missions! Satan is thwarting the expansion of God's kingdom and the future potential of His being glorified among the nations through a simple war of attrition upon the doctrine of God's people.

People have a tendency to assert their independent, self-centered thinking by espousing the priesthood of believers and autonomy of the local church, neglecting to acknowledge that these foundational convictions are based on the lordship of Jesus Christ and the authority of God's Word. The result is churches mimicking society, choosing humanistic thinking, cultural accommodation, and theological compromise at the expense of abiding and eternal truth that would compel us in our mission task.

Speaking at conferences and in churches I (Jerry) often attempt to portray graphically those who live in unreached people groups and have never even heard the name of Jesus. First, it is difficult for most people to comprehend any people in our world today are so isolated culturally and geographically that they have not heard of Jesus Christ.

After all, we can see news events as they occur anywhere in the world simultaneously on our newscasts. Yet researchers have identified more than a billion people who are isolated culturally and geographically in places where there are no churches, no Christian believers, and no Christian resources. They live a lifetime and die without ever knowing a Savior came and died for them.

> *Churches [are] mimicking society, choosing humanistic thinking, cultural accommodation, and theological compromise at the expense of truth that would compel us in our mission task.*

I have illustrated this in relating the tragedy of the earthquake and devastating tsunami that swept the coasts of eight Asian nations in December 2004. Up to a quarter of a million people perished instantly. I am invariably challenged when I say they were swept into hell—not because they had rejected Jesus Christ, or because they did not have spiritual needs that would lead them to embrace the gospel, but because they had never heard the gospel. They lived in places where missionaries had never been allowed, and they never had the opportunity to hear and respond to the gospel.

Many Christians object to that conclusion, rationalizing that if they never had an opportunity to hear of Jesus and be saved, and they followed their own religion with sincerity and faithfulness, surely a loving and merciful God would not condemn them to hell. Actually, this reasoning would be somewhat correct. God does not condemn them to hell; they are condemned by their sin. That is what separates them from a holy and righteous God for eternity. The Bible says, "All have sinned and fall short of the glory of God" (Rom. 3:23), and, "The wages of sin is death" (Rom. 6:23). Jesus Himself said, "I am the way, the truth, and the life. No one comes to the Father except through Me" (John 14:6). The followers of Jesus who knew Him and witnessed His death and resurrection declared, "There is salvation in no one else, for there is no other name under heaven given to people by which we must be saved" (Acts 4:12). We would totally have to reject the witness of Scripture to contend that anyone might be saved by any other means than repentance and faith in Jesus Christ. This is why we must wage warfare by avoiding speculations and bringing our thinking in conformity to the Word of God.

For the sake of argument, let's suppose that there was some remote possibility of people being saved without ever hearing of Jesus, due to the fact that they did not have the opportunity to hear and respond to the gospel. After all, they have not consciously rejected Him. Our most effective mission strategy would be silence! If we resolved never to mention the name of Jesus again, we rationalize that those who have never heard might be the recipients of God's mercy and compassion due to their ignorance. Perhaps He would accept them into heaven because they followed the only religion they knew in sincerity. If this line of thinking were true, Jesus would have given the Great Commission as "stay in your homes and be silent."

But that's not what the Bible tells us to do. The message of God's Word from Genesis to Revelation is to declare His glory among the nations and to proclaim His salvation to the ends of the earth. The pages of the Bible reverberate with the urgency to witness to God's grace and make disciples of all peoples because there is no other way. There is no hope apart from Jesus Christ. How quickly the passionate commitment to God's mission is eroded when Satan obscures our thinking about God's Word.

Satan Leads Us to Selective Interpretation of God's Word

Most Christians have not abandoned or denied the truth of God's Word, so Satan leads us to apply it selectively. Writer and lecturer Bob Sjogren, former mission mobilizer for Frontiers, says that we often approach the Bible as we did our yearbook in school. The first thing we did upon receiving our yearbook was to look through it and find our own picture! That's the way we approach the Bible. We readily accept the Scriptures that affirm our salvation and the grace of God forgiving our sin. We latch on to Jesus saying, "Come to Me, all of you who are weary and burdened, and I will give you rest" (Matt. 11:28). We claim Romans 8:28, "We know that all things work together for the good of those who love God: those who are called according to His purpose." We choose to identify with every promise of blessing and any passage guaranteeing the benefits that accrue to being a Christian.

But we readily overlook those passages that hold us responsible for God's mission. We rationalize that the call of God to go to the nations only applies to those with a unique calling to become "professional missionaries"—whatever that means. Everyone else may consider themselves exempt. Alluding to Acts 1:8, one pastor argued that the Bible tells us to be witnesses in our Jerusalem, *then* in Judea and Samaria, and *then* to the ends of the earth. But there is no "then" in the passage. This historical sequence was fulfilled in the book of Acts, leaving us with the task of reaching the ends of the earth. We tend to make Acts 1:8 an analogy to concentric circles of our hometown, the surrounding province, cross-culturally throughout North America, and then overseas. Of course God wants us to be His witnesses and declare His glory everywhere, especially where we live, but we have to indulge in considerable hermeneutical gymnastics to use this passage to justify a lack of responsibility to reach all peoples with the gospel.

When one takes a careful look at Acts 1:8 and the surrounding context, critical ideas emerge. Jesus had spent the previous forty days preparing His followers to be a part of a worldwide movement. As we watch the developing picture, it is obvious that something big was about to happen. Jesus needed to teach them core issues for an impending movement. What did the preparation experience look like? Luke reports that the disciples needed to see and experience "all that Jesus began to do and teach until the day He was taken up, after He had given orders through the Holy Spirit to the apostles whom He had chosen. After He had suffered, He also presented Himself alive to them by many convincing proofs, appearing to them during 40 days and speaking about the kingdom of God" (Acts 1:1–3). Information, application, and experiences make our journey meaningful. The disciples received all this, and more, as Jesus prepared them for the years to come.

A powerful point is hidden in Acts 1:8 if we treat it as a challenge and inspiration only. Jesus answered an important question that we do not intuitively know. What will it look like when My Holy Spirit falls on My people? How will My people behave? Keep in mind the disciples, as we often do, were thinking in the "now." After He has invested all this time (over three years) with them, they still reduced the purpose of Christ to short term. His purpose was His followers' needs and the help they needed with life. The disciples asked, "Now this kingdom thing sounds really great; we are starting right now, right?" The disciples thought small. Jesus thought big. Jesus helped them see the future. Acts 1:8 was a command to act on the vision Christ had for their future. Jesus let them in on an unfolding secret, "But you will receive power when the Holy Spirit has come upon you, and you will be My witnesses in Jerusalem, in all Judea and Samaria, and to the ends of the earth" (Acts 1:8). If being a missionary is joining God where He is working, then Acts 1:8 tells us where that is—everywhere.

Christians will always be on the move, going everywhere all the time, simultaneously calling people to faith in Him. When we are living missionally, when we are joining Him, then we will not work a linear strategy. Christians will be everywhere. The devil would love for us to be overwhelmed by the commands of Jesus in Scripture and begin to downsize them to what we feel we can reasonably do. God's people are called to engage all nations now. We are born again with the weighty responsibility of every man, woman, and child in the world upon us. God invites us to join His work fully understanding without Him we can do nothing.

Many neglect the pervasive mandate of Scripture compelling us to engage a lost world in fulfilling the mission of God and seek to accommodate self-indulgent teachings to justify ethnocentric church fellowships. They are like those spoken of by Isaiah: "Do not prophesy the truth to us. Tell us flattering things. Prophesy illusions" (Isa. 30:10). Such churches refuse to be confronted with the tragedy of a lost world and exhorted to the commitment expected of them to reach the lost. To ignore God's mission is to be among those who "have rejected the instruction of the LORD of Hosts, and . . . have despised the word of the Holy One of Israel" (Isa. 5:24). Instead, we as God's people should take delight in the Word of God and find joy in obedience to what He tells us to do. "Your words became a delight to me and the joy of my heart, for I am called by Your name" (Jer. 15:16).

> *The devil would love for us to be overwhelmed by the commands of Jesus and downsize them to what we feel we can reasonably do.*

Certainly all that we do in humanitarian and social ministries is in obedience to God's Word telling us to minister to orphans and widows, be compassionate toward the needy, and minister to the "least of these." Our efforts to disciple and nurture new believers are unquestionably aligned with what the Scripture instructs us to do as God's church. There is no doubt that God is pleased when we as His people gather to worship, sing His praises, pray, and listen to exhortation from His Word. But to do all this and neglect the mission for which He has called us as His people is to be victimized by the enemy who seeks to deprive God of His glory among the nations by our selective application of Scripture.

The Word of God Demands Obedience

The church must decide her primary purpose. If the church doesn't, Satan will happily do it for us. People on mission say our greatest priority is obedience to Christ. People who are not on mission often focus on the goods and services the church provides. The goods and services either consciously or unconsciously target insiders. Let's face it; people who are looking for Christian goods and services are . . . Christians. Although on occasion programs attract lost people, unless there is a great deal of intentionality, they are not even designed to meet the needs of the lost.

What happens is, their lives begin to be shaped by programs rather than by the Savior. Satan's strategy is often just to get us busy. He is perfectly content to have us concerned about our own needs, our own things, and our own programs. The result is a church which is unconsciously prioritizing obedience to the needs of believers rather than the mission of God. The purpose of the church is to equip and teach you to live out a life of obedience to Jesus. People on mission prioritize obedience to Christ.

John 14:15 says: "If you love Me, you will keep My commandments." Love God, do what He says. That's the answer. Simple. Simple is in, right? Google splash page? Simple. *Simple Church*. Simple. *Real Simple* magazine. Simple. People on mission. Simple. Do you want to solve all the world's problems? Do you want to solve all your problems? Love God and do what He says. When that happens, you are reshaped. Normally Christians lose this simple focus.

My (Ed) friend, Bob Logan, repeats a defining moment in his relationship with God and his father. His father was an engineer and in Bob's words "a very wise man." Bob asked his father to define success. His dad gave him a simple but unforgettable answer: "I did not want to go all the way through life and get to the end and realize I had missed it. So I pondered this question for several months, and I finally boiled it down into one sentence: Find out what God wants you to do and do it!"[2]

What is success to you as a Christian? People on mission are focused on obedience. As people on mission begin to create and populate local churches, the churches as a whole will live by the same value of obedience. Love God, do what He says. But love for Christ must come first. Once there is love, obedience flows naturally and abundantly.

First John 5 provides an obedience flowchart for the lives of people on mission: "Everyone who believes that Jesus is the Messiah has been born of God, and everyone who loves the parent also loves his child" (1 John 5:1). This is born again: you believe (trust in, rely on, cling to) Jesus as the Messiah, He is the Savior, you are born of God. Here is where the flow begins through people on mission: *Everyone who loves the parent also loves his child.* People on mission believe certain things are true about God, His Word, and His mission in the world. As a result, people on mission behave a certain way. What does that behavior look like? "This is how we know that we love God's children when we love God and obey His commands" (1 John 5:2). There it is again; love God; do what He says. Now here's the reality of this: when love comes first, ministry to others is natural and abundant. When love comes first, prioritizing others above you is natural.

When people get distracted from loving God, the results are obvious. The platform (the local church) gets corrupted, the glory of God is covered, and Satan wins in spite of the apparent programmatic successes. But when you have a church filled with people saying it's not about me, they get on the offensive against the gates of hell—God's mission to rescue humanity. Prioritizing obedience to Christ results in going along with Him to rescue your neighbor, both the one next door and the one around the globe.

When King Josiah found the Book of the Law in the temple, he acknowledged the consequences of not obeying what was written in its entirety. "For great is the LORD's wrath that is poured out on us because our fathers have not kept the word of the Lord in order to do everything written in this book" (2 Chron. 34:21). Should we not apply all that God has commanded us to do as Israel did as they prepared to take possession of the promised land? "You must not add anything to what I command you or take anything away from it, so that you may keep the commands of the Lord your God" (Deut. 4:2).

> *Anyone who misses or neglects the mission message of the Bible is deceived.*

Anyone who misses or neglects the mission message of the Bible is deceived. Jesus asked, "Are you not deceived because you don't know the Scriptures or the power of God?" (Mark 12:24). We should recognize who the deceiver is. If Satan cannot keep us from faith in Jesus Christ and serving Him, all he needs to do is deceive us into missing the central thrust of Scripture that compels us to take Christ to the nations. The power of God is the power of His Word doing its work in every believer and in the world. When we pick and choose what we want to believe and follow, we emasculate the power of God's truth to empower our witness and transform the world. As the book of Acts reports the growth of the church and the spread of the gospel, we are told, "The Word of the Lord was growing mightily and prevailing" (Acts 19:20 NASB). When Paul reflected on the receptivity of the gospel among the believers in Thessalonica, he said, "For our gospel did not come to you in word only, but also in power, in the Holy Spirit, and with much assurance" (1 Thess. 1:5). Satan would readily erode our confidence in

God's Word and obedience to it because it represents the power to overcome His dominions and bring the reign of Christ on the earth.

It should not be surprising that Satan would attack the authority of God's Word in our lives, using his access to our minds to cause us subtly to rationalize God's truth in a way that would divert us from His mission. Again, in speaking of those in Thessalonica, Paul said, "When you received the message about God that you heard from us, you welcomed it not as a human message, but as it truly is, the message of God, which also works effectively in you believers" (1 Thess. 2:13). Later, he said, "Pray . . . that the Lord's message may spread rapidly and be honored, just as it was with you, and that we may be delivered from wicked and evil men" (2 Thess. 3:1–2). Is this not why Jesus observed in His high priestly prayer concerning His disciples, "Sanctify them by the truth; Your word is truth" (John 17:17)? It is the power of God's Word and one's obedience to it that sanctifies. Holding forth the truth of God's Word keeps us from evil, and the power of God's Word penetrates sinful hearts, changing lives and transforming a lost world.

Is it any wonder that one of Satan's schemes is to erode the truth and authority of God's Word? "For the word of God is living and effective and sharper than any two-edged sword, penetrating as far as to divide soul, spirit, joints, and marrow; it is a judge of the ideas and thoughts of the heart" (Heb. 4:12). Humans stiffen their necks at the idea of being judged. Our culture once valued John 3:16 above all other verses. Now Matthew 7:1 seems to be the favorite: "Do not judge, so that you won't be judged." Satan is seeking to back the church down by convincing us that sin in small doses is acceptable. Sometimes even deserved.

The prophet Isaiah declared, "The grass withers, the flowers fade, but the word of our God remains forever" (Isa. 40:8). God gives confidence to the witness of every believer: "So My word that comes from My mouth will not return to Me empty, but it will accomplish what I please, and will prosper in what I send it to do" (Isa. 55:11). God goes on to say, "I will look favorably on this kind of person: one who is humble, submissive in spirit, and who trembles at My word" (Isa. 66:2). Perhaps that might be the starting point for some: learn again what it means to tremble at God's Word. Become humble, once again, at the reading and hearing of God's eternal truth expressed in Scripture.

Satan's strategy is deception. If he cannot get us to doubt, ignore, or rationalize away God's Word, he attempts to persuade us to believe it without doing anything about it. Not to tremble at it. This is why James exhorts us, "But be doers of the word and not hearers only, deceiving yourselves" (James 1:22). Can the Bible really be true and reliable? Personalize the question: Does the Bible matter in your life? Satan's strategy calls us to doubt God's trustworthiness. The serpent introduced the questions to Eve but continues to ask them to us today. Did God mean it? Can God be trusted?

We trust the Scripture because we trust the Scripture's author. Each word is inspired by God and written by people. How did we get the Bible? God addressed this question through Peter: "First of all, you should know this: no prophecy of Scripture comes from one's own interpretation, because no prophecy ever came by the will of man; instead, moved by the Holy Spirit, men spoke from God" (2 Pet. 1:20–21). How did God move men to write on His behalf? The Holy Spirit breathed the words into the writers, like a wind fills the sails of a ship. The ship of His inspired Word landed in the perfect place, safe and sound for us to embrace.

When you study Scripture closely, you discover unique settings and people who influenced the Bible story. So we know that God did not put His writers in a mystical trance. No evidence exists that we received our Bible through channeling. As we read the Bible, we look through the historical realities of the writers and their settings. Yet the miraculous delivery of God's Word was, is, and will always stand singularly unique. Different writers, multiple continents, various languages, given over thousands of years hardly were a conspiracy. One God wrote, one God moved men to write, and so one story is delivered.

Although the subject of the delivery of the Bible may not seem basic for a book addressing spiritual warfare, don't miss the point. God's Word provides the orders and authority to run to the nations with the good news of Jesus Christ. Regardless of the internal and external obstacles, God's army marches forward in faith. Why? Because God has ordered us to do so, and His Word is trustworthy. People who value God's Word are biased. They interpret the world as God does. If God says, "Go to the nations," we go. If God says, "People who have never heard need to hear and know Me," we tell. We tell even though at times it is uncomfortable, impractical, and politically incorrect. What does God want? What does God say? Those questions drive people of the Book.

Going Deeper

1. How could you make your daily quiet time with the Lord more enjoyable and effective? What is the major obstacle to consistent time in prayer and His Word? How can you address that obstacle?

2. Have you had a tendency to accept the blessings and promises of the Bible and ignore the challenges and calls to sacrifice and commitment? Have you distorted the missionary message of the Bible to apply only to select Christians rather than to the people of God, including you?

3. In what way should the Bible be authoritative in compelling us to do whatever it takes to reach all nations for God's glory?

4. With a group of friends, memorize a passage of the Bible that highlights the vital nature of God's Word and the importance of relying upon it. Consider memorizing passages such as Ephesians 6:10–20; 2 Timothy 3:10–17; Genesis 3:1–7; or Luke 4:1–13.

CHAPTER 9

SATAN'S STRATEGY:
DISTORT THE CALL OF GOD

It has been my (Jerry) privilege to lead the largest evangelical missionary-sending agency in the world. The International Mission Board has been a mobilizing force to challenge Southern Baptists to consider the call of God to missionary service. Each year hundreds respond to a personal sense of God's call to plant their lives in foreign countries while others take leave from their vocational commitment to serve for two or three years in short-term assignments. It is commendable that some are willing to lay down their personal aspirations, leave the comfort and security of their home country, face the challenge of cross-cultural adjustment and a potentially deprived lifestyle to make Jesus Christ known to other nations.

However, the perception of that special call of God has been twisted by the enemy to convince most Christians that they have no responsibility toward fulfilling the mission of God. It is not unusual after a mission conference or emphasis in a church or on a seminary campus for someone to say to me, "Dr. Rankin, I would be willing to go as a missionary, but God has not called me."

I have trouble responding to that tactfully! We have a lost world that God desires to save, and here is a dedicated Christian who is convinced that he would be willing to go share the gospel with a lost world but the reason he doesn't is that God has chosen not to call him. We forget that the task of missions belongs to the church—the people of God.

We have established a false dichotomy between those who are chosen to go and those permitted to stay. The real matter is finding one's place in God's mission. Certainly there is a specific, personal call and leading of God, but many reason that if they haven't seen a burning bush or been blinded by a bright light on the Damascus Road, then they are exempt from declaring God's salvation among the nations. They feel free to pursue their own plans, blaming God for their not going to the mission field. But we cannot blame God for our personal neglect of His mission to reach the nations!

The Bible speaks of many heroes of faith being called of God to a specific task. Abraham was "called" by God to leave his home and follow, even though he did not know where God was leading. Moses was "called" to lead Israel out of bondage in Egypt and to the promised land. Jeremiah said, "The word of the LORD came to me: 'I chose you before I formed you in the womb; I set you apart before you were born. I appointed you a prophet to the nations'" (Jer. 1:4–5).

Examine the call of Isaiah. He had acknowledged that God had a plan and purpose for his life, even before he was born. In Isaiah 6:8 he recounts this encounter with God: "Then I heard the voice of the Lord saying: 'Who should I send? Who will go for Us?' I said: 'Here I am. Send me.'" This wasn't a personal call. God did not tap Isaiah on the shoulder and say, "OK, you are the one; I am calling you to go to a people in darkness." No, it was a generic call. Isaiah heard the heart of God crying for someone to send, for someone who would be willing to go to a people lost and in darkness. Isaiah did not wait to be selected and excuse himself if that mystical experience never occurred. He took the initiative and invited God to send him!

Why do people today not respond to awareness of a lost world as Isaiah did—knowing people need to know Jesus Christ, knowing someone needs to go and tell them? All we have to do is turn on our television newscast or read our newspaper headlines to see the sinfulness, lostness, despair, and spiritual darkness throughout the world. It grieves the heart of God that most of the world does not know of His love while many in our churches sit idly by. Do we comprehend how the heart of God yearns for the peoples of the world to know and worship Him? Why do we not bow in surrender, saying like Isaiah, "Here I am. I am available. Lord, let me be the one to go and tell them the good news of salvation"? Could it be that Satan has twisted our thinking to believe that only a select few are called to go, and the rest of God's people are free to follow their own plans with no responsibility for reaching a lost world? We are deceived to believe that we have a right to our own life and what we want to do.

> *Satan has twisted our thinking to believe that only a select few are called to go, and the rest of God's people are exempt.*

When our denomination reached five thousand missionaries in 2001, it was considered to be a "bold mission thrust," but that number represented only .03 percent of church members and potential witnesses. Less than one out of every three thousand take the Great Commission seriously enough to become an international missionary for even a temporary time in their lives. If Southern Baptist churches sent just 1 percent of their members to reach the nations and peoples of the world, instead of five thousand there would be 160,000 missionaries (according to our reported membership of sixteen million in 2009). The support should not be a problem—not financially, logistically, or in human resources. Could not 99 percent of the church adequately support the 1 percent sent to the nations to fulfill the mission of God? Dare we dream of what would happen if 10 percent of our denominational members truly believed its mission was to disciple the nations? That would be 1.6 million involved at some level. But Satan doesn't want that to happen, so in his knack for lies and deception, he convinces most Christians that they are not called and have no responsibility to obey the mandate of our Lord. And God continues to be deprived of His glory among most of the peoples of the world.

Succumbing to Myths—Denying the Call

Even those who give their lives to Christian ministry tend to put a geographic restriction on their "call" and never consider the proportionate need for laborers. When one calculates that there are pastors serving forty-three thousand Southern Baptist churches and then adds the multiple ministry staff in many churches—as well as associational staff, state convention staff, and those serving denominational entities—there would be at least a hundred thousand full-time workers devoted to serving an area where overlapping denominational layers seek to serve and reach only 5 percent of the world's population. Meanwhile, five thousand missionaries are seen as all God has chosen to take the gospel to the rest of the world; never mind that that amounts to one missionary for every 1.6 million people!

Satan has distorted the thinking of God's people to give priority to serving God where they are rather than being a force for kingdom advance to the ends of the earth. The deception is evident in the thinking of many. Many have succumbed to the myth that we are only responsible for witnessing to those where we live and within our realm of contacts. Others make excuses as did Moses, saying, "I'm not qualified," or, "Let someone else do it." But the Scripture tells us in response to these efforts to excuse himself, "Then the LORD's anger burned against Moses" (Exod. 4:14). Do we realize we are incurring the wrath of God when we are disobedient to His call as the people of God to declare His glory among the nations? We need to be reminded that God does not call the qualified. He qualifies and equips the called. Those who offer themselves in obedience like Isaiah will receive the power of God's presence. They will find God guiding their path, opening the doors, leading the way, and empowering their witness.

Jesus told His disciples, "The harvest is abundant, but the workers are few. Therefore, pray to the Lord of the harvest to send out workers into His harvest" (Matt. 9:37–38). This is a rather perplexing instruction. If God is the Lord of the harvest and the One who calls, then He is capable of calling out the laborers to bring in the harvest. After all, He is sovereign over the nations and should be Lord over our lives. In an effort to provide an explanation, I have often said that we are instructed to pray for the laborers because God wants us to be those laborers. If a believer is truly burdened for a lost world, intercedes for the nations, and pleads with God for missionaries to go into the fields, it is not unlikely that God will move upon the heart of the one praying to sense that he should be the one to go. We have had many new missionaries give such a testimony of God's call.

However, there might be another perspective on why we are encouraged to beseech God to thrust out the laborers into the harvest. It is because there is an enemy that is inhibiting the flow of laborers into the harvest, stifling the conviction of God's call, and causing potential missionaries to rationalize away the personal responsibility to go. I (Jerry) once received a letter from someone who explained they were fervently praying Matthew 9:38 in response to the awareness of the many unreached people groups that needed laborers to proclaim the gospel. He asked, "Why isn't God answering my prayer to call out the missionaries that are needed to reach the whole world? Why isn't He faithful to do what He promised to do if we would pray?" In response, I recalled reading of a nineteenth-century missions advocate replying to this same question. He said that God is calling out the laborers, just as He said He would do, but the laborers are not responding. They are not responding to the call because of a closed mind, a calloused heart, or a reluctant will.

From where do such barriers arise? Certainly not from God! We may rationalize that it is just a natural tendency to hold on to one's own plans out of concern for one's welfare, but is that not the nature of the self-centered flesh rather than one dying to self and yielding to the leadership of God's Spirit? God is not glorified when we call the shots and determine the context in which we are willing to serve Him. Are we reluctant to trust God and follow His leadership because He might lead us to Africa? Are we fearful we might have to give up our beautiful new home or be separated from family and loved ones? When such attitudes dominate our thinking, we can be assured there is an influence other than the Holy Spirit speaking into our life. When we get so caught up in our comfortable lifestyle that we become indifferent to those who are lost, we have lost touch with the Lord of the harvest!

> *God is calling the laborers into the harvest, but the laborers are not responding because of a closed mind, a calloused heart, or a reluctant will.*

We are susceptible to Satan's devious influence because of his capacity to speak to our minds, distort our values, and lead us contrary to God's call. He creates doubts—"Has God really said?"—making us believe we are just experiencing an emotional moment in response to a missionary's appeal. He makes us feel unworthy due to past sins or a carnal lifestyle or convinces us we are not "holy" enough to be a missionary. We are vulnerable to such deceit designed to squelch the flow of laborers into the harvest; therefore, we need to pray that the Lord of the harvest will overcome Satan's lies. Almighty God is able to stand against Satan, reminding him that he is a defeated foe and his strategy will not prevail. He is the one that can bring the convicting truth of God's call and enable us to see the potential of our obedience in terms of His promised power and assured grace.

It is not uncommon for dedicated Christians to be conscientious about serving God and seeking His will. However, even our prayers often reflect an egotistical perspective as we pray, "Lord, what is Your will for my life?" We should be praying, "Lord, what is Your will?"—period! And once we come to understand God's will, then we can begin to get an understanding about what His will for us personally will be. God's will for each of His children is in the context of His mission, that universal plan and purpose to be known and worshipped among every people, tribe, language, and nation. For some it will mean to go. For others it is to be senders, mobilizers, and supporters. For all, it is to witness to those from the nations that He is bringing into our cities and communities.

But no one is exempt! To say, "I'll serve God where I live and ignore the need of the nations to know Jesus," is a deceptive scheme of Satan to divert believers from God's mission. To reason that I have no responsibility for the salvation of remote tribes and peoples because "God has not called me to go" is to express a demonic lie born in hell for the purpose of locking the nations of the world into the kingdom of darkness!

> *To serve God only where we live and ignore the needs of the nations is a deceptive scheme of Satan to divert believers from God's mission.*

Christians who are conscientious about missions often find many ways to support and encourage missions and avoid going, but our Lord expected us to go. We don't go out of a sense of obligation—somebody has got to do it, conscripted into service against our will—but as a privilege to be an instrument of God's power to touch the nations. Those who opt out on the basis of the lack of a personal call are literally implying that God has not commanded them to go. Actually, He has not commanded anyone to go. If you are familiar with the grammar of the Great Commission in Matthew 28:19–20, there is only one imperative verb, and that is "make disciples." The rest of the verb forms are participles. How does one make disciples? By baptizing and teaching them. Well, how does one make disciples of all nations? Obviously by going to them in order to disciple them. But it is not a command to go; it is an expectation. What Jesus literally says in this passage is, "As you are going, make disciples of all nations." When one is aware of a lost world needing to know Jesus and has come into a relationship of submissive lordship to Him, there should be a desire to go or do whatever it takes to reach and disciple the nations for Him!

It is necessary to go so that a lost world can see the reality of a living Savior in our lives. He declared in Ezekiel 36:23, "The nations will know that I am Yahweh . . . when I demonstrate My holiness through you in their sight." A world in darkness and despair needs to see and observe the reality of a victorious Christian life in their midst. It is the life lived among them that will earn credibility for a verbal witness and testimony. Therefore, we are expected to go as His disciples. Satan has inhibited the flow of witnesses to the ends of the earth by successfully propagating the myth of the call.

Called to Change the World

Every Christian is called to change the world. God has the world on His heart and desires the nations to worship Him. No one necessarily argues against God's desire to change the world, but we do argue about how it will be accomplished. The question comes, "Whom will God use to change the world and what will they do?" But we have too easily believed Satan's lie that only a special, elite group of Christians is prepared to do ministry, go out on mission, and change the world. We must live in a way that is prepared to change the world.

Many people sit, soak, and eventually sour in local churches, underchallenged because of the lie. Satan presents a "hall pass" to everyday Christians, excusing them from the real mission of

God. He convinces them that the call to missions or ministry is exclusive territory reserved for God's best. Our churches are structured in a way that perpetuates the lie. The pastor is the CEO, the church staff is special assistants in charge of customer service, and church attendees are the customers. At best, our responsibility is to pay going out the door, leave a nice tip for missions around Christmas, and convince our friends this is a great place to do business. The pastoral ranks have actually propagated the lie that feeds their own sense of self-importance. They appear as highly skilled, trained, answer men and are admired each week by hundreds if not thousands of parishioners. The customers come, bring their friends, and an "expert" tells them about Jesus. We create environments that feed the lie, "You need something, you come, and we'll take care of it."

We have believed Satan's lie that only a special, elite group of Christians is qualified to go out on mission and change the world.

Ministry professionals have unintentionally caused you to believe the lie. The lie is, you can't be in ministry, and you can't live on mission because you do not have the proper qualifications. And mission agencies have propagated the lie by establishing idealistic, narrow criteria for who is worthy of being approved for missionary service. We protect our narrow parameters of character, experience, and doctrinal preferences at the expense of a lost world hearing the gospel. Yet serving God on mission is exactly what Jesus called every believer to do. You are key players in God's heart for the world. Scripture is clear that we're all called to ministry. We're all sent on mission. The only question is, where and among whom?

God calls all believers to ministry and sends them on mission. "Called to ministry" is a phrase often used by pastors. When I (Ed) applied for seminary, one important request in the application process was to tell the story of how God had "called" me into ministry.

Ministers have been refused entry to school and ministry assignment opportunities because of their inability to articulate "the call" sufficiently. The implications are frightening. Is there a possibility that I am called to the ministry and you're not? The Bible does not support that perspective. God does speak, send, and direct His people. He assigns and reassigns those who love and follow Him. But this does not excuse any Christian from the ministry and missions call received upon salvation through God's Word.

The apparent three-class system in the local church is Satan's preferred system. Why? Because the two-class system is inefficient and ineffective. One of the reasons the American church is getting such poor results can be traced to the three-class system. The system keeps lost people lost and saved people disengaged. Here is what the system looks like: it's my job (clergy) to do ministry and your job (nonclergy or laity) to receive ministry. And it's those special people (missionaries) who do the really hard work of going overseas. Let me review God's preferred, biblical system: "Our" job (all of us) is to engage in ministry, serve one another in a lost world, and go to the nations in the name of Jesus. *Our job is to live on mission and in ministry as a missional people.* We are to live out what Jesus commanded in Acts 1:8 because of the Holy Spirit's arrival in Acts 2. Jerusalem, Judea, Samaria, and the ends of the earth are the domains where all Christians invest in God's mission and ministry. And we do it all of the time.

Satan wants you to see through a faulty lens of a dichotomy: owner—customer, player—fan, performer—audience. When God directs, our perspective changes. All are responsible (owners) to be on God's team (players), to glorify God (performers) among the nations for the rest of our lives. Let me show you how that looks in the Bible with three challenges Jesus gave in John 20.

You Are Sent, So Go!

Jesus is speaking to a group of disciples in the Gospel of John. The disciples had been commissioned and mentored by Jesus.

Now, in an anxiety-filled moment, Jesus adds to their apparent burden the mission of God. We are today's version of that group of disciples. All of us have different backgrounds, passions, and abilities. All of us have a natural fear and anxiety when we face greater roles in His mission. Notice Jesus entered the room with compassion, "In the evening of that first day of the week, the disciples were gathered together with the doors locked because of their fear of the Jews. Then Jesus came, stood among them, and said to them: 'Peace to you.' Having said this, He showed them His hands and His side. So the disciples rejoiced when they saw the Lord. Jesus said to them again, 'Peace to you! As the Father has sent Me, I also send you'" (John 20:19–21).

Jesus gives all of us the same commission. Jesus tells us we are "sent" as an identification of who we are. The original word comes from the source of our word *apostle*. We are not talking about a special office or position. We are talking about an action. "Sent" denotes a business or employment agenda, but our job assignments are all the same. Because we are sent by Jesus, we are all tent makers as was Paul. We are full-time apostles. We generate income through a career or job assignment but leverage our lives and resources for the mission of God. Once sent, always sent—all the time, every day, with every person.

What is Jesus' mission? We are sent just as Jesus was sent. Two passages in Luke's Gospel help us see how Jesus described His mission in the world. "The Spirit of the Lord is on Me, because He has anointed Me to preach good news to the poor. He has sent Me to proclaim freedom to the captives and recovery of sight to the blind, to set free the oppressed, to proclaim the year of the Lord's favor" (Luke 4:18–19). "For the Son of Man has come to seek and to save the lost" (Luke 19:10). What will the mission of Jesus look like in today's world? The mission will look like the two passages from Luke. Although culture and settings change, the needs of mankind do not. We are to serve like Jesus.

Commonly we describe the mission of Jesus through two "Greats" in Scripture. Many churches now have incorporated these ideas in their mission statements or guiding documents. The Great Commission and the Great Commandment provide another clear picture of how missionaries are to live. Matthew 28 records what we call the Great Commission. "Jesus came near and said to them, 'All authority has been given to Me in heaven and on earth. Go, therefore, and make disciples of all nations, baptizing them in the name of the Father and of the Son and of the Holy Spirit, teaching them to observe everything I have commanded you. And remember, I am with you always, to the end of the age'" (Matt. 28:18–20). Jesus said, "Go and make disciples." We are sent to make disciples of all nations. Now this is the reality. We've heard this a thousand times, and in all likelihood we've ignored it a thousand times. There's no nice way to put this. We are likely addressing an audience, the majority of whom are not engaged in making disciples of all nations. The vast majority of Christians have never shared their faith. Most Christians have never been a part of leading somebody to faith in Christ. We have talked ourselves out of the fact that you and I own the Great Commission. Satan has convinced us the Great Commission is someone else's job.

> *Satan has convinced us the Great Commission is someone else's job.*

I (Ed) want to apologize that we (clergy) have actually played into that lie. What we have said to you is this: "Bring your friends to church, and we'll seal the deal." We would let you lead them to Christ, but you would probably mess it up somehow. You have never been to seminary. You missed our last soul-winning training seminar. We'll tell them the gospel, and they'll come to Jesus. What we should have said, and what I'm saying now, is that *you own the Great Commission.* You're to go and make disciples of all nations. Don't just bring them here to come and see.

I understand the spirit of the "invest and invite" emphasis. Many growing churches have made this focus popular and successful. The motivation behind invest (in relationships with lost people) and invite (lost people to church) is to reach more lost people. That is a good thing. And, it is not likely a sin of speaking, but it could be a sin of hearing. Church leaders would never tell believers to stop sharing their faith in lieu of someone hearing it from the stage. But believers already hold a limited view of their role in God's mission, so we want to drive home their ability to engage fully in God's work in the world.

When Christians choose to measure their participation in God's mission by how many people they delivered to a church service to hear the preacher, the vision of Jesus for world evangelism comes to a screeching halt. The Great Commission becomes limited to how many friends (small number) you can reasonably make, how many of your friends (smaller) will come to church, and how many of them will be saved (smallest). Just in case, I propose a new contemporary version of invest and invite. I think I will call it "invest and invest and invest again." Keep on investing. Invest beyond your yearly prayer and sacrificial gift to the missions offering. Invest in someone everywhere you go. Teach and show others how to invest. Go to new places, far from here, to find new people in whom to invest. Sent ones behave that way. Sent ones are tools of God to change the world.

We are also sent for the Great Commandment. Jesus is addressing a question from the scribes meant to entrap Him. They asked which command of the law is most important. Jesus trapped them when He said: "'This is the most important,' Jesus answered: 'Listen, Israel! The Lord our God, The Lord is One. Love the Lord your God with all your heart, with all your soul, with all your mind, and with all your strength.' The second is: 'Love your neighbor as yourself. There is no other commandment greater than these'" (Mark 12:29–31). Jesus calls us to engage the Great Commission. He calls us to live in and through the Great Commandment. So what do we do? We *share* the good news of Jesus Christ, and we *show* the good news of Jesus Christ. Share and show . . . that has a nice ring to it. Could it be another alternative to invest and invite?

We share through the Great Commission; we show through the Great Commandment.

American Christianity has become "clergified." It is dominated by professional clergy. Our tendency toward this approach to church has seemed innocent and in some cases well intended. But the ramifications to the mission of God are devastating. Three levels of Christianity exist in some parts of the church world today. We are following a Middle Ages type motif of peasants, priests, and monks in order of importance. The peasants (laypeople) don't do much; they're just there. The priests (professional clergy) are spiritual leaders a step above the peasants. The monks (international missionaries) are an elite class of their own, choosing to give up all the essentials of life to serve God 24/7. We admire them; we just never want to be them. We've got laypeople, we've got clergy, and we've got missionaries. The analogy may sound funny, but the implications are worse than you think. For the kingdom of God and the body of Christ, everybody loses with this mind-set. What is God's most plentiful earthly resource? Everyday Christians. But they end up at the bottom of the spiritual food chain being told to just wait and see what the professionals will do next. Pay, pray, and get out of the way is the normal set of expectations for the average layperson. A quarterly stay in the church nursery is added for the most dedicated pew saints. "Called to ministry" is a phrase we should eliminate from Christianese.

I (Ed) am with international missionaries often in my current ministry roles. From sharing conference platforms, to leading local churches, and traveling the world myself, interaction with these "most admired" in the kingdom is common. We have hosted missionaries at the churches I served. They always wear funny clothes, typical of the country where they serve. Stories often begin with, "You know I was eating a bug the other day at dinner," or, "You know, I found a poison snake in my bed last Thursday." We nervously chuckle through the stories. During the invitation we are challenged to hear the call and go. Often we end up thanking God that He never called us and asking Him to keep not calling us if that is OK with Him. You have just heard from a real, live missionary again, just like last year. Something you will never be but always admire is that real, live missionary. Follow the thought here all the way through. You are just as called as the bug-eating, snake-ducking, funny-dressed, real-live missionary. You are as responsible as he is to find God's spot and embrace your call.

In the three levels we've created, laypeople are called to nothing. Pastors are called to the "ministry." Missionaries are called to the "mission field." This lie from hell has been perpetuated in the American church by the adversary (1 Pet. 5:8) for years. Maybe it is Satan's most believable lie because it seems to be working so well for us in America.

We have franchised the church, particularly in suburban America. Like McDonald's, you can go into the majority of suburban churches to be greeted with a kind voice as you look upward toward the menu, "Welcome to Super Church; how may I serve you?" You scratch your head and say, "I'll have the middle-school ministry, hold the lock-in, easy on the mission trips; uh, one small group for baby boomer married adults with light Bible study, one night a month; and add interesting preaching with contemporary worship and movie clips." "Great! Anything else sir?" You then collect your courage and ask, "Could you supersize the middle-school ministry?" The kind voice replies, "Why of course, that will be 10 percent of your household income, if your personal journey allows that, and oh, by the way, at Super Church we gladly take net or gross!" "Wow, how about that, honey, they take net or gross! We have just discovered Six Flags over Jesus!"

To run such a franchise successfully takes employees, long hours, and lots of cash flow. The reality has much deeper ramifications than the tremendous cost of Super Church. As we continue to grow and franchise the church, we create environments totally oblivious to the compelling call of God on the life of every Christian. We have de-obligated ourselves to the debt of lost humanity. At best we may "volunteer" some place to do God and the church a favor. The American church is its own greatest obstacle to an incredible movement of God that will change friends, communities, and nations.

From this moment on, consider yourself called! All of us are called to the nations, not just to give, pray, and thumb through mission magazines, but to go. If we claim the name of Jesus Christ, we are called to the ministry the day we meet Jesus. He calls us to Himself, and then He sends us on mission through the Great Commandment and the Great Commission. All of us are called to God's global work among the nations. All of us are called to serve the poor and the hurting. All of us are called to change the world for Jesus' name. The only question is where and among whom? Some are missionaries to the Pequot in Africa, to the Quechua of the Highlands of Peru, and then there is you. You may be sent on mission to the factory where you work, the office where you serve, or the school where you attend. All of us are called to the community and neighborhoods where we live. Do not wait for an out-of-body experience to confirm that call. Disobedience against God is the only way to bypass His irrevocable call. So the wrong question is, How do I know if God is calling me? The right question is, Where will I embrace the call He has already placed on my life?

> *The question is not, How do I know if God is calling me? but Where will I embrace the call He has already placed on my life?*

Part of the confusion over the call has been clergy driven. I want to apologize on behalf of pastors everywhere that we have considered ourselves indispensable when only Jesus is indispensable. Why? Because I'm not the one who has to tell your friends about Jesus; you are. I'm not the one who needs to serve the hurting in your community; you are. I need to do those things in my community, and that's what I work toward; that's what I seek to do. But you are sent, so go.

You Are Empowered, So Serve!

Do you ever feel overwhelmed by it all? I mean, you have your life, your family, and your job. You sincerely want to matter for God, but you feel so overmatched. You don't feel overmatched on Sunday morning. That is home court and the home team. You have a church full of cheerleaders who love you and make you feel good. The head coach is on the platform, teaching and encouraging you. Occasionally he yells, but you don't mind. At times you deserve it, and you know it.

Remember part of your testimony is who you are in Christ, as well as who you are not. Look at the disciples in John 20. They were hiding in a room after Jesus' death. We can sound brave because we have the whole story; they didn't. Jesus gave them the story, but at the time it was way over their heads. Jesus entered the room with compassion. There was no name calling, no yelling, only compassion. The postresurrection word to an overwhelmed, overmatched group was *peace*. Notice what Jesus did not say: "You guys need to find some peace, for crying out loud. You are acting like babies. You should know better. You are making Me nervous!" Jesus walked in the door to give them something they could not find otherwise. When I think of five billion lost people in our world, I have a hard time finding peace. When I think of facing radical Islam, growing atheism in America, and increasing disdain for anything remotely Christian in our culture I am afraid. But enter Jesus, the Author and Finisher of our faith, who can turn cowardly men into those "who have turned the world upside down" (Acts 17:6).

Jesus does not stop with the gift of peace. He gave them His ongoing supernatural presence in the person of the Holy Spirit. Jesus did something that at a glance seemed bizarre. "After saying this, He breathed on them and said, 'Receive the Holy Spirit'" (John 20:22). But when you see the original setting and understand the Holy Spirit, you discover the incredible impact He had on them. How personal and deep is our own breath? Have you ever been so close to a spouse or a child that you can hear or feel them breathe? Breath means life. The breath of Jesus not only means life, but it means supernatural ability and closeness to Him. In the breath of Jesus, He delivered the Holy Spirit to believers to work with divine power.

Do you ever, just for a nanosecond, feel that the expectations of Jesus of His followers are a bit unreasonable? Maybe *ridiculous* would be a better word. Is it reasonable to think we can manage our lives, relationships, and responsibilities well? In addition to managing our family, jobs, and home, we have responsibilities with our church. Beyond our churches, there's one more thing . . . we also need to change the world. Oh, and I forgot, be sure to be home in time for dinner. Jesus did not ask us to do anything we could reasonably do in our own power. We must be empowered by God's Spirit. Then with His power comes His glory, not ours. The defining moment becomes when those who have never met Him ask two life-changing questions: How do they do that? Why do they do that? We are to live in such a way that unbelievers naturally ask what's different about our lives.

Zechariah was facing intimidating obstacles to his mission from the Lord to rebuild the temple. Enter again Satan himself at the right hand of God, trying to foil the mission of God: "Then he showed me Joshua the high priest standing before the Angel of the LORD, with Satan standing at his right side to accuse him. The LORD said to Satan: 'The LORD rebuke you, Satan! May the LORD who has chosen Jerusalem rebuke you! Isn't this man a burning stick snatched from the fire?'" (Zech. 3:1–2). Behind every man or woman that has a great vision to join the mission of God, Satan is there to remind them why it can't be done. The tempter (1 Thess. 3:5) will not stop short of questioning the integrity of God. The roaring lion wins most of his battles by sheer intimidation. Is there a demon behind every bush to oppose the mission of God and His people? Maybe not, but the thought of Satan's opposition should stir us to a new level of dependence on the breath of Jesus. As the Spirit fills us, believers gain courage from Him.

The Holy Spirit empowers us with God's energy and strength. But the Holy Spirit further equips people on mission with supernatural gifts. "There are different gifts, but the same Spirit. There are different ministries, but the same Lord. And there are different activities, but the same God is active in everyone and everything. A manifestation of the Spirit is given to each person to produce what is beneficial" (1 Cor. 12:4–7). Researching the deeper meaning of this passage to see what God truly meant by the phrase "each person" uncovers an interesting discovery. I looked up "each person" in the Greek, and it means . . . "each person." If you are a Christian, you are given a manifestation of gifting from the Holy Spirit. His gifts enable us to live out the Great Commission and the Great Commandment. So you and I are called, given a gifting of the Holy Spirit to produce what is beneficial.

> *The awareness of Satan's opposition should stir us to a new level of dependence on God's energy and strength.*

Christians who disregard the mission of God are often those who have ignored the empowering nature of God. Satan's pride caused him to rebel against God. In the same manner, prideful people of God ignore His mission. The battle is spiritual. More relevance or contemporary music will not convince people to come to Christ. More excellence will not convince people to come to Christ. Less churchy language is not the problem. Christianity is not growing in America for more spiritual reasons—we are not involved in the mission. And the "we" means you.

God is not weak, and Christianity is not flawed. The prophet Zechariah's leadership and mission were directly opposed by Satan. The prophet got the final word in one of his visions from God. The word was counterintuitive. The rebuilding of the mission of God was facing incredible odds. I am sure Zechariah and King Zerubbabel thought of the most obvious solutions: "We need more people, or we need stronger people to work harder." How can you argue with that thinking? Isn't that what we think? We are witnessing the derailment of the mission of God in America by thinking we just need to work harder. The word from God was this, "So he answered me, 'This is the word of the Lord to Zerubbabel: "Not by strength or by might, but by My Spirit," says the Lord of Hosts'" (Zech. 4:6). Neither larger armies nor stronger soldiers were the answer. The Holy Spirit of God on a people completely surrendered to Him will produce impossible results.

You are mentoring people all around you, either intentionally or unintentionally. You are mentoring your children and grandchildren. You are mentoring your spouse and friends. Samuel Clemens (Mark Twain) once said, "Church is good people standing in front of good people telling them how to be good people." Basically we all come to church because good people come to church and bad people don't go to church. Positive peer pressure exists in the body to attend, throw a few bucks in the offering plate, and help out once in a while. But at the end of the day we go because we want to appear as good people. We're not involved in changing the world. We ignore the Great Commission and the Great Commandment. We are driven to the lowest possible level of motivation. We are here because we're supposed to be here. We believe, but we do not do. We have ignored God's empowering presence and subsequently created religious structures for unspiritual people. And we teach others that changing the world is either unimportant or something to be accomplished by human effort.

Basically good people standing in front of good people telling them how to be good people is not compelling. I (Ed) grew up in a highly religious, Roman Catholic neighborhood in New York. We didn't think that at the time, but that's exactly what it was. Church was the right thing to do. I thought the strange phenomenon must be unique to New York. And then I moved to Tennessee and found that the church brands changed but the cultural impulse did not.

Good people go to church; bad people don't go to church. You go to church, and you don't commit big horrible sins. Basically you go to church because it is a cultural expectation to do so. Now it may not be Roman Catholic. Your brand may be Baptist, Church of Christ, or Methodist, but the cultural expectation is there. Good people go to church and bad people don't. The gospel of Jesus Christ sends us on mission. Believers who are truly changed embrace the "sent" part of the mission of God rather than becoming moral observers to quaint homilies.

Satan can't keep us from Jesus. What can he do to hinder the mission of God and keep lost people lost? Satan could whisper in our ears that all we need to do is go to church, be good people, and be nice. Christians can be "Christian" and yet ignore the things God wants us to do. Here's why. Nice people do not bring up awkward subjects. Good people do not want to make other people uncomfortable with their views. The reason most of us are not engaged in the Great Commission is because we want to be nice and not offend people. Once empowered by the Spirit, we can move into the lives of the lost with only one offensive thing—the cross. And we should happily do that.

If lost people look at us and see the sum total of Christianity as being a better person, then we are losing the battle. What kind of gospel are you living? If you choose to live the false gospel of going to church because that is what good people do, it will not work even to assure future generations of church attendees. Your children will reject it, or they will stick with it only because of social pressure. Eventually they will move away from it because no life change was witnessed and no world transformation was witnessed. The gospel of Christ is compelling to those who hear and empowering to those who accept it.

We have already seen two great challenges from Jesus in John 20. The first challenge was, "You are sent, so go." The second challenge was, "You are empowered, so serve." One more challenge is left.

You Are Responsible, So Care!

How could God's people join Him in mission and seemingly not care for other people? When you observe John 20:19–23, you can see the drama. But I also see some extremely awkward, surprising moments in the story. First, the anxious group of people formerly known as Christ followers (He was dead now) were hiding and scared. What do you think they felt when He showed up? Confusion, shame, and more fear could have been some responses. Happiness, relief, and surprise could have been other responses. Then He comforted them and told them to receive the Holy Spirit. It would have been a powerful and unforgettable moment with the Master.

The final surprise is when Jesus gave His followers power or authority to deal with other peoples' sin. Why is that surprising and awkward? Maybe more questions might help. Why someone else's sin? Shouldn't my own sin be my first concern? Why should I believe everybody has to deal with sin and forgiveness my way? Does this mean that my sin is other people's business too? People in other countries have their ways; I have mine.

Look again at what Jesus said, "If you forgive the sins of any, they are forgiven them; if you retain the sins of any, they are retained" (John 20:23). Jesus was telling His followers of their strategic role in delivering His will to people. Jesus purchased their forgiveness. But He chose the delivery system to be from person to person, mouth to mouth, life on life. You have to wonder what they thought at such a moment when an incredible responsibility was given to them.

Jesus was handing His followers a scorecard. And it is radically different from the one we are using in the modern church. What is your bottom line? What does success in ministry look like to you? Jesus calls us to get deep into His redemptive work. He wants us not only to participate in the mission but care deeply about the results of the mission in the lives of men, women, and children. If we are sent to people, we must care about people.

If we can reduce the most basic problems, they all evolve from sin and the need of forgiveness. Making wrong, anti-God, self-centered choices is sin. Embracing our debt of sin and God's payment is forgiveness. All other issues—emotional aches and pains, addictions, relationships, finances, desire for God—evolve from sin and forgiveness. We relate to God, either good or bad, through our understanding of sin and forgiveness. Now here is the deep truth: *Christians have been given the full responsibility for the proclamation of the forgiveness of sin for everybody in the world.* Stop, go back, and read that again. Pray this time that God would give you the ability to understand and embrace what that means. In short it means, Christians have been given the mission of God. Why else could Paul have said, "I am obligated" to take the gospel to everybody (Rom. 1:14)?

> *Christians have been given the full responsibility for the proclamation of forgiveness of sin for everybody in the world.*

I am not at all suggesting that we do the forgiving. Yet John 20:23 puts more responsibility on us for the mission of God than we can comprehend. Forgiveness is what only God through Christ offers every person. But the responsibility of communicating forgiveness has been left up to us. To tell people they can be forgiven, you must first care about them. If you don't care, then why tell them they can be forgiven.

Any ideas on what that might look like? Forgiveness is a person; His name is Jesus. Forgiveness looks like Jesus. You have been given the responsibility in every conceivable way to make the connection between Jesus Christ and the needs of the people you know. You have also been given the same responsibility for every language, tribe, and nation.

A second word in verse 23 is an equal responsibility yet potentially polarizing. From the heart of God, there are two types of people in the world. No matter whether you think America is a cultural tossed salad, pancake, or waffle, God sees two types of people. These two types are the forgiven in Christ and the unforgiven. Our responsibility is to help people embrace the forgiveness of Jesus and move on to the mission of God. However, to help people understand the "unforgiveness" of God is tricky and not as popular.

Now granted, oftentimes the Christian position on sin in culture comes across as dysfunctional and does damage to the cause of Christ. When the insane bomb abortion clinics or the hateful picket public events with "God Hates Fags" signs, they undermine the gospel. How unredeeming can an alleged Christ follower be? It is safe to say that no one reading this book has done anything as criminal as these acts. But chances are, we have all thrown obstacles in the way of a lost person's understanding of the gospel by the way we spoke or lived.

Here is a multiple-choice question: Who did Jesus address in the following statements? "'You are from below,' He told them, 'I am from above. You are of this world; I am not of this world. Therefore I told you that you will die in your sins. For if you do not believe that I am He, you will die in your sins'" (John 8:23–24). Pick one: (1) a gay rights parade in Jerusalem; (2) abortion doctors international convention in Rome; (3) pornographers trade convention in Nineveh; (4) the most religious people on the planet—Pharisees. If you picked 4, you were correct. Now positionally, the message applies to any group. But Jesus addressed the issue of hell and eternal damnation more to the religious people than the irreligious. We have left lost people with the perception that we hate them, and if there is a hell, we could care less that they might spend eternity there.

What does Satan think about the church's perception of lost people? If his mission is to keep lost people lost, he does not need to keep us hateful. He simply wants us to be apathetic. He will convince us there is an abundance of answers to sin and forgiveness worldwide. Other people's lives and choices are none of our business. How will people know they need to step across what Bill Hybels called "the line of faith" if we are unwilling to show them the line? How do we apply this truth as we join God's mission? Without apology, clearly and strongly we need to draw a line between the forgiven and unforgiven. But the motivation we have when we draw the line matters.

Remember the challenge, "You are responsible, so care." What then should we care about? The standard between good and evil, or the people who are on the wrong side of the standard? The answer is both. But it is easier to care about the former and not the latter. The line is supposed to be a clear one, so drawing it in a caring way can be difficult. Here are a few questions to use in how you participate in God's mission:

Do I really love the people to whom God has sent me as if they were Christ Himself?

Are they projects for my résumé or people for whom Christ died? Am I caring so I can feel good about myself? Am I caring because I have experienced an abundance of the love and grace of God?

How I care matters. How I care will also affect my real influence in the lives of other people. Our care for the lost should result in a bid to convince them that One has died for them. Living as "the forgiven" should be compelling to them because of our heart. As we think about convincing people about their need for forgiveness to join the mission of God, there is a sales principle worth considering. What happens when you are trying to sell something to someone you know they don't have, but they think they do? An experienced salesman was in a mentoring conversation with a younger salesman. As they debriefed, the young salesman bemoaned the fact that the person to whom he was selling thought he already owned what he was selling. The experienced salesman scolded him saying, "If he thinks he already had what you were selling, that was not his fault that was yours!" It is sad today to confess that people far from God actually feel they may already have what we are "selling." Is it because they are spiritually blind?

Well, that is one reason. But could the other reason be that we are living no different from them? Our lives as the redeemed should be so deeply different, so utterly passionate that they cannot help but realize they do not have what is ours in Christ.

Isaiah relayed the words of God and the vision of His redemptive plan. He described a dream scenario for those who deeply care for the sin and forgiveness of the people: "So you will summon a nation you do not know, and nations who do not know you will run to you. For the LORD your God, even the Holy One of Israel, has glorified you" (Isa. 55:5). Can you see that? God is telling His people what their mission to "live forgiven lives" would look like. The passage contains a rare case where we actually get glory! But notice the glory is not to our credit but to God's. *Glory* means to "put on display" or "draw attention to." When God puts a "forgiven life" on display, the heart hunger of the "unforgiven" will be realized. The word *nations* in this context was not necessarily a geographical description but a spiritual description. The heathen and pagan people of the day were of other nationalities and people groups. Could I live in a way that people and nations will run to me, to find out how and why I am who I am? Remember, you are responsible, so care!

The name Bernard L. Madoff will be famous in U.S. history. His name will be linked with dishonesty and mismanagement. Madoff stole the trusted resources of thousands of people. On June 29, 2009, the Wall Street investment guru was sentenced to 150 years of jail time and required to pay 170 billion dollars in restitution. As I followed the numerous news reports recounting the extent of the scandal, I became angry. Innocent people, businesses, and institutions trusted Madoff with everything they had. He exploited that trust for many years, mismanaging his way to an estimated rip-off worth $64.8 billion. How could Madoff sleep at night? How could he look into the faces of people on a daily basis from whom he was stealing? Not only was he stealing, but he was enjoying life while others around him were on the brink of financial devastation. For years, thousands of people felt that all was well with their money and their future. How did the victims feel when they were informed of the truth? District Court Judge Denny Chin described Madoff's behaviors as "extraordinarily evil."

Madoff issued the following apology in the courtroom after his sentencing:

> I cannot offer an excuse for my behavior. How do you excuse deceiving investors . . . and 200 employees? How do you excuse lying to my sons and two brothers? How do you excuse lying to a wife who stood by me for 50 years and still stands by me? There is no excuse for that. I have left a legacy of shame to my family and my grandchildren that is something that I will live with for the rest of my life. I apologize to my victims and I will turn to face them.[1]

Before I get too self-righteous, I must look at the mismanagement of the American church. The reality is that millions of people in America and billions worldwide are being victimized. Like Barney Madoff's clients, lost people have no idea they are lost. People who are being stolen from by Satan are totally unaware there is anything to fear while we play religious games in our spiritual havens. We, like Madoff, turn and face the victims of our inaction each day, where we live, work, and play. We owe them either a shame filled apology or a life obsessed with the Great Commission and Great Commandment. Our integrity before God demands a deeper sense of our responsibility for sin and forgiveness of the world. Our integrity before God demands better management of the spiritual resources God has provided for us to join Him on mission. Our integrity demands that we hear His call to worldwide missions. Feel manipulated? How about convicted? Join Jesus on His mission. As a Christ follower, you will find purpose.

You may be surprised to discover that is where we were destined to be all along!

Going Deeper

1. What ways have you acted like a customer in your local church? What will it look like when you transition to an owner? When will you do that?

2. What are your spiritual gifts? How can you learn more about them through serving? How might they influence how you live out the Great Commission and Great Commandment? (Go to www.placeministries.org for a spiritual gifts assessment and other assessments that will help you).

3. What does it look like to live a "forgiven life"? Discuss this with your family. Decide areas where you are not living a forgiven life. What steps will you take to make amends? When?

4. What distractions or obstacles do you have that allow you to deny God's call to impact all the nations with the message of redemption? What positive steps can you take to ignore the distractions or overcome the obstacles to global disciple making?

5. Have you been promoting and/or accepting the three-class system in your local church? How can it begin to change in your congregation so that all believers will learn that they can effectively serve and engage in kingdom-focused ministry?

CHAPTER 10

SATAN'S STRATEGY: ERODE THE FAITH OF GOD'S PEOPLE

The nation of Israel is an example of how the people of God can so easily be led astray from the mission of God. His calling and purpose for His chosen people was clear. In His providence He had brought them to Egypt where for four hundred years they were protected and prospered and grew to be a mighty nation. He led them out of Egypt, delivered them from bondage, and set before them a mission to possess the promised land and become a witness to all the peoples of the world. As Moses reviews their history in Deuteronomy, he reminds them of God's commissioning, "See, I have set the land before you. Enter and take possession of the land the LORD swore to give to your fathers Abraham, Isaac, and Jacob and their descendants after them" (Deut. 1:8).

When they finally reached the borders of the land of Canaan, twelve spies were sent in for reconnaissance. They came back affirming that it was a land flowing with milk and honey and even brought back fruit and produce as evidence of its prosperity. But they went on to report, "However, the people living in the land are strong, and the cities are large and fortified. We also saw the descendants of Anak there. The Amalekites are living in the land of the Negev; the Hittites, Jebusites, and Amorites live in the hill country; and the Canaanites live by the sea and along the Jordan" (Num. 13:28–29). They concluded the report with a dismal assessment, "We can't go up against the people because they are stronger than we are. . . . The land we passed through to explore is one that devours its inhabitants, and all the people we saw in it are men of great size" (Num. 13:31–32). In spite of the contrary opinion of Caleb and Joshua, in faithlessness the people succumbed to fear and turned their back on the mission of God.

It Takes Faith to Engage the Nations

Many churches today are like the children of Israel in that they clearly understand the Great Commission task, but they don't have the faith to move out and give priority to personal involvement in fulfilling God's mission. In fact, they cower in the security of their church building, enjoying the nurturing fellowship of believers, insulated from even impacting the cross-cultural secularism in their own community. Like Israel, seeing the pagan tribes to be confronted, we are made aware of the numbers of unreached people groups around the world. There are the Sereer and Kanuri in West Africa, the Quashkai and Mazandarani in Central Asia, the Zuang and Hui in China, and thousands of similar unreached people groups that have no access to the gospel. Media and our travels may expose us to the massive cities of Istanbul, Cairo, Shanghai, and Sao Paulo, fortified by religious history and traditions that appear to make them impregnable to a Christian witness. We are overwhelmed, feeling we are like grasshoppers among giants. We figuratively throw up our hands in dismay, concluding we can do nothing. We are too small; we don't have the resources or know what to do. We will just try to be good witnesses where we live.

Such lack of faith to trust God and His promised empowerment to be His witnesses to the ends of the earth is an obvious and devious tactic of Satan. It keeps the majority of God's churches from unleashing the resources to storm his strongholds around the world and claim them for our Lord. The contrast was the minority report of Joshua and Caleb who believed God and said, "We must go up and take possession of the land because we can certainly conquer it!" (Num. 13:30). God was angry with the people, and the consequence was their meaningless wandering in the wilderness for forty years as He replaced a faithless generation. Many churches are wandering in the wilderness, trying to find their way, in futility searching for relevance and direction, because they have rejected the priority of their mission. God commended Caleb, saying, "But since My servant Caleb has a different spirit and has followed Me completely, I will bring him into the land" (Num. 14:24).

Many churches rationalize that they are too small and don't have the resources to get involved in mission outreach beyond their own community. They see giving to missions as competitive with the more urgent priority of supporting their own programs. They are unresponsive to a few mission champions seeking to enlist members for mission trips and challenging the church to a global vision. They are lacking the spirit of Caleb who was committed to following God completely.

While participating in a recent mission conference at a church with an average attendance that seldom exceeded three hundred, I was amazed to hear reports of strategic partnerships in half a dozen places around the world. These were not just promotional announcements of another mission trip, but they reviewed the involvement of the church through prayer and multiple mission projects over several years. The coordinators for each partnership described the opportunities and vision for what teams from their church would do in working with missionaries, or in some cases engaging a people group where there was no missionary partner. After hearing what the church was doing in Belarus, China, India, the Ukraine, Mexico, and Brazil, the pastor got my attention and apologetically explained that they had decided to focus only on these six countries because they were such a small church with limited resources! In the course of any given year, more than half their members would participate in one of these overseas opportunities. But most churches are overwhelmed by the task of impacting a city, a people group, a culture far removed from where they live, and the nations remain in darkness, unclaimed by those our Lord commissioned to take possession of them for His glory.

Actually, all a church has to do is pray for the peoples and nations of the world, and God has promised to claim them as His possession. "Ask of Me, and I will make the nations Your inheritance and the ends of the earth Your possession" (Ps. 2:8). God is sovereign over the nations and will deliver them to the lordship of Jesus Christ, for either judgment or salvation; should not we intercede and pray for them that God would open their culture to a channel of witness and their hearts to His saving grace? But such prayer is born out of compassionate hearts that are burdened for a lost world, stirred in response to the Great Commandment of our Lord.

Isn't Satan clever! He knows that if we prayed for the Baluchi in Pakistan, the Pamir in Tajikistan, the Kurds in Turkey and Iraq that enemy strongholds would crumble and these people would be penetrated with the gospel. Satan is a fallen angel, a messenger, who has access to our minds to distort our perceptions and values. So, if we are going to be a people of prayer, he influences us to center our praying around our own interests, focusing on personal concerns—our needs, our family, our church, our community. How much time do we spend lifting up to the Father our pleas for the salvation

> *People are unreached and remain the strongholds of Satan when we center our prayers around our own interests instead of interceding for the nations.*

of Hazara in Afghanistan or the Bejas in Sudan? Is it any wonder they remain unreached? Not only does God work in response to our intercessory prayers; those prayers move us to be involved and do something about reaching a lost world.

It is not how big a church is or how many resources it has at its disposal but whether or not a congregation has a heart to follow God and His heart for the nations. Paul expressed concern for the believers in Corinth, "But I fear that, as the serpent deceived Eve by his cunning, your minds may be corrupted from a complete and pure devotion to Christ" (2 Cor. 11:3). Where is evidence of faith and devotion to Christ when we excuse ourselves as being too small and fail to trust Christ to guide, empower, and use us in whatever one's place may be in fulfilling God's mission?

Faith Is a Journey of Believing and Following God

Many Christians overlook the critical role of faith in the mission of God. Obedience to His mission is compelled by faith in believing God when He said, "I am God, exalted among the nations" (Ps. 46:10). In spite of the obstacles and apparent barriers, we must believe, "All the nations You have made will come and bow down before You, Lord" (Ps. 86:9). The opposite of faith is not just doubt but is also fear. Satan attempts to get us to see all the obstacles and opposition and question whether or not a certain people group can be reached. We encounter hardened hearts and even antagonistic response and doubt the power of the gospel to save certain segments of society. Or out of fear, concern for our own safety and welfare, we do not have the faith to take the risk and do whatever it takes to take the gospel to the nations, choosing the option of serving God in the security of our comfort zone at home. Infected with skepticism and doubt, we forget that we serve a sovereign God who bestows the power of a risen Christ upon those who will go in faith declaring His glory to the nations.

The majority of the time when God calls, He calls into empty space! One familiar example is the invitation of Jesus to Peter. Jesus invited him from apparent safety (a boat) to certain death (a raging sea). Jesus was teaching Peter an unforgettable lesson about faith. The disciples were on a boat in the middle of the night, experiencing a violent storm. In principle we see environments where people learn to follow Jesus in faith. The episode was intense. Life and death were in the balance. The disciples were unable to recognize Jesus as He walked across the water. When reading from Matthew's Gospel, note the use of words like *fear, courage, faith,* and *doubt.*

"Immediately Jesus spoke to them. 'Have courage! It is I. Don't be afraid.' 'Lord, if it's You,' Peter answered Him, 'command me to come to You on the water.' 'Come!' He said. And climbing out of the boat, Peter started walking on the water and came toward Jesus. But when he saw the strength of the wind, he was afraid. And beginning to sink he cried out, 'Lord, save me!' Immediately Jesus reached out His hand, caught hold of him, and said to him, 'You of little faith, why did you doubt?' When they got into the boat, the wind ceased. Then those in the boat worshiped Him and said, 'Truly You are the Son of God!'" (Matt. 14:27–33).

God invites us to empty space, to the unrepentant cultures, language groups, tribes, and nations. He invites us, humanly speaking, where there is no place to put our feet. The episode in the life of Peter demonstrated certain signs that Peter was maturing. At first he did not recognize Jesus, but when he did, he asked Jesus to let him move out of the boat with Him. We also see the obedience paradox. Watch as Peter struggles between two extremes: courage and fear. Peter had just witnessed possibly the greatest miracle of Jesus at that time. Jesus had taken a small amount of food, a serving for one. He blessed and broke it. The next thing you know, a serving for one becomes a serving for more than five thousand. Faking that type of miracle would have been impossible. Peter was inspired. In Peter there was a growing heart hunger to be with Jesus, no matter the risk, wherever Jesus wanted him to be.

For the Christian, faith and courage are the two edges of a sword. They are accompanying partners in our battle, never to be separated. When God assigns, He expects obedience. Where He expects obedience, He empowers our faith and courage. Jesus taught this lesson to His disciples, "I am the vine; you are the branches. The one who remains in Me and I in him produces much fruit, because you can do nothing without Me" (John 15:5). True faith is God empowered. God's assignment will never make sense from a natural perspective. Your own family may doubt because of the perceived value of a decision versus the cost. Friends may question your intelligence. I wonder what the other disciples thought of Peter's desire to climb out of a boat (little hope) to walk on the raging sea (no hope).

Courage is a corresponding behavior of empowered faith. Empowered faith is focused on the omnipotent God of the universe. Courage is the action of faith. As people consider the assignment and reassignments of God, Satan will highlight every possible doomsday scenario that could transpire for obedient Christ followers. Satan is the master discourager, attempting to reverse the courage you feel in the moment of obedience to God. Satan seeks to twist courage into shame and discouragement.

Have you ever listened to a strong sermon or experienced true worship that inspired you? God spoke to you. You made certain commitments, in the moment, as a result. Yet when you left the building, you felt paralyzed in fear of following through. Your commitment might have been in the moment as, "I am going to ask my wife to forgive me for the way I acted this week," or, "I am going to tell my neighbor about Jesus this afternoon." Your commitment might have been as significant as moving to another country or city for the sake of Christ. Yet you felt afraid and even paralyzed when it came time to follow through. The experience of inspiration to commitment without follow-through is common to all of us. At times we dismiss those times in which we lose confidence in God as being only human. But when we realize the consequences of disobedience to the mission of God, the origin of this paralysis is easy to trace back to Satan.

The late Ron Dunn said it this way, "A man will never trust God until he has to." Obedience to God's assignment will almost always be counterintuitive. Satan's role is to intimidate the faith out of us. He points out the waves, highlights the nothingness, and displays the risk. Faith is the bridge between God's assignment and our obedience. Without faith in God's supernatural ability and resources through us we will not consistently get out of bed for Him, much less move to Calcutta. The mission is God's mission, not ours. Faith trusts Him for the details that surround our simple obedience.

> *Faith is the bridge between God's assignment and our obedience.*

The real need for people who are considering God's assignment is encouragement. Notice you have the same root word in *encourage* as *discourage* but a different prefix. *En* means "to put a person in a place or a condition" . . . of what? Courage! Courage is essential to obedience and is a by-product of faith. It should be taught by the church and embraced by the people. If you are a church leader, immerse God's people in an environment that truly values His activity around the world. Special sermons and services are a part of the environment. Ultimately its source must be rooted in the Word and experienced through the Spirit's filling. The value of missions should saturate everything that happens including decisions, publications, staffing, budget, and decor. The result will be God assigning and reassigning people from the church around the world. God is speaking. God is inviting. Create and be in the environments that challenge people to hear and obey.

The first time I (Ed) ever walked into Northwood Church in Keller, Texas, I experienced a missions environment unlike any I had ever seen. As I entered the lobby, I noticed the walls were covered with maps of the world, complete with pictures and specific target areas. The church was ethnically diverse, as was the staff. When I began to read the program for the day, I noticed reports from mission trips, requests for prayer for those currently on trips, and advertisements for different mission opportunities. A missional church produces environments that value the responsibility of Christians for every tongue, tribe, and nation. The environment is something God uses to give each Christian the courage and support to embrace His agenda for the world. The missional church overcomes the satanic obstacle of small dreaming and stimulates a can-do faith to believe God and change the world.

In his own book, the pastor, Bob Roberts, described the phenomenal work of God in the Northwood environment:

> In our present day congregation in Texas, we
> have a growing number of businesspeople, lawyers,
> doctors, and the like who are all going into the
> ministry in our church. The majority of these people
> have been agnostic or atheists. I can't explain it
> other than to say people are moving to our bedroom
> community and technology based area, and God is
> capturing their hearts. They are being transformed
> to such a degree that they want to leave their jobs
> and their vocations to start churches. In fact, one of
> my biggest problems is trying to keep doctors in the
> medical field and lawyers in the legal fields instead of
> leaving their training behind for the mission field. We
> encourage them to use their jobs, not leave their jobs,
> because their job is their venue into the very mission
> field they love. That is the living example of the early
> church.[1]

Satan is not threatened by churches that acknowledge missions simply as another program, a special Christmas emphasis, or a particular line in the budget. Where is the faith and risk in missions as one of many things we care about? The lack of focus produces mediocre results at best. We reduce the mission of God for the nations to a special affinity by a select few. In many churches missions is the passion of older ladies and children (thank God for them) instead of the burden of every Christ follower. No wonder embracing the mission of God is perceived by many as an option. Satan is intimidated by the church that storms the gates of hell by challenging every man, woman, and child with the responsibility of engaging the nations. Churches that take the mission of God seriously, like Northwood Church in Keller, really do not have time to worry about consumers, rumors, and squabbles.

Missional congregations, like Northwood, have an environment similar to an airport. People only land for a short time to rest and be refreshed before moving on to the next place. As comfortable and impressive as some airports are, no one is there to stay. If you've had to stay overnight in one, you know that is true. The mission of the airport is to keep people moving. Successful takeoffs are celebrated. Delays are the enemy of a well-run airport. Large screens posting flight arrivals and departures are strategically placed throughout the airports to help passengers know where and when to leave or meet guests. Advertisements for places to go and airlines to choose are along the walls.

On the other hand, resorts are built differently. A resort is designed for you to lose track of time so you will stay longer. Amenities are available for your convenience. Pillows are fluffed every day. A room with a view is prized. Clocks are scarce. They want you to lose track of time so you will feel relaxed. After all, it is your destination vacation. Is your congregation like an airport or a resort? When you walk the halls of your church campus, it should shout, "Serve! Care! Glorify! Go!" What kind of mission environment exists in your congregation? Our congregations should challenge people each week to embrace God's heart for the nations. Our messages should challenge them to listen to God concerning their current assignment and future reassignment. Our prayers should reveal the church's strategy for the nations. When people walk into your building for the first time, what would they say you really value?

The collective faith journey of a church ought to show up in everything you do. From the Sunday sermon to what appears the most trivial announcement sheet in Sunday School, faith should be evident. A believer's life should be the same. Faith is to color our view of the world and season our language. As we are filled with the Spirit each day, our faith opens the gate to courage, and courage will give way to the kingdom's victory in battle.

Breaking the Satanic Code

We always want more information about what things might look like. If Satan is opposing and intimidating, how can I defeat him? Give me the formula. Give me the steps. People often desire concrete formula-based approaches for satanic opposition. Yet even when a formula is given, as in 1 Peter, the devil is described as unpredictable in his schemes. His greatest asset is the uncertainty of when and where he will attack. Satan's goal is for you to be terrified by him all the time. Your satanic obsession will be a great advertisement (remember, there is no such thing as bad publicity) for his cause. Trinkets, formulas, sayings, and bumper stickers have little influence on our deceptive foe. As you struggle with the faith required to obey the Lord, you must develop a deeper understanding of Satan's alternative plan. Faith, or the confidence and persuasion that God is reliable, is the simple formula to defeat Him. Is there a constant state of readiness formula? Yes. "Be sober! Be on the alert! Your adversary the Devil is prowling around like a roaring lion, looking for anyone he can devour. Resist him, firm in the faith, knowing that the same sufferings are being experienced by your brothers in the world" (1 Pet. 5:8–9).

The Scripture describes Satan as being "like a lion." He is not a lion, but he works like one. The lion has an uncanny ability to surprise its prey. The large, soft pads on his paws silence his every footstep. So, like a lion, Satan does not give a warning before he comes. In the least likely of circumstances, he attacks. He roars to intimidate. A lion's roar can be heard up to five miles away. The deep growl of the male lion freezes his prey in their tracks so he can devour. What does it look like when Satan devours a believer seeking to obey God? Satan devours believers through temptation to sin or to doubt God. Discouragement and depression are flaming arrows that devour. Disunity weakens the body of Christ, devouring their focus on communities and nations. The Greek verb tense of the word *devour* indicates a lack of definition and predictability of action. When and where the devil will attack cannot be anticipated. The force of the teaching by Peter is that you can count on the fact that Satan will attack and he is able to devour. Be ready!

People who see Satan everywhere are his greatest ally. Satan is not omnipresent. He is limited by space and time. We get a picture of Satan's boundaries in his conversation with God in the Old Testament. "The LORD asked Satan, 'Where have you come from?' 'From roaming through the earth,' Satan answered Him, 'and walking around on it'" (Job 1:7). When we picture the devil as ever present, we carry on his work for him. Neither he nor any of his demons need to attack, as we are already constantly obsessed with him.

The formula for our success is faith. The best defense is a good offense. Any coach can tell you that you can prevent the other team from scoring, but if your team is not putting more points on the scoreboard than your opponent, you will be defeated. We can only resist Satan when we are firm in our faith, believing God, claiming His Word, and allowing His power to overcome the subtle attacks of the enemy. Placing our faith in the true omnipresent One gives us assurance of our position of victory. Satan cannot resist such faith. His only hope is to scare faith out of you. Resist Satan in faith, knowing he is no match for the God of the universe. John described the controlling spirit of the Antichrist, already in their world, but encouraged readers by saying. "You are from God, little children, and you have conquered them, because the One who is in you is greater than the one who is in the world" (1 John 4:4).

If we are to claim the victory, the place to begin is to assess our faith. Faith-deficient Christians are an obstacle to the mission of God. How can we discover more and deeper faith in God? Growth is critical if we are to move out of our comfort zones and safe places. Satan exploits our immaturity and distracts us with spiritual attention deficit disorder. We are stirred but quickly distracted by short-term goals. Often we feel that changing the world is the job for the people featured in our mission magazines and brochures. At times even short-term mission trips become a substitute for what God really wants in our lives. Remember, there is no substitute for all-out obedience to God and joining Him on His mission. This was reflected by the new generation of Israel when, under Joshua's leadership, they were ready and equipped to fulfill the mission of God in claiming the promised land. "Everything you have commanded us we will do, and everywhere you send us we will go" (Josh. 1:16).

Bob Logan and Charles Ridley designed an extensive interview to assess church planting candidate couples. Valuable insights on how to assess faith emerged from the process. The purpose of the interview is to make a prediction concerning how well candidates

> *The best defense is a good offense. We resist Satan when we are firm in our faith, believing God, claiming His Word, and trusting His power.*

may perform as church planters. Thirteen behavioral categories were determined as keys to fulfilling God's mission through church planting. The uniqueness of the process is that evidence of these behaviors was determined by going into a candidate's past instead of the future. Logan and Ridley believed the greatest single indicator of future performance was previous behavior.

Although the church planter assessment interview was not flawless, over the years it has proved to be a helpful tool. What may not always be true in the lives of people, however, is always true with the God of the universe. The greatest single indicator of what God will do in the future is what He has done in the past. Although basic, this truth is a critical starting point if you desire to mature in your faith. Prayerfully research the issue. If you pack up your family and move across the world, how do you know what God will do? Go backward. See what He has done in the lives of others He has reassigned to difficult places. Listen to their stories. Go back in your past. List ways He has worked through challenges in your life. Go to God's Word. What did He do in the past? Let the characters of the Bible mentor you in the area of faith. Read Hebrews 11–12, the greatest running commentary on faith in the Bible. Pray through the Scripture and ask God to deepen your faith. What do you see in the stories? What can you learn? Where can you apply God's truth to your situation?

When taking on a task so incredible for God, normally there is a preparation process to develop the heart and skill of candidates. Topics include flexibility and adaptability, ability to cast vision, history of working with people from diverse backgrounds, and more. The last category in the interview is demonstration of faith. Often God moves deeply in many of the interviews during the discussion about faith. Many tears are shed as the Holy Spirit reminds and affirms the candidates of difficult times and facing insurmountable odds when God has come through.

The devil often accuses God's people who are considering high-risk, dramatic assignments for Him. He tells them things like, "God will not come through for you," or, "You don't have enough faith to serve God in that new place." Give the devil his due in these matters. He gives part of the truth but changes it into a diabolical lie, "You really don't have *enough* faith." At times it will seem that God is doing what you thought He should. Those are the times God invites you into deeper water with Him. At those times when He comes through, you will have no doubt it was Him. Then God gives you another story to remember the next time that will encourage your faith.

God provides encouragement to His people who struggle with faith. However, the challenge of trusting God does not make faith an option. Paul goes so far as to say, "Everything that is not from faith is sin" (Rom. 14:23). Faith must inform every choice we make, both large and small. We will not sugarcoat it. The choice to be out on mission with God is huge. It is both frightening and exhilarating all at once. Your level of faith will control your level of commitment to God's mission, not just faith in having trusted Jesus Christ as Savior but faith to believe the Word of God, all that He has said, and accept it as reality.

You may have seen the messages on the "from God" billboard series. The signs are meant to draw positive attention to God and provide a chuckle at the same time. One of my favorite billboard messages from God said, "Looking for a sign, here it is." Wow, wouldn't it be nice if God would show us where and how He wanted us to live out His mission on a large, black-and-white, roadside billboard? For some reason, the people of God sometimes struggle for clarity of God's direction in our lives. Part of the struggle is God's process of sending undeniable clarity. If God spoke to you on a billboard that disappeared the next day, would you question what you really saw? Yet when clarity from God comes from a prolonged labor and delivery process, His breakthrough is undeniable. In assessing our faith, we should find that we have a listening faith that is patient to hear all God says over a lifetime of assignments.

Do you desperately desire a sign from God to boost your faith? Your heart may hunger for something concrete through which God can communicate His will. The Bible records the story of Gideon (Judg. 6), who was so weak and intimidated by God's enemies he continually needed supernatural signs. Gideon requested a sign in the middle of a conversation with God, and God delivered. God did not seem to be put off by the request. Gideon whined about the good old days. "God, You did this for previous generations. Why won't You do it now?" was the essence of Gideon's challenge. First Gideon needed a sign that it was really God who spoke. Then he needed signs that God would help defeat the enemy. Even Gideon knew he was stretching God's patience. Gideon said, "'Don't be angry with me; let me speak one more time. Please allow me to make one more test with the fleece. Let it remain dry, and the dew be all over the ground.' That night God did as Gideon requested:

only the fleece was dry, and dew was all over the ground" (Judg. 6:39–40). Gideon could have gone back to the altar He had already constructed in honor of God. He really did not need a sign; he already had one.

Jesus dealt differently in the New Testament with people who were hungry for signs. He knew people were so needy that they would always need more signs. Eventually they would forget the last sign. The request for signs does not always emerge from pure motives. Take the Pharisees for example. Mark's Gospel recorded, "The Pharisees came out and began to argue with Him, demanding of Him a sign from heaven to test Him. But sighing deeply in His spirit, He said, 'Why does this generation demand a sign? I assure you: No sign will be given to this generation!' Then He left them, got on board the boat again, and went to the other side" (Mark 8:11–13). This context is different from Gideon's situation. The Pharisees motives were not pure. Yet as we compare the two episodes, what can we discover about real faith?

First, God does not bind Himself to work miracles in order to get us to obey Him. If He chooses to provide supernatural evidence of His will, celebrate! But, never excuse yourself from the already revealed will of God through His Word. We have been given God's Holy Spirit to lead us and His Word to inform us. Must God send snow on the Fourth of July, or change your cat into a goldfish in order for you to obey Him? If your need for a sign turns God into a circus act instead of God Almighty, then a faith assessment is in order.

> *God does not bind Himself to work miracles in order to get us to obey Him.*

Second, the sign God has given us may be in our past. Gideon was a real man with real fears. Yet Gideon was coming off of an irrefutable encounter with God. He built an altar and declared God the God of peace. The same God was calling Gideon to battle. Gideon enjoyed a long conversation with God and saw the fire of God fall. Yet it is almost as if Gideon became addicted to signs. Remember, the greatest single indicator of future performance is previous behavior. Spend extended time writing a "this is your life" journal. What has God done in your past that might reveal His will for the present and future? Signs are encounters or experiences that can often be forgotten. When Satan really frightens us, in our panic we may forget the past. Our faith journey with God will include our past encounters with Him. The extreme, however, is to become obsessed with them as our only source of inspiration.

Third, we may miss the signs God has placed in our current situations. Notice there was an obvious sign that Abraham might have taken for granted right under his nose (or maybe above his head). God gave Abraham an object lesson that left a permanent impression: "He took him outside and said, 'Look at the sky and count the stars, if you are able to count them.' Then He said to him, 'Your offspring will be that numerous.' Abram believed the LORD, and He credited it to him as righteousness" (Gen. 15:5–6). Abraham was beginning to doubt God's ability to keep His previous promise. God pointed to the heavens and said, "I am doing something really big through you." The stars became the lesson and a supernatural sign to help Abraham through a doubting phase. Although Abraham had seen the stars countless times before, they took on new meaning from that day on. God may speak through common, everyday night objects, changing them into unforgettable supernatural signs of His purposes for us.

Finally, determine what you are seeking is a way forward, not a sign. Never assume that your desire for a sign is sincere. Someone once described the unlimited potential of God's people who never get to the mission field as, "Willing to go but planning to stay." Our hearts are deceitful. What you may be searching for is a "no sign" from the Lord, especially when it involves personal sacrifice in order to be on mission with God. Obviously the Pharisees did not endear themselves to Jesus by their request for signs. Why? The Pharisees were attempting to disprove Jesus the Messiah, not prove Him! Jesus will never be manipulated by people with insincere motives.

Answer these two question as you seek direction from God: (1) If He performs a supernatural, inexplicable miracle right in front of me, will I obey Him immediately with no hesitation? (2) If He speaks clearly through His Word, His Spirit, or an ordinary circumstance of life, will I follow immediately with no hesitation? If you are not sure of the answer, that is the place to start your search for His assignment. Jesus was described in the Gospels as being able to see into the hearts of men. Jesus' supernatural vision goes beyond what we might say or do to the "heart of the matter." Personal time seeking Him for answers is vital. He knows you better than you know yourself. Should you reconsider your current assignment? Notice again, I did not say calling. I refuse to say calling. You have been called. You may not have embraced your call. Unless you believe a lie from Satan, you have been commissioned and sent already. Remember the lie from the previous chapter—only a special group of Christians is prepared to do ministry, go out on mission, and change the world. The question is, Where and how does God want me to live out His call? So what is your next step?

Faith Leads to Obedience

Obeying God with no promises of health, wealth, or happiness is the distinctive part of your journey with God. Isaiah experienced no promises when God invited him to go (Isa. 6). People who were interested in following Jesus were told the reality of obedience. Jesus told them, "Foxes have dens, and birds of the sky have nests, but the Son of Man has no place to lay His head" (Luke 9:58). This is another example of an invitation into empty space. Faith is the abstract that God turns into the concrete. Faith is God given and God energized. Faith overrules sight. The writer of Hebrews said, "Now faith is the reality of what is hoped for, the proof of what is not seen. For by it our ancestors were approved" (Heb. 11:1–2).

God speaks to His people with great clarity at the right time. His people do not need any more reality or proof than they already have through faith, once they have heard His voice. So the wrong question is, Do you have the faith to follow Him anywhere? The right question is, What is God saying? Your problem may not be in a flawed faith but an issue of hearing Him.

The distinguishing factor in the lives of Christ followers is that they hear His voice. That mark elevates Christianity from a traditional religion or philosophy to a personal relationship with the God of the universe through Jesus Christ. Jesus compared His relationship with His people to a shepherd's relationship with his sheep. He said, "My sheep hear My voice, I know them, and they follow Me" (John 10:27). Real sheep learn the voice of their shepherd. Following the shepherd is the natural result of hearing the shepherd. The sheep should instinctively follow the shepherd anywhere, trusting every turn. The assessment of our faith is done according to the length at which we will follow His voice.

How is faith measured? Faith is measured by action. God presented what has been known as a faith hall of fame in Hebrews 11. What a perfect place to do research and find faith mentors! Paul invited Christians to live their lives like he lived his (Phil. 4:9). I think it is OK to behave with faith even when you don't feel all warm and fuzzy. You can imitate the people of the Bible. In it you will see how people of faith behaved.

God does us a favor when He invites us to follow Him to new places and join Him in big things. The interruption of our plans and patterns is difficult and will require adjustments. But God cares enough to conform us into His image for His purposes. One faith example from which we can learn is from the life of Noah. He followed God on a mission. A part of His faith story is recorded in Hebrews 11. Noah was not a perfect man (that's encouraging), yet his faith was extraordinary enough to be mentioned in this chapter. Could Noah become a faith mentor for us? A quick overview of his life provides invaluable lessons from which to draw.

First, we see Noah took chances. There will always be risk involved in stepping into new places for God. The world was in a dismal state. God's assessment of the situation was dramatic. "When the Lord saw that man's wickedness was widespread on the earth and that every scheme his mind thought of was nothing but evil all the time, the Lord regretted that He had made man on the earth, and He was grieved in His heart" (Gen. 6:5–6).

> The distinguishing mark of Christ followers is they hear and follow His voice. Faith is measured by action!

God asked Noah to take a step into an empty space. Noah had never seen rain come from the sky (Gen. 2:5–6). Neither had Noah ever seen the judgment of God. Noah had never seen an ark, much less built one. He was called to experience new things. The principle remains true today. God's desire from the time of Adam was to have relationship with man. Man's fallen nature continued to draw him into an anti-God mind-set. God was on a mission. He invited Noah to join Him. Noah had nothing or no one to trust in this assignment but God Himself.

The Bible does not give us the deeper thoughts of a man like Noah. No question he saw the terrible things there were going on through the people of his culture. Maybe at a dark moment Noah questioned God, maybe not. No matter his thoughts, Noah had the same choice to make that we do: step out or play it safe. What would "playing it safe" have looked like as Noah deliberated about what he should do? He could try to pray more to delay starting the assignment—for clarity of course. He might ask for a different assignment that would take him out of the current circumstance. To "do something on a local level" sounds nice. As with Noah, so it is with us. Safe is risky! Choosing the option of safety is to risk your engagement with God's kingdom. It is never worth the choice.

What about current realities in America? Researcher David T. Olsen made the following observation in his book *American Church in Crisis*: "Approximately 55,000 churches will close between 2005 and 2020, while 60,000 new churches will open, producing a net gain of 4,500 churches. However, to keep pace with population growth, a net gain of 48,000 churches will be needed. In those years the American church will fall short of this mark by almost 43,500."[2]

The argument here is not a panicked, "What can we do to save or preserve our churches and denominations?" There is no question that some churches and denominations will disappear. The grim reality is, however, we can't be effective in God's mission for every tongue, tribe, and nation as local churches crumble before us. How can we finance and man our part of the mission of God worldwide without Great Commission churches in America thriving, growing, and multiplying? How can we rescue the perishing while we are drowning in spiritual mediocrity? Don't misunderstand the warning here. The suggestion is not that we suspend our commitment to the nations in order to repair the American mother ship. Part of our decline could well be the judgment of God upon comfortable American Christians who worry more about programs than people. I am saying if we are not afraid or even desperate, we are not paying attention to reality.

To play it safe is the most risky decision we could make. To risk is the safest decision we can make with God. No matter the short-term implications, we must obey God with reckless abandon. Changing the scorecard, our faith compels us to hear God's solutions and be willing to make it about absolute obedience. And by all means, the American church must stop looking in the mirror, self-absorbed and self-affirmed, while the world goes to hell. The call of God is to move from primping to proclamation.

When people of God gain a deeper understanding of the plan of God, geographical or vocational reassignment soon follows. From air traffic controllers to church janitors, dramatic shifts in the what, where, and how of God's call are seen. During their struggle we ask, "If you knew you could not fail, what would you do for God?" The question is common, but deeply flawed. One faulty assumption is that the assignment is all about the one assigned. What do I love to do? What am I passionate about? The second faulty assumption is that my definition of success and failure will be the issue that informs my decision to obey God. Why take any risk at all if I knew I could pray myself into a place of great passion and guaranteed success? I am seeking God for something that does not exist. Moving forward with God in faith is risky.

The second lesson we discover is that *Noah embraced God's purpose.* We call that vision. Vision is a picture of the future. Vision is big. In partnership with God, His vision will always be bigger than ours. If we intend to be included in His mission, we must always be stretched to embrace the vision of the God of the universe. When we embrace God's vision, we embrace His ability to work in us to accomplish His mission. When we are unsure about God's vision, it says what we believe about His ability, not what we believe about our ability. Paul described the vision of God in these terms: "Now to Him who is able to do above and beyond all that we ask or think—according to the power that works in you—to Him be glory in the church and in Christ Jesus to all generations, forever and ever. Amen" (Eph. 3:20–21). Our vision, devoid of faith, will be small. We will be satisfied with reaching a few, breaking last year's statistical records, or incremental growth. One or two people who respond to God's invitation and reassignment will be enough for us. But God has an entire world on His heart. We will be overwhelmed at the complications and frustrations of day-to-day ministry if we don't see what God sees. We will be intimidated by opposition and criticism. The roars of the lion will take away our courage. By faith we must embrace God's vision for the world. The wrong question is, What can we do for God? The honest answer to that question is, not very much. The right question is, What does God want? When that question is answered, then we are given His unlimited strength and resources to get the job done.

"God liked what He saw in Noah" (Gen. 6:8 *The Message*). What kind of person does God use to change the world? In Noah, God picked a man He could trust. God picked a man who would in turn trust Him. God uses people who watch the world with eternity in mind. How humbling is that truth? God has confidence in us to deliver His invitation to the nations. When you look at the way we in America have mishandled the gospel, it is nothing short of embarrassing. God believes in mortal man more than mortal man believes in Almighty God. No doubt, God knew who He was talking to when He invited Noah on mission. God did not want the story to end with Noah's generation. God's plan was not for the world to end at that point, and so there was one man He trusted. Noah walked with God and was in relationship with Him. God did not override Noah's will because Noah had given his will to God.

The third lesson of faith we discover is *Noah obeyed the details*. God gave Noah specific plans in Genesis 6 of what obedience to Him would look like. The chapter ends with the following observation: "He did everything that God had commanded him" (Gen. 6:22). Here is what really matters to God . . . everything He asks us to do for Him. The vision of God was to save the world through judging the world. The mission of God matched the vision of God. Sometimes the mission of God is not as dramatic as God's big vision, yet it is as important. Noah's task of building and gathering was daunting. Noah and his family, along with the two-by-twos were part of carrying on God's purposes. Faith extends to taking everything God says as important and productive.

Embracing the bigger picture of God can have a downside. We can articulate God's vision through impressive mission conferences, brochures, and film clips. But at the end of the day, we must embrace it individually. We are responsible to be Christ in our current assigned location on the planet. Let me say it another way: we do not deliver the message of the gospel; we are part of the message. The evangelistic debate of the ages is between witnessing with words or deeds. Let me settle the debate once and for all. Satan would love for us to spend time arguing while the world is hungry for both words and living epistles. We usually are either trying to defend our brashness or bashfulness in our long, tired arguments. To separate the message from the messenger is impossible. We speak with one voice. We should be able to tell believers and unbelievers alike that we are an example of how God intended people to live. Why don't we? Because usually we are not the example of how God intended for people to live. John 1:14 says, "The Word became flesh and took up residence among us." In the same way, Christ is in us, living among people so they can see His glory.

You have heard the old adage, "The devil is in the details." The devil is working to sabotage the mundane part of obeying God. However, God is in the details, particularly when it comes to living your life like He intended. Mother Teresa responded to the idea that God would not give us more than we can handle. She said once, "I wish He didn't trust me so much." God trusts you to be and to do His will. He has given you the resources you need to get it done. Now, as the famous Nike marketing campaign says, "Just Do It!"

Remember, Satan has a mission too. The mission of Satan is to keep lost people lost. He is not all-powerful, but this is all he has left to do. If Satan can do anything possible to distract God's chosen delivery system (us), he will. He will even resort to causing us to take our eyes off lost people and to put them on him. Opposition to the mission of God is not flesh and blood opposition. Opposition against the mission of God is "against the rulers, against the authorities, against the world powers of this darkness, against the spiritual forces of evil in the heavens" (Eph. 6:12). This was Paul's argument supporting the need to be armed. All armor is critical to the success of the person who joins God on His mission. But against the "flaming arrows" (Eph. 6:16), the defense is "a shield of faith." Faith that moves forward aggressively, sees God's vision for the future, and obeys Him in great detail is what puts the Christ follower in the position of victory in the battle.

We need to respond as the children of Israel under Joshua's leadership as they prepared to go into the promised land and fulfill the mission of God. "Everything you have commanded us we will do, and everywhere you send us we will go" (Josh. 1:16).

Going Deeper

1. Develop a system to continue learning about several different "unreached people groups" (UPG). Commit to learn about a new UPG each month for the next twelve months.

2. Spend extended time praying, meditating, and journaling through Hebrews 11.

- Create a list of lessons learned about faith.
- Rank the lessons in order of your own need to grow deeper.
- What will you do to grow deeper in faith?
- Who or what can help you?
- When will you begin the journey to deeper faith?

3. Spend extended time carefully creating a "This is your life with God" journal.

- List every significant event in your life.
- List times He came through for you in undeniable ways.
- What did you learn as a result?
- How can those lessons help you in the future?

4. Initiate conversations with your family or closest friends about taking a mission trip together. Consider how your trip might touch one of the unreached people groups you are learning about.

5. What "empty spaces" have you noticed around you? With God's help, what would it take for you to step out of the place of comfort and safety into that "empty space"? How could you take an initial step of faith in that direction?

CHAPTER 11

SATAN'S STRATEGY: DESTROY THE SPIRITUAL VITALITY OF THE CHURCH

I f Satan cannot get us to neglect our mission responsibility due to lack of faith, he successfully emasculates our witness by eroding the distinct witness of a dynamic, spiritually transformed people of God. Even in our own country, churches have little vitality for engaging culture in an attractive, positive witness that would draw people to Jesus. Unbelievers may even attend our worship and observe shallow, meaningless ritual that fails to speak to their life needs and even discourages them in a search for God. The lost see Christian neighbors loading the family into their SUV and making the Sunday morning pilgrimage to church but observe their squabbles, conflicts, and indulgence in a self-serving lifestyle that obscures any reality of a vibrant faith.

We are inundated with blatant expressions of sin and carnality in our world today. In a previous generation society seemed to acknowledge and be committed to basic moral values. Church held a prominent place in the community, and biblical teachings were respected as the norm for relationships and life. We lived the

"Ozzie and Harriet" suburban myth in which children respected and obeyed their parents and everyone followed the Golden Rule. There was a seedy side of life, but we had to go out of our way to see the depraved enticement of bars, gambling, and the sly, clandestine circulation of pornographic materials. That is no longer true, as acceptable entertainment, award-winning movies, and a steady flow of television sitcoms confront us with the sensual side of life.

Unfortunately many Christians compromise their walk with the Lord by adopting the carnal values of the world, yielding to the temptation for fleshly gratification that comes from a materialistic and hedonistic lifestyle. The Holy Spirit is grieved and God is deprived of His glory when people become in bondage to Internet pornography, allowing infidelity to destroy a sacred marriage covenant, or engage in fraudulent business practices. Sexual innuendoes and vulgar language become such a normal part of television entertainment and the workplace environment that we dismiss it as meaningless and even participate lest we be perceived as prudish. We fail to realize how the enemy of our souls is devastating the spiritual vitality of a life that has been redeemed to reflect the glory of our Lord.

Satan knows that most Christians are repulsed by the blatant disregard for God's Word and the unrighteous values promulgated by society, or at least they should be. So he subtly leads us astray in other devious ways to destroy or nullify our witness. Most churches faithfully hold forth the Word of Truth and seek to nurture members in the faith, but they are unwittingly distracted from recognizing its calling to a global mission and diverted from its task of exalting God among the nations.

Israel continually fell into sin along the way to fulfilling God's mission. Their halfhearted devotion to the task, while longing for the comforts of Egypt, is reflective of the attitude of many today. Their complaining about the sacrifice entailed in being the people of God discouraged even Moses. Even after they gained possession of the promised land, their continual attraction to the high places of pagan altars and inclination to worship Baal compromised any hope of being the people that would exalt God among the nations and proclaim His glory to the ends of the earth. They even engaged in carnal revelry and turned from God to worship the golden calf along the way. It is instructive to read the apostle Paul's reflection on this incident.

> Now I want you to know, brothers, that our fathers were all under the cloud, all passed through the sea. . . . For they drank from a spiritual rock that followed them, and that rock was Christ. But God was not pleased with most of them, for they were struck down in the desert. Now these things became examples for us, so that we will not desire evil as they did. . . . As it is written, "The people sat down to eat and drink, and got up to play." (1 Cor. 10:1, 4–7)

What an indictment and powerful alert for us! The people of God were anointed for a special mission that came from none other than the preincarnate Christ. They were led under a covering of God's Spirit, benefactors of the miracle-working power of Almighty God. But they were rejected and struck down because they were more interested in enjoying life, feasting and playing, than pressing forward in obedience to fulfilling God's mission.

To think that in God's providence, what that was all about was an example to the New Testament church and God's people today. You don't mess around with a sovereign God who has called you to be His people and appointed you to a mission of glorifying Him among the nations. Our time-consuming church fellowships and costly activity centers, created for our own enjoyment, reflect something of the values that brought judgment on Israel in the wilderness.

In Samuel Moffett's book, *The History of Christianity in Asia*, he traces the expansion of the Syrian church and the Nestorian sect across Asia and into what is now China. Archeological evidence reveals how phenomenally widespread the church in the East had become, even in the third and fourth centuries. However, its witness by the end of the first millennium had vanished in comparison to the spread of Christianity across Europe and to the West. Among the reasons the church became practically extinct in Asia, even as it began to encircle the globe to the West, was due to geographical isolation, numerical weakness, persecution, and the encountering of well-entrenched Asian religions. However, in spite of these formidable obstacles, Moffett observes that the primary reasons the Christian witness did not flourish was ethnic introversion, internal divisions, and theological compromise. "A case could be made that in Asia, as everywhere, Christians have always been their own worst enemies. In the final analysis, the deadliest obstacle to any community of Christians is to be found not outside it, but within it." Heresy and syncretism and reports of discreditable behavior diminished its attraction and moderated the favor of the church among political leaders.[1]

Missionaries, in the expansion of Christianity in the seventeenth and eighteenth centuries, rode the coattails of European colonialists and imported a spiritually irrelevant Western model of the church. In earlier centuries the institutionalization of the Roman Catholic and Orthodox churches represented a ritualism that had no spiritual vitality that would appeal to a pagan world. In fact, even the Protestant ecclesiastical presence of early missionary efforts simply reflected the ethnic superiority and arrogance of colonial governments, slave traders, and the economic exploitation they represented. Those from "Christian nations" and cultures brought disease, drinking, and debauchery to peoples suffering for centuries in spiritual darkness separated from God.

When a lost world observes dissension among competitive, self-serving missionaries or modern media makes them aware of the carnal lifestyles in "Christian nations," the life-transforming power of the gospel is obscured. Any attraction to a verbal, biblical witness is eroded by behavior that doesn't match one's testimony. We should not be naive in failing to realize that Satan is deliberate in his insidious strategy to attack the witness of the church from within. Why would a church be motivated to engage in global missions when they are not effectively engaging a mission field of lostness in their own community? How can God's mission be fulfilled around the world when the church's theology is diluted to eradicate a compelling conviction concerning the lostness of those without Christ and its eternal consequences?

The Local Church—Good and Bad

Satan opposes the mission of God by opposing local churches. He has a vested interest in what is going on at your church. Satan would love to keep churches self-absorbed, blind, and inward focused. If he can only stop us in the parking lot, then the lost in our communities will never see or hear the gospel. He would love to stop us before we can get started. So Satan will attack the health of the local church and its members. He will attack relationships; he will draw people into sexual immorality and create a false sense of wellness, all to keep the mission of God stalled.

> *Any attraction to a biblical witness is eroded by behavior that doesn't match one's testimony.*

The revelation of John was addressed to seven churches. The amazing thing about these churches was how good they were and how bad they were at the same time. Churches as a whole, like people, can be spiritually schizophrenic. We can be really good and really bad, on the same day, in same hour. When you look at the churches in Revelation as a group, strong patterns emerge. All seven churches were good at something (although Laodicea's strengths were not clear). Really, that is an understatement. All seven churches were impressive, pacesetter type churches that would easily fall into the category of "most admired." But five were thoroughly reprimanded by the Lord. As always, however, a clear path to vitality and right standing with God was provided. None of the five churches were considered hopeless, or broken beyond repair. Five churches were considered really sick, that is all, except for the case of Sardis who was informed "you are dead" (Rev. 3:1). Thud! When we look at the current realities of local churches in North America, direct, prophetic words are critical. Recognizing the strengths of churches is needed in difficult times. But ignoring spiritual sickness and deadness will have eternal ramifications.

The apostle John knew the church in Ephesus well. It was his hometown. The church at Ephesus was complimented for hard work, patience, and a strong stand against evil, yet their motivation was in question. The church was under tremendous pressure. Compromisers were trying to become church members. Others like John had been politically exiled from the city because of their commitment to Christ. Within the church, love for God and people had slipped considerably. They had lost their first love. Is it possible to do the right things for the wrong reasons? Does it matter? Can you achieve excellence in church programming but not be serving God because your heart is far from Him? A case study of the Ephesian church confirms it is possible. Churches can be right and committed but ineffective because their motivation is wrong. Orthodoxy is never an end into itself. Without a passion for God and people, spiritual power is absent. The matter was serious enough for a call to repentance. Ephesus Community Church had lost their direction and influence. They were so good and so bad at the same time.

> Satan would love to keep churches self-absorbed and inward focused; if he stops us in the parking lot, the lost will never hear the gospel.

Two of the five churches were accused of corruption and compromise. Pergamum had experienced the martyrdom of one of their leaders and was located in an incredibly corrupt culture. Yet this church, who was standing strong in the worst of circumstances, evidently was struggling with the flesh. Members were in relationships that were spiritually and sexually immoral. Thyatira was described as having faith, patience, service, and love. Yet as with Pergamum they were being led away in immoral sexual relationships. Laodicea had the unenviable position of receiving no compliments. Nothing seemed right about the current state of the Laodicean church. Laodicea was known for piping water into their city from six miles away. Cold water was refreshing. Hot water was cleansing. Lukewarm water was nauseating. The Laodicean church nauseated God.

Most of these churches were under incredible pressure from their cultures. Satan is constantly cited as the source of false teaching, immoral decisions, and compromise in the church. As a result, the mission of God was suffering. The influence on their respective cultures diminished. Midcourse corrections in these five churches were critical. We can talk about missions, pray for missionaries, and take impressive mission offerings but be spiritually sick at the same time. Our doctrine can be on target biblically, but we could care less about the marginalized in our community. We can show a high level of commitment and hard work yet compromise clear moral mandates from the Bible.

Why do these kinds of environments exist in our churches? First, Satan creates external pressure on us in groups and as individuals when we attempt to live Christianity in our respective cultures. Notice the overarching message needed for the church that is feeling the pressure of culture. The entire book of Revelation assures us that the pressure is not imagined; it is real. The drama and intensity of the revelation of John goes from beginning to end. The intensity is not temporary, but as a church continues toward their rightful place among the nations, the intense opposition will grow. The flaws of the church will be exposed under pressure. So what does success look like under pressure? God not only provided hope by giving a clear path for the five sick churches, but He also provided the examples of two who were doing well. Smyrna Church was encouraged but also heard the reality of the persecution they were about to suffer. Philadelphia

Church had an open door but was suffering intense pressure. God is able to make churches succeed for Him. The circumstances in Smyrna and Philadelphia were difficult, yet they, to that point, had not compromised and were being useful to God.

The second challenge is the internal pressure we feel as a result of our "natural-born sinner" disposition. Can we blame the devil all the time? If you sleep in when the church has a ministry going on at an adoption center, it wasn't the "pillow demon"; it was you. Though Satan is always looking for someone to devour, we provide him a great working environment at times.

We can be so good and so bad at the same time. Authenticity is the key to growth. Healthy churches are filled with healthy Christ followers. Healthy Christ followers never excuse their struggles, but they will always admit them. James's prescription for a healthy church environment was seen as he encouraged believers to "confess your sins one to another and pray for one another, so that you may be healed" (James 5:16). A church has a collective identity with God that can be compromised through individual sin and self-centeredness.

How can you discover what people really believe? Will you discover my belief system by how I answer a true-false test? Will you discover what I believe by a theological position paper, a lecture, or a sermon? The true test of my beliefs is how I live. What do I talk about? What do I do? How do I spend my time and my money? People live what they believe. Behavior is a mirror of our real belief system. Thus, if the "father of lies" (John 8:44 NASB) can convince us to believe lies, then we will live accordingly. Our spiritual vitality becomes nonexistent as we design our own customized version of Christianity. Then Satan, in turn, accomplishes his mission of hiding the glory of God and opposing the expansion of gospel influence.

Unholy Living Sabotages Mission

When Christ followers make bad choices, the glory of God is covered, and it hinders His mission. If Satan can disconnect us from the Word of God, our lives will follow their natural tendencies. What are those tendencies? Terrible, self-centered, destructive choices we call sin.

Few people enjoy shopping for new cars. Yet the reality of life is that car shopping is as inevitable as death and taxes. One common practice while you are test driving a car is to take your hands off the wheel for a moment to see if there are any major alignment issues. If the frame of the car has been damaged in a previous accident, it will pull to the right or the left. Guess what? Our frame has been bent by sin. As we grab hold of God's Word, God gets hold of the wheel of our lives. When we refuse His influence, we fall prey to our own natural, badly bent tendencies. To serve the Lord, or to profess to be a Christian, while at the same time making ungodly choices, has dire consequences. Satan uses us as his "witnesses." He tells people far from God that we are hypocrites and are not to be trusted; thus, God is not to be trusted. We are telling the world how they should live, while at the same time swerving all over the road with our moral and spiritual lives out of control. No wonder, when Jesus prayed in John 17:19, He included the plea for His people to be "sanctified by" God's truth.

How does God want His people to live? He wants us to understand how much our sin damages our lives and His mission. Stop trying to convince yourself that secret sin in your life and in the church will not hinder the mission of God.

The prophet Ezra ministered in an era when God's people were under siege from the forces of darkness. Satan pressured God's people from the outside. Babylon, the evil superpower, had taken Israel into captivity and destroyed Jerusalem. But Babylon was not the only obstruction to the glory of God. God's people had been disobedient to God and suffered the consequences. Ezra described the situation, "Everyone who trembled at the words of the God of Israel gathered around me, because of the unfaithfulness of the exiles, while I sat devastated until the evening offering. At the evening offering, I got up from my humiliation, with my tunic and robe torn. Then I fell on my knees and spread out my hands to the LORD my God. And I said: 'My God, I am ashamed and embarrassed to lift my face toward You, my God, because our iniquities are higher than our heads and our guilt is as high as the heavens'" (Ezra 9:4–6). The Word of God was revealed to His people. Extreme conviction, brokenness, and repentance followed. From politicians to preachers, no one seems to confess until they are caught. No one cries and is honest until he is exposed. The Word of God will always convict us before, during, and after we sin. So, if Satan can keep us separated from the Word, the probability of sin and its consequences is much greater.

Our bad choices hurt us, our families, and our churches, even if no one knows what we are doing. God is calling us to live gospel-centered, repentance-filled lives. As a pastor, I (Ed) have heard it time and time again: "My sin does not hurt anyone else." We need to realize that there are no "small" sins. God refers to all sin as an affront to His righteousness. All sin brings separation.

Growing up in a nominally Catholic home, I heard about venial and mortal sins on Christmas and Easter. Venial sins are taught to be the "little ones" like gossip about a trivial matter. Mortal sins are explained as bringing about spiritual death because of their serious nature. But Scripture makes no such distinction between venial and mortal. Paul taught the Galatians, "Now the works of the flesh are obvious: sexual immorality, moral impurity, promiscuity, idolatry, sorcery, hatreds, strife, jealousy, outbursts of anger, selfish ambitions, dissensions, factions, envy, drunkenness, carousing, and anything similar, about which I tell you in advance—as I told you before—that those who practice such things will not inherit the kingdom of God" (Gal. 5:19–21).

I am not having an affair, and I am not a warlock, I have those covered . . . right? But look at the rest: "hatreds, strife, jealousy, outbursts of anger, selfish ambitions, dissensions, factions, envy." *But I hate the deacons at church or coworkers at the office, lust after a bigger house, and envy someone with a better salary—let alone committing adultery in my heart.* "Drunkenness, carousing," *I don't even drink wine with my pasta,* . . . "or anything similar . . ."

But just in case you missed it, "anything similar" is in the list. Enough said. "About which I tell you in advance—as I told you before—that those who practice such things will not inherit the kingdom of God" (Gal. 5:21).

There is no difference in God's eyes between being a warlock and a pastor envying a larger church, lusting in your heart after what's on the cable channel, and hating some of your neighbors. They all keep you out of right fellowship with God. It's sin. It saps spiritual power. It kills you, your spiritual life, and the spiritual life of your church. It brings about disconnection with the work of the kingdom. The glory of God is covered.

How quickly and comfortably we have found the ability to highlight other peoples' sins. We roll off the names of Swaggart, Baker, and Haggard . . . but I wonder how your neighbors and mine might speak our names. How about our spouses, children, and coworkers? How do they speak our names? But we often forget: if Satan cannot compromise our beliefs, he is happy to settle for our character. And that is what he is doing in the lives of both leader and parishioner in the church today. Truth spoken from a compromised life is like a light shining from behind a curtain, only residual effects are made.

We need gospel-centered and repentance-filled lives. The gospel is not something you get over; it is something you live in. A cross-centered and resurrection-powered life doesn't get saved and then live on our own power. We, instead, die daily. And it is repentance filled because that is how we respond to a sin-sick world—by quickly and readily repenting.

Here are four principles to consider as you order your life around holiness before God. The first is: *Secret sins are only that way for a short time.* Sin might be kept secret for a season but in its time will give rise to death. God does not keep silent about the secret sins of his leaders. God's people should feel no need to act as superheroes who must maintain a secret identity. In fact,

God Himself is the only real hero of the Bible. The apparent success of His people was all about Him. Choose one; they were all miserable failures who made decisions that thwarted the mission of God: Noah, Abraham, Moses, David, Peter, and others. Moses warned his people that sin will be exposed: "But if you don't do this, you will certainly sin against the LORD; be sure your sin will catch up with you" (Num. 32:23). It has been said, even the king of an empire cannot hide his sin once God is ready to confront him with his deeds. Stop trying to convince yourself that secret sin in your life and in the church will not hinder the mission of God. Instead, live a gospel-centered, repentance-filled life.

The second principle is: *Private sin can deliver the community of faith into public defeat.* Satan's lie is that my sin is private and does not affect the community of faith. Your sin saps your church's spiritual power. It does not matter if you are the pastor everyone knows or the quietest person in the congregation known only by a few, your sin affects the entire body. We see this principle demonstrated in the story of Achan's sin resulting in the defeat of God's people at Ai. The entire community was blamed for the sin of Achan. But ultimately Achan "started it" when he took God-forbidden valuables from Jericho. He could never have imagined the devastation he would cause and the glory he would cover. We are called to live out our faith in community. For Israel to have success in the promised land and fulfill God's mission, sin had to be rooted out of the camp. Just as faith is most effectively lived out in community, so is sin. Faith gives rise to mutual boldness. Sin gives rise to mutual weakness. Again, stop trying to convince yourself that secret sin in your life and in the church will not hinder the mission of God. Instead, live a gospel-centered, repentance-filled life.

> *For Israel to have success and fulfill God's mission, sin had to be rooted out of the camp.*

The third principle to consider as you live out holiness: *The church's toleration of sin leads to a communal rejection of the mission.* Christians in the Corinthian church were reprimanded: "It is widely reported that there is sexual immorality among you, and the kind of sexual immorality that is not even condoned among the Gentiles—a man is living with his father's wife. And you are inflated with pride, instead of filled with grief so that he who has committed this act might be removed from among you" (1 Cor. 5:1–2).

The Corinthian Christians not only tolerated the sinfulness of the man, they were even proud of it! No wonder the Corinthians were so off base. They needed to be educated in right living for God. When you tolerate open sin in your church, you are not being loving. You are being naive. Paul tells the whole church how to handle what today's culture would have termed a "private, family matter." Your church lacks spiritual power if it does not practice church discipline. Disobedience to Christ is a rejection of His missionary endeavor to others. Stop trying to convince yourself that secret sin in your life and in the church will not hinder the mission of God. Instead, live a gospel-centered, repentance-filled life.

The final principle is: *A return to God's mission begins with repentance before God's standard.* The church at Corinth is an interesting case study about the sin cycle and its effect on the mission of God. Remember, Paul warned the Corinthian Christians through the failure of Israel in the wilderness in the Old Testament: "Now I want you to know . . . God was not pleased with most of them, for they were struck down in the desert. Now these things became examples for us, so that we will not desire evil as they did. Don't become idolaters as some of them were; as it is written, 'The people sat down to eat and drink, and got up to play'" (1 Cor. 10:1, 5–7).

Sin is serious business. Often we use our humanity and our desire to be "real" as an excuse to permit all types of compromise to enter the body of Christ. We trust ourselves too much. We overestimate our own spiritual maturity. From the Internet, to relationships with the opposite sex, and even to the movies we watch, we act bulletproof. We are deeply flawed. John Calvin said, "The heart is an idol factory." That's why every day you and I have to die to self in order to live for Christ. I am going to need to repent today. I am going to need to repent tomorrow. So far I have never had a day where God said, "Nope, you're good . . . thanks for checking."

Jeremiah puts our sin potential in perspective. He said, "The heart is more deceitful than anything else and desperately sick—who can understand it?" (17:19). He compared the condition of our hearts to a mountain range. Inside us are incredibly high and beautiful peaks that give way to deep dark valleys. Self-awareness is a key. Who are you? Where are your deep dark valleys? Whom have you confided in about those valleys?

> *If Satan cannot get us to doubt, ignore, or rationalize God's Word, he persuades us to believe it without doing what it says.* ᧁ

God's most powerful instrument for ministry on the earth is His repentant people. The satanic lie: secret sin in your life and in the church will not hinder the mission of God. God's solution: live a gospel-centered, repentance-filled life.

Healthy Disciples, Healthy Churches . . . God's Mission

Healthy churches are populated with healthy people. How can you tell when people are healthy? You can tell people are healthy through their relationship with Jesus Christ. Healthy people are passionate about the things Jesus is passionate about. Healthy churches, in turn, are always involved in the mission of God, everywhere, much to the dismay of our adversary, the devil. Never confuse healthy with perfect. But never confuse imperfect with irresponsibility or spiritually dead!

Spiritual warfare is about the clash of kingdoms—the kingdom of light and the kingdom of darkness. Immediately after Jesus had experienced the temptations by Satan, He announced the kingdom of heaven had come. Notice the last offer Satan made to Jesus, "Again, the Devil took Him to a very high mountain and showed Him all the kingdoms of the world and their splendor. And he said to Him, 'I will give You all these things if You will fall down and worship me'" (Matt. 4:8–9). All the kingdoms of the world belonged to Jesus. Satan ignored the fact that Jesus was King of *the* kingdom. All the kingdoms Satan claimed to own are not worth the eternal kingdom of the King who was in his presence. What Satan was requesting from Jesus the King was the one thing Satan refused to give to the worthy Lamb of God—worship. What twisted and delusional values were demonstrated by Satan on that day. The same twisted satanic value system keeps men in the kingdom of darkness today.

The Gospel of Matthew focuses on Jesus the King and His kingdom. In Matthew 4:12, following Jesus' baptism and temptation, the public ministry of Jesus began. The clarity of Jesus' kingdom message was established immediately: "From then on Jesus began to preach, 'Repent, because the kingdom of heaven has come near!'" (Matt. 4:17). The middle part of the chapter featured the calling of the disciples. Then the last part is a summary of the rest of Matthew: "Jesus was going all over Galilee, teaching in their synagogues, preaching the good news of the kingdom, and healing every disease and sickness among the people. Then the news about Him spread throughout Syria. So they brought to Him all those who were afflicted, those suffering from various diseases and intense pains, the demon-possessed, the epileptics, and the paralytics. And He healed them. Large crowds followed Him from Galilee, Decapolis, Jerusalem, Judea, and beyond the Jordan" (Matt. 4:23–25). Kingdom Christians are spiritually healthy and make up the membership of a spiritually healthy church. From this passage we can learn how kingdom Christians are supposed to live.

Kingdom Christians live a universal message, the gospel of the kingdom. "The people who live in darkness have seen a great light, and for those living in the shadowland of death, light has dawned. From then on Jesus began to preach, 'Repent, because the kingdom of heaven has come near!'" (Matt. 4:16–17). The gospel of the kingdom is powerful. The way to recognize the presence of kingdom gospel is through the life-changing results. The kingdom gospel changes everything. It changes you. It changes those around you. As Jesus began His ministry, He fulfilled a prophecy spoken centuries earlier: "The people walking in darkness have seen a great light; on those living in the land of darkness, a light has dawned" (Isa. 9:2). The "darkness to light" transition was dramatic.

In Isaiah, the promise represented hope in the middle of a miserable life situation. The enemy (Assyria) held Israel captive. Overwhelmed and helpless by life's circumstances, people needed a reason for hope. Our enemy, Satan, blinds the minds of unbelievers and holds them captive today. Some are held captive by their own false religious beliefs. Others are held captive by their confidence in unbelief. Jesus and the kingdom gospel are introduced into their darkness. Jesus is greater than a religious preference or denominational affiliation; He is the "light of the world" (John 8:12). Described as moving from the "shadowland of death" and seeing a "great light" dawning was a foreshadowing of the ministry to the Gentiles, what we do today.

Jesus slipped silently into the world as an innocent baby. That's the theme of the beginning of Matthew, a King born in an obscure place. But he announces His ministry with a profound declaration, "Repent, because the kingdom of heaven has come near!" (Matt. 3:2). The universal message includes a radical call. The radical call is not a religious one but personal . . . repent. We don't like the word; it feels ancient and dreadful. However, repentance is the only proper response when the eternal kingdom arrives. As clear as Jesus was about the radical message, He could not force or demand repentance. He could only invite people to the place of a personal relationship with Him. They could not stay in darkness and follow Jesus at the same time. To relocate to the light required a radical U-turn. The universal nature of this message is clear. Regardless of Jew or Gentile, religious or not, righteous or sinful, darkness is darkness. Repentance (radical relocation from one direction to another) is the only way to enter into a relation with the King and to become a citizen in His kingdom.

We talk a lot about the gospel and the kingdom. What is the gospel? Here is the definition I (Ed) use: The gospel is the good news that God, who is more holy than we can imagine, looked with great compassion upon people. People are more sinful than we would possibly admit, so God sent Jesus into history to establish His kingdom and reconcile people and the world to Himself. Jesus, whose love is more extravagant than we can measure, came to die sacrificially for us. Through His grace we now gain what the Bible defines as eternal life through His death and resurrection. We now can know the only true God and take hold of this present life by the direction and abundant strength afforded to us through the Spirit. We must never lose sight of the enormity of that message.

> *The kingdom gospel is universal, personal, and local and will make a deep, substantive change in you.*

But our culture has unfortunately become inoculated to the message of the gospel. To most people, it is no more than a message of "be good and go to church." We proclaim the gospel message as the antidote to the prevalent false gospel of moralistic deism. Moralistic deism suggests that there is a god who started all this, who is not really involved, but who just wants you to be good and go to church. Wouldn't Satan love for us to think that way? The gospel of the kingdom is a big and universal gospel that changes (and recreates) everything. The gospel is not a do-gooders creed but a declaration of the kingdom's arrival in the finite existence of men.

What had come near? The kingdom had come near in the person of Christ. The gospel is a message of God's reign everywhere. The expansiveness of the gospel is overshadowed only by the eternality of its King. Living the universal message of the gospel requires a willingness to go to the ends of the earth with the message. Remember, people in darkness have only one solution, the light of the world, Jesus. The kingdom gospel changes everything.

Kingdom Christians live a personal message, the gospel of transformation. "As He was walking along the Sea of Galilee, He saw two brothers, Simon, who was called Peter, and his brother Andrew. They were casting a net into the sea, since they were fishermen. 'Follow Me,' He told them, 'and I will make you fish for people!' Immediately they left their nets and followed Him. Going on from there, He saw two other brothers, James the son of Zebedee, and his brother John. They were in a boat with Zebedee their father, mending their nets, and He called them. Immediately they left the boat and their father and followed Him" (Matt. 4:18–22). The kingdom gospel changes everything (universal), changes you (personal), and changes those around you (your neighbor). Kingdom Christians are clear that the message means change. As they grow in a healthy relationship with Jesus, they grow deeper in living out the message.

When Jesus came upon Peter and Andrew, he said, "Follow Me, and I will make you fish for people." How radical was this call? How personal was this call? Notice what the call was not. Jesus did not say to them, "Keep fishing. I want to make you a better version of yourself." Neither did Jesus say, "Could I please hang out with you and follow you around? You will really like me, I promise." Keep in mind, too, fishing was not evil. Fishing was common, honest work. Yet Jesus was not asking His disciples if He could do life with them. Jesus was inviting them to do life with Him. He was inviting them to do life substantively different than they had ever imagined or experienced before. For them to follow Jesus would involve repentance. Complete and substantive relocation from one place to another is what is required. That message goes from making my life better to making my life new. How personal is that? The big, universal kingdom gospel now becomes a transformational gospel. The personal call was: come, follow, leave everything, and fish for men.

Paul's letter to the Ephesians addressed our identity as Christians. Our identity of "in Christ" is the fulfillment of Eden's call, "Adam, where are you?" What a gift! Someone who cares enough to ask us the right question at the right time brings life change. Dozens of times in the New Testament, the phrase "in Christ" is used to describe the life of a believer. Remember Paul's words to the Romans: "So, you, too consider yourselves dead to sin, but alive to God in Christ Jesus" (Rom. 6:11). Because of your new identity, you have moved from death to life, from darkness to light, from wallowing in humanity to touching the divine. But it also calls us to leave things behind. Peter, Andrew, and all of us must leave our nets behind in order to become better fishermen. You will have to walk away from what you have in order to gain all Christ has for you.

Philip Nation and I (Ed) wrote a book entitled *Compelled by Love*.[2] The picture of the missional church in our book is described by the missional Christian motivated by the love of Jesus who is part of that church. The church is often seen as an impersonal institution that is supposed to do and be something. Normally the pastor is perceived as a negative coach of your worst nightmare, always yelling and dissatisfied at the behavior of this underachieving monster, "the church." He is angry, but we do not know exactly who or what makes him angry. We know it can't be us. Well then, it must be the church. The healthy church is made up of healthy, responsible Christ followers. I call them people. The face of the church is your face and my face, not the building, church address, or the denomination.

Compelled by Love is based on the detailed and personal description of the people of God from 2 Corinthians:

From now on, then, we do not know anyone in a
purely human way. Even if we have known Christ
in a purely human way, yet now we no longer know
Him like that. Therefore if anyone is in Christ, there
is a new creation; old things have passed away, and
look, new things have come. Now everything is from
God, who reconciled us to Himself through Christ
and gave us the ministry of reconciliation: that is,
in Christ, God was reconciling the world to Himself,
not counting their trespasses against them, and He
has committed the message of reconciliation to us.
Therefore, we are ambassadors for Christ; certain
that God is appealing through us, we plead on
Christ's behalf, "Be reconciled to God." He made the
One who did not know sin to be sin for us, so that
we might become the righteousness of God in Him.
(2 Cor. 5:16–21)

If you follow Jesus, then He will make you into something
new in your identity and activity. Jesus will do something deep
and personal. Being moral and kind is only one part of the transformational work of Christ. The value system you hold deep and
personal will be literally turned upside down. The things you used
to love, you will see as mere shadows compared to Christ and His
kingdom. The things you rebelled against, you will love. Why?
Because you are moving deeper in the kingdom of light. Your work
will begin personal but go public. You are now His ambassador, or
highest ranking human representative, of one country to another.

*Kingdom Christians live a local message, the gospel for your neigh-
bor.* "Jesus was going all over Galilee, teaching in their synagogues,
preaching the good news of the kingdom, and healing every disease and sickness among the people. Then the news about Him
spread throughout Syria. So they brought to Him all those who
were afflicted, those suffering from various diseases and intense
pains, the demon-possessed, the epileptics, and the paralytics.

And He healed them. Large crowds followed Him from Galilee, Decapolis, Jerusalem, Judea, and beyond the Jordan" (Matt. 4:23–25). The kingdom gospel is universal, personal, and local. The kingdom gospel is for all fishermen, in every nation. That same gospel will make deep, substantive personal changes in you.

The third arena is often the toughest. Our neighbors are engaged by the daily travel rhythms of our lives. Our life, work, and play acquaintances are most commonly seen and least commonly engaged with the gospel. How awkward does it feel as we attempt to talk about such a personal issue as faith to people we are with all the time? It is oftentimes easier to travel around the world to discuss faith with people we will never see again than the ones across the street we see daily. Holding real spiritual conversations every day is the great challenge to many Christians. Keep in mind that these conversations will always be the most uncomfortable. No matter what you memorize or how experienced you are, don't expect any real relief. Satan and the forces of hell are aimed against your next spiritual conversation with someone you know. Satan knows the power of an ongoing narrative between two people, one person on the journey, another genuinely seeking. Satan knows that multiple conversations over days, months, and years might be what it will take. Satan is not OK with our caring and praying for the lost. But he truly loathes it when we personally engage them in conversation. The talking part is what he wants to stop. Satan knows the power of an unbeliever's seeing a real Christian as well as hearing the gospel.

The presence of Christ can change your community. Look at Jesus in action in Matthew 4:23. Jesus was:

- Preaching: strong declaration of the gospel like a prophet.
- Teaching: grace-filled conversations of the gospel like a priest.
- Healing: touching life needs because of the gospel like a physician.

Kingdom Christians live a dynamic message, the gospel for all peoples. "Large crowds followed Him from Galilee, Decapolis, Jerusalem, Judea, and beyond the Jordan" (Matt. 4:25). One of the great themes for all of the Gospels is that the gospel is for everyone. Satan will do everything possible to keep us from a universal declaration of the gospel. But God has called us to it. He has given us all we need to overcome our self-imposed hindrances. He has provided every resource needed to get the job done. How will we respond?

This passage introduced who Jesus is and what He does in the rest of the book of Matthew. The missional church is to join Jesus in His mission. God calls you and me to be Jesus to our friends. The completely healthy Christian, who makes up the healthy, missional church, is a be, do, and tell Christian. "Preach the gospel at all times—if necessary, use words" is the often used quote from St. Francis. Nice, warm, and fuzzy but wrong. And he most likely never said it. Instead, we should be, do, and tell the gospel at all times. It should be inherent in every thought, word, and action of our lives. As we live out the kingdom of light in the middle of the shadowlands, the gospel must burn brightly from our lives.

The church is the base camp from which we launch to change the community. Jesus ministered in real places among real people. The message of the gospel is not an ethereal idea. It carries the weight of judgment and the joy of forgiveness. And it is for you and your neighbors—and it sometimes calls us to new neighbors around the globe, but we join Jesus on His mission to preach, teach, and heal. Christ in your neighborhood is the message of the gospel. Christ where you live, work, and play sounds healthy and right, just as Jesus planned it.

Resorting to Our Own Efforts and Ingenuity

After the children of Israel turned back in faithlessness from pressing forward to fulfill God's mission and take possession of the land, the Scripture says that God was angry with the people and vowed to destroy them. In response to the intercession of Moses, God relented "for the sake of His fame among the nations" and declared that, with the exception of Joshua and Caleb, all of those twenty years old and above would perish and not have the privilege of participating in the blessings of His promised reward. Moses shared with the people the consequences of their lack of faith and disbelief in the power of God, and the Scripture tells us they were overcome with grief. So they got up the next morning determined that they would go into the land and engage the Amalekites and Canaanites in battle.

"They got up early the next morning and went up . . . saying, 'Let's go to the place the LORD promised, for we were wrong.' But Moses responded, 'Why are you going against the LORD's command? It won't succeed. Don't go, because the LORD is not among you and you will be defeated'" (Num. 14:40–42). And of course the people were routed. They considered themselves to be doing what God wanted them to do, but it was not in God's timing and God's way, and He was not with them.

We dare not presume to fulfill the mission of God in our own methods and think our resources can accomplish anything apart from God's power. Many churches respond to the challenge of global missions but lose sight of the fact of the spiritual nature of the task. For a lost world in Africa, Latin America, Asia, and secularized Europe to come to saving faith in Jesus Christ, and lives and society changed for the glory of God, the gospel must be communicated in a culturally sensitive way that allows the power of God's Spirit to bring conviction of sin and truth. Paul laid down this basic, foundational truth when he declared, "For I am not ashamed of the gospel, because it is God's power for salvation

> *We dare not presume to fulfill the mission of God with our own methods and resources . . . apart from God's power.*

to everyone who believes, first to the Jew, and also to the Greek" (Rom. 1:16). But a lot of mission efforts have no evidence of the power of God, nor does the incarnational witness and good works of mission teams communicate cross-culturally the message of good news that will draw people to become followers of Jesus Christ.

A lot that churches do overseas is designed to make them feel good about having gone on a mission trip when there are no lasting results. Certainly, as Christ followers, we are to minister to those in need. Feeding the poor, ministering to those who are suffering, and rebuilding disaster-hit areas are appropriate; and the compassion demonstrated by a godly love unknown in communities and cultures that do not know Jesus does make an impact. But Satan would make us satisfied with a sense of sacrifice of having given our time, contributed significant expenses, and helped a lot of people without ever introducing them to the One that can give eternal hope. One of our public health workers, reflecting on the success of projects bringing sanitation and rehabilitating villages, expressed his sense of failure that the people had not come to faith in Christ with the observation, "Healthy in hell doesn't count for much." Doing good deeds may fulfill our sense of obligation and make us feel good, but such deeds alone do not extend the kingdom of God to the point of His being exalted among the nations.

Satan may also be engaged in causing us to have a narrow perspective on missions that inhibits God's larger mission purpose from being fulfilled. The potential for reaching every tribe, people, language, and nation and giving all the peoples of the world an opportunity to hear, understand, and respond to the gospel in their own culture requires an indigenous mission strategy. There will never be enough cross-cultural missionaries and mission teams to reach all the people in the world. The gospel must be shared and planted in a way that it can multiply among those who are receptive. Churches must be bodies of believers drawn together into worshipping, witnessing fellowships by the Holy Spirit without dependence on superfluous elements for their existence that would inhibit their reproducing.

Many have expressed skepticism regarding International Mission Board reports of church-planting movements and the rapid reproduction of church fellowships because we in America are so ingrained in a corporate Western model of programs, organizations, and facilities. We forget that when one's life is radically transformed by the gospel, it is a message that cannot be contained. As the gospel is shared within extended family networks and from village to village, new believers are nurtured in the Word of God. They become a nucleus of witness that goes beyond that of a Western missionary or church planter. Their witness grows in a reproducing pattern that has the potential of making the gospel accessible throughout a city or people group.

What better way could Satan devise to inhibit such a growing, multiplying witness—clearly demonstrated in the book of Acts—than to create dependency on outside leadership or resources. Many have gone overseas to build church buildings, presuming they are providing a service that will strengthen a local church and ministry. But what happens is to propagate a model that a church cannot really exist and be effective without a building as a special place of worship. That local church seldom has the resources or capacity to reproduce such a model, so no further outreach and expansion occurs until overseas benefactors are found to build another church building. The congregation comes to see resources beyond their means as necessary to function as a church rather than learn that spiritual resources from God are all they need.

When the former Soviet Union began to disintegrate, we observed the rapid multiplication of the church with the new freedoms that came to the republics in the Commonwealth of Independent States. In one of the countries of Eastern Europe, Baptists from the United States established a partnership in which they agreed to assist in church planting. Stateside churches rallied to build church buildings for the impoverished believers who didn't have the resources to provide places of worship. The Americans even provided support for the national church planters and pastors, and in five years fifty new churches had been planted. Of course, when the subsidy and aid were eventually withdrawn, the inherent weakness of such help was evident. Many of the churches did not survive, and their witness was anemic because others did everything for them. Meanwhile, in the same time frame more than a thousand churches spread across a neighboring republic. The good intentions of mission teams were not unlike the children of Israel who decided to engage the battle themselves, with their own resources rather than in the power of God and with His leadership.

One of our staff told about participating in a pastors conference in Russia several years after the country had opened to Westerners. One of the participants commented on the constant flow of Americans coming to lead conferences, training them in various programs and methodology of church growth. He said, "Back during the repressive days of the Soviet Union, we were persecuted and had nothing. Our perspective was that Jesus was all we had, and He was all we needed; we had Jesus or died. Now it seems that Jesus isn't enough!"

We need to be aware that Satan is indeed subtle and devious. He can take our good intentions to engage in, what appears to us to be an effective mission strategy. But if it is based on what we do and the resources we provide without the power of God's Spirit to impact lostness in a way that goes beyond our brief trip and financial investment, Satan has gained the larger victory. It is amazing how American pastors want to jump on the bandwagon when reports come of an emerging harvest. Many relish being able to participate in crusades where they can preach to massive crowds and come home reporting on thousands of conversions—all for the glory of God, of course.

But are we not deceived in denying that there is a lot of ego and personal gratification in being a part of a movement of God and something He is doing with or without us? If Satan can get us to interpret our mission task as populating heaven with as many people as possible, we will resort to going only to those places of receptivity and harvest and neglect doing what is needed to reach the unreached and penetrate the dominions of darkness with the light of the gospel. We need to be cautious about choosing the least expensive and easy places to engage in missions, while justifying our neglect of areas that are isolated, hostile, restrictive, and where we have no assurance of response. By what criteria should any people be deprived of an opportunity to hear and respond to the gospel? We dare not seek to fulfill God's mission in our own way, exporting programs and Western methods or for our own sense of gratification in lieu of being a channel for God's Spirit.

Going Deeper

1. What are you becoming in Christ? How has God changed you in the last year?

2. On a 1 to 10 scale, where are you in your relationship with Jesus Christ? Where would you like to be? What would it take to move you closer? When will you take those steps? Who can help you?

3. What area in your life is being influenced by the devil? Is there someone who could help you? When will you talk with them?

CHAPTER 12

THE FINAL VICTORY: WILL WE BE FOUND FAITHFUL?

When our strategy team for the Persian world suggested that I take a trip to Iran, I (Jerry) wasn't too enthusiastic about the proposal. I am usually excited about adventurous destinations and opportunities to go to new places, but we don't get a lot of positive news about Americans and Christians out of Iran. I suggested that we consider deferring the trip for a year or two, or maybe ten! Perhaps tensions will have settled down and more positive relationships restored with our country by that time. However, the team insisted that this was the time; we had to see personally how God was at work through all the political upheaval and fanaticism of the ayatollahs. We enlisted a group of businessmen who were willing to explore investment opportunities and survey the rich historic and cultural sites of the country.

We were amazed at the hospitality of the Iranian people and how well we were received as we traveled throughout the country for ten days. Every day God did something to reveal how He was at work among the people. We were surprised to find on our itinerary the tomb of Esther and Mordecai. As we were making our way on the bus toward Hamedan, where the tomb was located, I read once again the book of Esther in the Bible since we were seeing the geography and terrain of the ancient Babylonian Empire where these events took place. The most familiar passage in this Old Testament book is Esther 4:14 where Esther is challenged by Mordecai to go in before the king and intervene on behalf of her people. He says, "And who knoweth whether thou art come to the kingdom for such a time as this?" (KJV).

We got a glimpse of that kingdom of ancient Babylon as we toured the Persian nation of Iran, but that was only a portion of a kingdom the Bible describes as stretching from Ethiopia to India. One day our itinerary took us to the exhibit of the crown jewels at the Central Bank of Tehran. The opulence and wealth were unbelievable. It wasn't just jewel-encrusted crowns and scepters, but there were saddles and bridles, furniture, and clothes embedded with rubies, diamonds, emeralds, and all kinds of precious stones. The displays of bracelets, necklaces, and rings from that ancient empire seemed endless.

But there is a coming kingdom of God that will make the kingdom of ancient Babylon pale into insignificance. It is a kingdom of far greater wealth and value than could be accumulated in terms of earthly jewels. Jesus spoke of this coming kingdom and sent His disciples to proclaim the good news of the kingdom to all peoples. I thought of this comparison when I found myself reading a part of the story of Esther in chapter 8. Esther had become queen of Persia and, at risk of her life, had intervened for her people. The conspiracy of Haman was revealed, and he was hung on the gallows prepared for Mordecai. However, the decree had already been issued, due to Haman's devious influence that all the Jews were to be destroyed. And the law of the Medes and Persians could not be changed.

So the king issued a subsequent decree. In this edict he warned the Jews of the pending threat and gave them permission to arm and defend themselves. It was a message of salvation for a people doomed to be destroyed. The Scripture tells us they sent couriers with the message translated into every language to the most remote regions of the empire. There was a sense of urgency. They chose the fastest horses from the royal stables as the couriers "rode out in haste, at the king's urgent command" (Esther 8:14).

As I read this account, I thought of several possible scenarios. What if they had forgotten about one of the minority people groups in a faraway province in the remote regions of the empire? Or what if they had not been able to find someone in the capital city to translate the decree into the language of some of the people? What if a courier had stopped along the way, or been diverted, and the people to whom he was sent never got the message? The people would have perished, not because a decree of salvation and deliverance had not been given but because they never got the message!

That is exactly what has happened in our world today. Jesus Christ came and died for the sins of the world so that whoever calls on the name of the Lord can be saved. But many of the peoples of the world have not heard that good news, and they continue to perish in their sins. Multitudes continue to die and enter an eternity in hell, not because salvation is not available but because they have never heard the news. Of the more than six thousand languages in the world, fewer than a thousand have the entire Bible in their own language. Only about twelve hundred others have the New Testament or some portion of Scripture; we haven't bothered to translate and deliver God's Word of the hope of redemption into most of the languages spoken throughout the world. We are the couriers sent to proclaim deliverance to all peoples, but we have stopped short. Instead of reaching the most remote regions, we have been diverted to caring for our own people and investing more in our own church programs than getting the gospel to all peoples.

But God's mission will be fulfilled. God is moving in providence and power to bring the nations into the kingdom. Mordecai had this sense of God's providence when he challenged Esther to recognize that God had uniquely positioned her within the palace to be the one to intercede before the king. We often miss the implications of the rest of that often-quoted verse. Mordecai goes on to say in Esther 4:14, "If you keep silent at this time, liberation and deliverance will come to the Jewish people from another place, but you and your father's house will be destroyed. Who knows, perhaps you have come to the kingdom for such a time as this." Mordecai remembered God's covenant with Abraham, the patriarchs, and the affirmation of His promise to the prophets of God who foresaw the fulfillment of that coming kingdom. He knew God would be true to His covenant promise. He would find a way to deliver His people that the Messiah would come and bring redemption.

He said to Esther, "If you don't step up to be the one that God chooses to use, you are the loser. You and your household will perish along with others, but God's purpose will be carried out through some other means and instrument." God's mission will be fulfilled. That day will come when those from every tribe, language, people, and nation will be gathered around the throne of God singing praises to the Lamb. The tragedy is the fact that many of God's people have forfeited the privilege of being the one used by God. Many have been unwilling to take the risk, holding on to their own security and comfort instead of recognizing we have been called into the kingdom for such a time as this.

> *Many of God's people have forfeited that privilege of being used by God, failing to recognize they have been called into the kingdom for such a time as this.*

We are called to be the faithful ones that have the privilege of extending the kingdom of God upon the earth. "The Lamb will conquer them because he is Lord of lords and King of kings. Those with him are called and elect and faithful" (Rev. 17:14). God is sovereign over the nations, and His kingdom will prevail. We need to recapture that vision that was so prominent among the Old

Testament prophets. "Arise, shine, for your light has come, and the glory of the LORD shines over you. For look, darkness covers the earth, and total darkness the peoples; but the LORD will shine over you, and His glory will appear over you. Nations will come to your light, and kings to the brightness of your radiance" (Isa. 60:1–3). "Nations will see your righteousness, and all kings your glory" (Isa. 62:2). "In the last days . . . all nations will stream to it, and many peoples will come" (Isa. 2:2–3); "The LORD alone will be exalted on that day" (Isa. 2:11). The Old Testament closes with the assurance from God, "For My name will be great among the nations, from the rising of the sun to its setting" (Mal. 1:11).

Satan's Lies about the Power of the Resurrection

The apostle Paul's passionate prayer for the church in the first chapter of Ephesians is a reminder that Christ promised us the power and authority to fulfill His mission. His resurrection and victory over Satan and death assured us the power of the Holy Spirit would indwell us for the purpose of an empowered witness in the world:

> I pray that the eyes of your heart may be enlightened so you may know what is the hope of His calling, what are the glorious riches of His inheritance among the saints, and what is the immeasurable greatness of His power to us who believe, according to the working of His vast strength. He demonstrated this power in the Messiah by raising Him from the dead . . . far above every ruler and authority, power and dominion. . . . And He put everything under His feet and appointed Him as head over everything for the church, which is His body. (Eph. 1:18–23)

A casual reading of this passage may lead us to be reminded of the truth that Christ is head of the church, which He is. But note that He is head over everything, and this power and dominion is *for* the church!

One major lie of Satan contains a grain of truth. The lie concerns the resurrection of Jesus Christ. Many professing Christians believe that the resurrection of Christ is not powerful enough to save and needs additional works to be effective; for others it is the power of salvation, and that is all. For many the resurrection of Christ is little more than a happy ending to a great Mel Gibson movie. Christians go to church and believe the resurrection of Christ is a historical reality. The resurrection of Jesus is much more than a historical reality. The greater reality is what we celebrate once a year, on Easter Sunday morning, and has incredible, year-round, worldwide implications. The Resurrection of Jesus Christ impacts, changes, and transforms everything from our lives to our world, including our churches.

Easter is a traditional holiday in the United States. Christians and non-Christians commonly acknowledge on that day that Jesus Christ resurrected from the dead. Our churches are filled with what has been called "E/C people" or Easter/Christmas-only attendees. Some pastors have been known to end their Easter Sunday service with a hearty "Merry Christmas" each year, telling attendees he would not see many of them until Christmas so he wanted to be the first to give them Christmas greetings.

I (Ed) remember my Easter experience as a kid in Levittown, just outside of New York City. My family would drag us to church on Easter Sunday. I have three distinct memories of Easter Sunday morning. My childhood Easter memories—chocolate, tight clothes, and profanity—are not exact matches with most "normal" people's memories. We were Irish. So Easter Sunday invaded our dysfunctional family system each year. My dad insisted we get up early and make our journey to church. He insisted on the same behavior for Christmas. We really didn't like it when we went. But we knew, if you are Irish and you didn't go to church on Easter, hell was pretty much guaranteed. So our family was dragged to church on Easter. Our parents, I remember, took us to this big building with painted windows and a lot of old people. We witnessed an angry man scream at us for twenty minutes (the priest) and then another would scream profanities at the traffic as we went home (my father). This awkward, unwelcomed family tradition had no real affect on our lives. We believed that Jesus was raised from the dead, but it was not a big deal. We bought into the lie of Satan. We did Easter and Christmas, but we did not let them interfere with the way we lived.

Early Christians engaged the event that changed human history, the resurrection of Jesus Christ, on a much deeper level. They often greeted one another with the phrase, "He is risen," to which those they greeted responded with, "He is risen, indeed!" More than a greeting, early Christians experienced the power of the resurrection to the point that they were willing to die for the cause of Christ. The belief of early Christians profoundly affected their passion, their purpose, and ultimately their behavior. Stephen, the first Christian martyr on record, experienced a deeper embrace of Jesus' resurrection. Stephen saw Christ alive. He was filled with the Holy Spirit and experienced the full glory of God. The Bible lets us witness Stephen's power at the moment of his martyrdom:

> But Stephen, filled by the Holy Spirit, gazed into
> heaven. He saw God's glory, with Jesus standing
> at the right hand of God, and he said, "Look! I see
> the heavens opened and the Son of Man standing at
> the right hand of God!" Then they screamed at the
> top of their voices, stopped their ears, and rushed
> together against him. They threw him out of the city
> and began to stone him. And the witnesses laid their
> robes at the feet of a young man named Saul. They
> were stoning Stephen as he called out: "Lord Jesus,
> receive my spirit!" Then he knelt down and cried out

with a loud voice, "Lord, do not charge them with this sin!" And saying this, he fell asleep. (Acts 7:55–60)

When it comes to the issue of spiritual warfare, the body of Christ (as with many issues) owns a variety of solutions. In fact, a quick Google search reveals that in the last year there have been almost a million new entries on the subject. YouTube, the incredibly popular video site, has around two thousand spiritual warfare video listings. Amazon lists more than twelve hundred books that address the issue.

The most sensational of all solutions to Satan and evil is known as a power encounter. This is a confrontational approach in which people are encouraged to cast out demons in a bold confrontation of the powers of darkness. Another common solution to overcome satanic schemes is considered a truth encounter. This position is held by many writers as overcoming Satan through a truth encounter; this is not coming face-to-face with demons and using certain formulas to command them to leave. A truth encounter confronts satanic opposition by learning and applying truth from God's Word. When it comes to spiritual warfare we tend to be stuck in ditches on opposite sides of the road. The first ditch contains those who ignore the devil, read the Bible, and try to be good Christians. As a result he will go away, only to torture lost people. The other ditch contains those who live each day implementing rituals, formulas, and nailing horseshoes over front doors to scare away the legions of attacking devils. The second ditch dwellers believe there is a demon behind every bush.

A balanced, biblical approach is featured in my (Jerry) earlier book *Spiritual Warfare: The Battle for God's Glory.* The Holy Spirit is our defense as Christians against demonic attacks. However, the influence of Satan in our lives is well documented in Scripture and confirmed in life experience. We are given clear action steps if, as Christians, we are experiencing oppression (hopelessness, doubts, discouragement, temptations). We are encouraged to recognize Satan's strategies and anything that is not of Christ in our behavior and attitudes, understand we have been given victory in Christ, and then by faith claim that victory, led by the Holy Spirit within us.

We need to have a truth encounter that will make a profound difference in our life. The answer to the devil's lie is this: the gospel is the power of God for salvation, right living, and spiritual maturity that empowers us for mission. The Christian who has a vital relationship with Jesus Christ will populate spiritually vital churches. The gospel is power. This power, through the resurrection of Jesus Christ, can save you and change you to be more like Jesus. The power of the gospel, by the way, is not exclusive to white Americans, born in Protestant homes, in suburban Atlanta, Charlotte, or Birmingham. The same gospel can be power to a dark-skinned teenage boy under a tree in Mbale, Uganda. The resurrection of Jesus Christ is power the first time a Japanese coed hears the message or power to a seventy-five-year-old man in Havana, Cuba. Your personal mission and desire to embrace the great mission of God to the nations will be profoundly influenced by your personal experience with the gospel.

> *The resurrection of Christ is the power of God for salvation, right living, and maturity to carry out His mission.*

Central to the gospel is the resurrection of Jesus. Central to the resurrection of Jesus is the corresponding power of God for salvation and for sanctification. Within the resurrection of Christ is all the power necessary for salvation, for living in faith, for growing in maturity. The gospel and its resurrection is the source of your salvation, strength for righteous living, and also for spiritual maturity.

Easter Sunday is an opportunity for Christians to relive the incredible story of the resurrection. We are all fluent in resurrection story trivia, yet the story is important to revisit. Plus, understanding the backstory will add a deeper dimension. To find that backstory, a study of 1 Corinthians 15 is important. The Gospel accounts of the resurrection tell you *what* happens. First Corinthians 15 tells you *why* it happens.

Paul's discussion of the backstory of the resurrection begins as follows: "Now brothers, I want to clarify for you the gospel I proclaimed to you" (1 Cor. 15:1). Paul is drawing his inspiration from the Holy Spirit. He felt a need to review the essentials of the gospel. One reason Christians are vulnerable to satanic lies about the resurrection is that they are overfamiliar with the details of the story but underfamiliar with the implications. Paul continued, "Now brothers, I want to clarify for you the gospel I proclaimed to you; you received it and have taken your stand on it. You are also saved by it, if you hold to the message I proclaimed to you—unless you believed to no purpose. For I passed on to you as most important what I also received: that Christ died for our sins according to the Scriptures, that He was buried, that He was raised on the third day according to the Scriptures" (1 Cor. 15:1–4).

What's first in importance? That Christ died, that He was buried and rose again on the third day. This is the story and the most important thing. The difficulty is when our spiritual life has no vitality as a result. Faith and church become that thing we do because we should. In turn people see an unimpressive and false representation of the life Christ intended for His followers.

Many of us grew up in families who struggled from paycheck to paycheck. Perhaps your family lives that way right now. Satan wants to keep you so focused on the struggles of life that you never connect the power of the resurrection to everyday living. When our whole focus is on the stuff of the earth, the relationships where the gospel is needed are the first to suffer. With Paul's declaration that Christ's resurrection is of first importance, we should all pause to test what has been in that spot in our lives.

The implications are real and intersect life. This is earth shattering and life changing. A lot of people have died, but God the Son became Jesus the Christ. When God raised Him from the dead, this is the most important thing. People often miss that. Three critical messages are contained in the teachings of Paul concerning the resurrection.

1. The Power of God for Our Salvation. So why believe in the resurrection? What are the implications of the resurrected Christ? First, the message of the resurrection is the power of God for our salvation. Many who profess to be Christians have never experienced this power. However, genuine salvation from Jesus Christ involves a supernatural and personal change. Without an infusion of power from the outside in, we remain the same people. God gets no glory in unchanged people who go to church. Unchanged people who go to church have no real passion to take the gospel to the nations. Enter Satan, the classic minimalist, who says Jesus is something but not everything. Tribes, tongues, and nations can follow their own gods. Jesus is your choice. You are an American.

Research and researchers continue to come to sad conclusions about the state of American Christians. Although we are not the only Christians in the world who live under the mandate of God to go and make disciples, we may be the least personally effective. The reason is our lack of vitality and commitment as disciples. Researcher George Barna captured the burden of Christians unchanged by their Christian faith:

> One of the greatest frustrations of my life has been the disconnection between what our research consistently shows about churched Christians and what the Bible calls us to be. Granted, we are sinful creatures and will never achieve perfection on this planet . . . however, if the local church is comprised of people who have been transformed by the grace of God through their redemption in Christ and the presence of the Holy Spirit, then their lives should be noticeably and compellingly different from the norm.[1]

We live in the era of large churches that offer much to attract people. *Outreach* Magazine, through LifeWay Research, audits the numerical success of churches in America each year. Reports confirm that at no other time in history have there been so many large churches. I thank God for the positive effect these churches have in His kingdom. Yet, as our churches become more attractive, Christianity has become less attractive to people far from God. Ultimately God gets glory when a person experiences a life change in Jesus Christ. His glory is what Satan hates and attempts in every way possible to sabotage.

Paul explained how the mission of God advanced through stories of individual life change. Paul's motives were questioned, and his life was threatened. Some of Paul's critics accused him of being just another philosophical con-man preying on people for his gain. His first argument and defense of his ministry was the substantive influence the message had in the lives of people:

> For our gospel did not come to you in word only, but also in power, in the Holy Spirit, and with much assurance. You know what kind of men we were among you for your benefit, and you became imitators of us and of the Lord when, in spite of severe persecution, you welcomed the message with the joy from the Holy Spirit. As a result, you became an example to all the believers in Macedonia and Achaia. For the Lord's message rang out from you, not only in Macedonia and Achaia, but in every place that your faith in God has gone out, so we don't need to say anything. For they themselves report about us what kind of reception we had from you: how you turned to God from idols to serve the living and true God, and to wait for His Son from heaven, whom He raised from the dead—Jesus, who rescues us from the coming wrath. (1 Thess. 1:5–10)

Can you make that argument from your ministry? How about your church? How is that defense clear from your own faith story?

I (Ed) remember when I came to Christ, August 13, 1977. Christ changed my life, and I responded to His work on my heart. I was one of those stories Paul talked about. I remember I was so excited. I could tell I'd been changed by the gospel. I knew that something had changed in me. I went home to my dad, and I said, "Dad, are you saved?" And he said, "Saved from what?" I said, "I don't know, but you've got to be." Well you know that we're saved. We're saved from being dead in our trespasses and sins. We've been made alive in Christ through the power of His resurrection. Although my spiritual journey with Jesus began over thirty years ago, I was changed. No question. And even greater, I am still being changed by the power of Jesus Christ. That is power. That is also attractive to those seeking reality in Jesus. Attractive Christians make attractive churches. Our mistake is we invest more in trying to make our churches attractive at the expense of the investment it takes to make vibrant disciples.

2. The Power of God to Live Righteously. The resurrection enables us to live righteously. The Bible says you are declared righteous when you become a Christian. God makes you righteous. You get the righteousness of Christ when you become a Christian. Through the power of the cross and the resurrection, we can live rightly. Why? Because the power that raised Christ from the dead and the spirit that raised Christ from the dead is now at work in us.

As we admire the practical wisdom of the Bible, we often make incredible claims about how God intended people to live. We say a person can take the advice and moral boundaries of the Bible for successful living, even if he is not a believer. Although there is some truth to that, we must never forget that the Bible is way too large with way too much advice to be able to live effectively without the power of God. When you add into the mix our own natural-born sinfulness, the probability for success is nil. I agree with the person who said the Christian life is not difficult to live;

it is impossible. The letters WWJD represent the question, What Would Jesus Do? T-shirts and bumper stickers abound with the reminder. The implications are, however, that a WWJD reminder makes living like Jesus 24/7 possible. Only Jesus can live like Jesus 24/7. For us to go deeper, we need His power working in us. We need supernatural power to make right choices, maintain right relationships, and fulfill the mission of God in our world.

Paul explained the relevance of the resurrection to our need for supernatural power. "And if the Spirit of Him who raised Jesus from the dead lives in you, then He who raised Christ from the dead will also bring your mortal bodies to life through His Spirit who lives in you" (Rom. 8:11). Paul had already presented in Romans that the gospel is "God's power for salvation" (Rom. 1:16). Now he says that the spirit continues with you to help you live right. The power of God that gives you spiritual birth (salvation) also gives you spiritual life (sanctification). The power of God that raised Jesus from the dead gives you the life you need to live the right way. That moves us well beyond Easter. That also moves us much deeper than a story in a book that became a movie. God has provided you the resources to live a resurrection-empowered life. The Bible assures us, "For His divine power has given us everything required for *life and godliness*, through the knowledge of Him who called us by His own glory and goodness" (2 Pet. 1:3, emphasis added).

Philippians 2:13 puts it this way: "For it is God who is working in you." Right, now because of the power of the resurrection, "it is God who is working in you, enabling you both to will and to act for His good purpose." You may say, "I've tried to live for God and I can't." What I would say to you is one of two things. First, consider the possibility that you have not yet experienced what it means to know Christ personally. The Spirit of Him who raised Jesus from the dead is not yet living in you because once He does, it changes you. If that is not the situation, consider another option. You have become so accustomed to pushing God's Spirit and promptings to the side you know nothing else. You are habitually selfish. You are living a powerless Christian life. Once again tap into the power of the resurrection. Be encouraged! The same Spirit that raised Jesus from the dead is now living in you. God is working in you, enabling you both to will and to act according to His good purpose. You can become habitually righteous by living a cross-centered, resurrection-transformed life.

3. *The Power of God for Our Maturity.* The cross and resurrection provide the foundation for maturity in my faith journey. *Journey* is one of those overused, feel good, spiritual terms that is growing stale for some. But, when we look at the phases of life for the Christ follower, a *journey* describes what should be taking place. A journey represents advancement and adventure. As we trace the literal three-year journey of Jesus' disciples with Him, we see all the metaphorical elements. From their calling to a new faith, to the powerful word pictures of the Sermon on the Mount, to the Passion, and beyond the empty tomb, we witness the spiritual transformation of the disciples. The victories, lessons, failures, obstacles, and celebrations were all a part of life with Jesus. But the big idea of the journey for Christians is that we always have some place new and deeper to travel with God. Satan prefers to stop our forward movement with Him. Then we become less attractive and believable to those who desperately need to see a transformed life.

One of the most effective lies Satan uses that hides the glory of God and the advancement of His mission is, "This is as good as it gets." Many Christians reluctantly accept that they have served God as well as they ever will. Also, the hurts, bad habits, and lack of spiritual growth are the current realities that must be accepted. But God's Spirit can give you hope again. He wants your journey with Him to be complete. He is calling you to new and deeper paths for His glory.

Robert S. McGee, professional counselor, lecturer, and president of Search Resources, explained four lies from Satan we believe. One is that "I am who I am, I cannot change, and I am hopeless."[2] If we will believe Satan's lie, then we can excuse ourselves from any responsibility to God. At that point our journey has ended. We are taking up space on the earth, waiting to die and meet the Lord.

Paul explained the platform for mature faith in 1 Corinthians. "So that your faith might not be based on men's wisdom but on God's power" (1 Cor. 2:5). Part of the difficulty is our own perception that Christianity is a religious choice or preference. People are identifying less with Christianity as a religious choice than ever before. Jon Meacham wrote a *Newsweek* article, "The End of Christian America," that was featured during Easter, April 13, 2009. Meacham reported the self-identified number of Christians in America is declining. Depending on whom you ask, poll data revealed about 75 percent of Americans say that they are Christians. The number, however, has declined about 10 percent over the last decade. I (Ed) received a call from Fox News Radio to discuss the article. In the interview I told them I did not think the decline was necessarily a bad thing. I am sure that was not the answer they expected from me, a Baptist preacher. If the meaning of the poll is that fewer people identify themselves by the word *Christian* it could be a good thing. The word *Christian,* is one of the most misunderstood and abused words in the world today. If 75 percent of Americans say they are Christians, I don't think it means three out of four people in the U.S. are genuine followers of Jesus. It has become a spiritual moniker, confusing the lost. Being a biblical Christian means to be one who follows Jesus. So what I told the radio audience was that I wished fewer people would call themselves Christians if they are not following Christ.

Maturity in my faith means I grow more and more to be like Jesus. Martha faced a defining moment on her spiritual journey when she experienced the death of her brother Lazarus. Jesus authenticated who He really was for her, as well as for me, in their graveside conversation. The Gospel of John gives us the opportunity to listen in on their conversation: "Jesus said to her, 'I am the resurrection and the life. The one who believes in Me, even if he dies, will live. Everyone who lives and believes in Me will never die—ever. Do you believe this?' 'Yes, Lord,' she told Him, 'I believe You are the Messiah, the Son of God, who was to come into the world'" (John 11:25–27). All of Martha's fears and doubts about Jesus seemed less significant in light of who He was. From Martha's personal encounter with Jesus, she matured rapidly from questioning Jesus' timing to proclaiming Him as Messiah for the world. A closer study of this passage reveals that maturity preceded miracle. The miracle of a transformed life and perspective was the greatest miracle that day. The resurrection of a dead brother from the grave added incredible meaning and drama to the episode, but that was not all. The extra miracle of resurrecting dead Lazarus was an indication of what was to come for the world through the powerful resurrection of Jesus the Messiah.

Paul addressed the resurrection issue again in 1 Corinthians 15:12: "Now if Christ is preached as raised from the dead, how can some of you say, 'There is no resurrection from the dead'?" The scandal in some early churches was the contention that Christ's body did not literally rise from the dead. The Holy Spirit always inspired God to speak to where believers struggled. Paul continued his reasoning in 1 Corinthians 15:13–14: "But if there is no resurrection of the dead, then Christ has not been raised, and if Christ has not been raised then our preaching is without foundation, and so is your faith." The environment, foundation, and platform for my maturity in Christ is His resurrection. Without the resurrection Christianity loses its real platform in my life or the life of anyone for that matter. "Satan, the one who deceives the whole world" (Rev. 12:9), would love to reduce Christianity to a religion without a resurrection. In spite of the morals and high ideals presented in the Bible, the completed work of Jesus Christ, including His bodily resurrection makes Christianity more than a religious brand. The empty tomb moves Christianity beyond an option in the worldwide religious landscape.

Popular culture has little room for such an exclusive faith. The "God is dead" culture of the sixties and seventies has given birth to the Oprahzation of spirituality in the new millennium. Oprah Winfrey's Spirit Podcast is one of the top ten downloads in the religion and spirituality genre on iTunes. Spirituality has become much more of a designer spirituality that makes the individual the power source of faith. Why such a big deal? Isn't it OK as long as you believe something?

Paul assessed the real value of faith without a resurrected Christ: "And if Christ has not been raised, your faith is worthless; you are still in your sins" (1 Cor. 15:17). A Christian religious preference that does not affirm the power of Christ and the resurrection is of no value. Where does that leave spirituality without any room for Jesus Christ? As we see Paul's words from God, we discover the incredible, eternal value of the resurrection. Since Christ has risen, your faith is worthy, rich, and substantive. My suggestion is to quit "celebrating" Easter and start living in the power of the resurrection. I am not sure the average Christian needs to hear the classic arguments that support the resurrection. I think we need to be convinced to live it! Faith is the victory.

The final part of 1 Corinthains 15:17 is the most sobering. We celebrate the resurrection in the Christian movement with everything from elaborate productions to cool T-shirts. But when Paul says without the risen Christ "you are still in your sins," he draws a dividing line between those who have trusted Christ and those who have not. If you are one who has experienced the forgiveness of sins in Jesus Christ, I hope that makes you feel blessed. But the blessing of His power and grace should come with a corresponding burden to draw the lost into the redemption we enjoy.

Resurrection Power to Fulfil God's Mission

The Global Research Department at the International Mission Board produces a research reference on the status of global evangelization. It is a thick computer printout listing the more than eleven thousand ethnic-linguistic people groups of the world. The database indicates whether or not there are churches and the estimated number of believers among each people group. There is information regarding the availability of Scripture in the language of the people and the status of Bible translation. Whether the *Jesus* film is available and radio broadcasts are accessible are indicated as well as a listing of mission agencies that are known to be engaging in strategies among each particular people group. As one thumbs through this volume of data, line upon line is highlighted in a bold, dark font which indicates a people group among which there are no churches, no Christian believers, no Scripture, and no missionary witness engaging them with the gospel. Many of these would have a relatively small population, but hundreds have a population of more than one hundred thousand people and several in excess of a million!

I (Jerry) don't have to open this reference material to know what it contains, but every time an updated version appears on my desk, my mind immediately goes to Revelation 7:9 where John envisioned the day Christ would return. He said that he saw a multitude from every tribe, people, language, and nation gathered around the throne of God and worshipping the Lamb. That puts our mission task in perspective. God's mission will be fulfilled. The only question is whether we, as His people, will be faithful and obedient in the task to which He has called us into His kingdom. In God's providence and sovereign timing, the gospel will reach the whole world, but like Esther, we are the ones who will suffer the consequences if we forfeit involvement in the mission of God.

> *God's mission will be fulfilled. The only question is whether we, as His people, will be faithful and obedient in the task.*

It is a unique privilege for me, as president of the International Mission Board, to be in a position to have a global overview of how God is working throughout the world. One notable impression I (Jerry) have gained is an awesome sense of God's providence. He is moving through history and global events to fulfill His purpose. We can choose to be a part of what God is doing and His mission in the world or not. God doesn't need Jerry Rankin and Ed Stetzer.

He doesn't need the International Mission Board and Southern Baptists. He is not dependent on your church doing anything about reaching a lost world. He is sovereign over the nations, and His purpose will be realized in His divinely ordained timeframe. But it would be tragic for any of God's people to be so self-serving or so narrow in their concept of missions to miss being a part of what God has called us to do as His people.

The culmination of history and the triumphant kingdom of God is a foregone conclusion in revelation of God's Word. God gave to John, the beloved disciple, special insight into the spiritual nature of the kingdom. In contrast with the Synoptic Gospels, the Gospel of John uniquely presents the deity of Christ. To John, in his later years, God revealed the revelation of the final days when Christ would return and establish His kingdom. The Child that was born would be the One who will "shepherd all nations with an iron scepter—and her child was caught up to God and to His throne" (Rev. 12:5). We are told of His might as the One who is righteous and true—"Lord, who will not fear and glorify Your name? Because You alone are holy, because all the nations will come and worship before You" (Rev. 15:4). In the sequence of end-times events, John reveals that the seventh trumpet blast will signal that the "kingdom of the world has become the kingdom of our Lord and of His Messiah, and He will reign forever and ever!" (Rev. 11:15).

Paul concluded the book of Romans with the assurance of this becoming a reality. The gospel is still a mystery, unknown by the peoples of the world. It is a "sacred secret kept silent" (Rom. 16:25), but it would be revealed by the proclamation of Jesus Christ just as it was "made known through the prophetic Scriptures, according to the command of the eternal God, to advance the obedience of faith among all nations" (Rom. 16:26). But don't miss the ultimate purpose of all nations coming to obedience of faith: "To the only wise God, through Jesus Christ—to Him be the glory forever!" (Rom. 16:27). It is for God's glory that the nations are to be brought to obedience to the faith and the kingdoms of the world become the kingdom of our Lord. Satan is adamantly opposed to God being glorified in our lives and among the nations. He is doing everything in His power to keep the gospel from being proclaimed to all peoples.

It is amazing that, after a rapid start in the first Christian century, the church and God's people were diverted from the mission of God and the task to declare His glory among the nations that all the ends of the earth would praise His name. The initial Jewish church was reluctant to recognize that those other than Jews could be a part of the kingdom of God. Within a few centuries the church became institutionalized, doctrines were diluted, and a clerical hierarchy distorted the hope of redemption, hiding the truth from the masses. The Reformation brought renewed hope and impetus to the spread of the gospel and response to a message of salvation by grace through faith alone. In fact, the Moravians were among the earliest to embrace the mission of God as the purpose of the church. At least 10 percent of their members went out to share the gospel among unevangelized peoples while more than half of the remaining congregations diligently focused on winning the lost where they lived. But it was the nineteenth century after Christ before a movement began to reach the whole world.

Yet, still, Satan's wiles were subtle and disastrous to the spread of the kingdom. Warfare, violence, and totalitarian governments allowed the prince of the powers of the air to inhibit a Christian witness in many parts of the world. His power over principalities, rulers, and dominions where Christ was not known barricaded much of the world to a message of hope and salvation. Missionaries rode the coattails of Western colonialists, but the church that followed failed to bridge effectively cultural barriers to indigenous expressions. Its forms and rituals, even on foreign soil, failed to reflect a testimony of spiritual transformation that had the power to penetrate a pagan world with a relationship with God. Until the final years of the twentieth century, Satan, as the great deceiver, had obscured the nature of Christian mission to reach all peoples. He deluded a rising tide of missionary efforts to presume a token witness in each country was fulfillment of the Great Commission, while most of the peoples of the world remained untouched by a Christian witness.

These tactics have been exposed, and God is moving to assert the resurrection power of the gospel in penetrating historical barriers and extending His kingdom to the ends of the earth. A changing global community, international relations, and communication technology have resulted in the gospel penetrating every nation on the face of the earth. Sociological research has brought people group awareness, exposing the nature of our mission task and stimulating a new impetus for global evangelization. Even Satan's efforts to bring persecution and suffering to God's people have served only to give evidence of the genuineness of faith and power to overcome. Even the indifference and self-centered nature of the modern-day church cannot deter God's kingdom being established upon the earth. Nothing has been so effective in Satan's arsenal as Christians consumed in their own programs and activities, celebrating their own comforts and prosperity, while ignoring the compelling appeal of our Lord to forsake all and follow Him.

Do we not risk losing the reward for faithfulness as God's people? What will be the consequences as we stand before the throne of God to give account for the deeds we have done and to be found lacking? How will we explain being recipients of God's grace and then neglecting to share it with the nations? Will we find ourselves trying to justify serving God where we live, providing lavish worship facilities and ministering to His people while multitudes never have an opportunity to hear and respond to the gospel? Rather than spreading the good news and multiplying God's kingdom resources, will we not be like the servant who received one talent but did nothing with it? He incurred the wrath of God who characterized his fear and indifference as one who was wicked and slothful. Do we really want to risk being identified with the one we know as wicked and is behind all the wickedness in the world?

God yearns for the worship and praise of all peoples. Will we be responsible for His being deprived of the praise and glory of unreached people groups because of self-centered concern in following our own plans and holding on to our own comfort and security? However, the real tragedy is to forfeit the joy and blessing in being found faithful and to have had the privilege of taking Christ to those who have yet to hear? Do we not hear the cry of a lost world calling out like the disciples on the storm-tossed Sea of Galilee, "Carest thou not that we perish?" (Mark 4:38 KJV). Will there be those still living in spiritual darkness with no hope of eternal life, struggling in sin and superstition who must be saying as the lost characterized by the prophet, "Harvest has passed, summer has ended, but we have not been saved" (Jer. 8:20)?

Even though the gospel will eventually touch every nation, people, and language, how many multitudes will perish without an opportunity of knowing the way to God and that eternal life is through faith in Jesus Christ? How many are waiting for someone to tell them the good news that salvation has been provided through God's grace rather than the futile rituals and efforts to attain personal goodness? Most of the world has yet to know that a victorious, abundant life and the assurance of heaven does not come in devotion to religious traditions but by faith in the Son of God. Yes, God's grace does extend to whomever will repent and believe on Jesus Christ. Paul tells us in Romans 10:13, "Everyone who calls on the name of the Lord will be saved." But then we are confronted with the question: "But how can they call on Him in whom they have not believed? And how can they believe without hearing about Him" (Rom. 10:14)? Yes, they may be lost, but God's people will be held accountable for every person that has never heard. More than two thousand years ago, our Lord made our calling clear. His mandate was unequivocal as He commissioned His people to go and preach the gospel to every creature.

The reality of the coming kingdom itself has been rationalized away by an interesting twisted eschatology. Acknowledging that the kingdoms of this world will become the kingdoms of our Lord and that all people, tribes, languages, and nations will be represented around the throne of God, many see that not as a result of our witness upon the earth but only in the new heavens and new earth in the millennial reign of Christ. But even if the fulfillment of God's mission will not come until the return of Christ, should we not be diligently pursuing the salvation of all peoples in the opportunity we have been given in this age? By what criteria can we justify allowing any people to die in their sin and face an eternity without Christ?

Neglecting God's Mission Is Sin and Will Entail Judgment

Let's go back to the experience of Israel in the wilderness and their failure to fulfill God's mission. Fast-forward forty years to a new generation that was now ready to follow God's leadership by faith, and in His power claim the promised land as His possession. During all these years of wandering in the wilderness, the tribes of Gad and Reuben (and half the tribe of Manasseh) had settled in the land of Jazer and Gilead on the east side of the Jordan River. They came to Moses and Eleazer the priest and leader of Israel with an interesting request. "The Reubenites and Gadites had a large number of livestock. . . . They saw that the region was a good one for livestock. . . . They said, 'If we have found favor in your sight, let this land be given to your servants as a possession. Don't make us cross the Jordan'" (Num. 32:1, 3–5). In verse 6 Moses replied, "Should your brothers go to war while you stay here?"

They were saying like many Christians and churches: "We understand the mission responsibility and need to claim the nations and peoples of the world for Jesus Christ, but we are comfortably settled here in the United States. God has blessed and prospered our businesses. This is where our children and families live. God is blessing our church and endeavor to serve Him where we live. We want to be exempt from the responsibility of crossing oceans and engaging other cultures with the gospel. Let others go, but we will serve God here!"

It is often a matter of wanting to hold on to comforts and security rather than embracing the sacrifice required to take the gospel to the lost nations of the world. We enjoy the finer things of life, but 1 John 2:15–16 admonishes us, "Do not love the world or the things that belong to the world. If anyone loves the world, love for the Father is not in him. Because everything that belongs to the world—the lust of the flesh, the lust of the eyes, and the pride in one's lifestyle—is not from the Father, but is from the world."

Most churches want to relinquish the task of missions to a mission agency to fulfill on their behalf. They reason that they will be responsible for evangelism and ministry to the people where they are located but will support someone else to do missions overseas for them. Local churches tempted to relinquish responsibility for the mission of God and simply express emotional or financial support face real spiritual dangers. The privilege of joining God as He moves in history and global events to plant the gospel and be exalted among all the peoples of the earth cannot be forfeited without endangering the nature of the church. Churches who re-interpret the mission of God in a narrow provincialism and their role as ministering to their community, nurturing their membership, and witnessing to the lost in the immediate vicinity of their church deny Jesus' vision and command for His followers.

> *If the church sees the mission of God as a sequential set of concentric circles, they will never move beyond the narrow core.*

Some leaders of such churches make Acts 1:8 sequential and say they are focused on reaching their "Jerusalem," their own city or town, and perhaps extend their witness in the larger surrounding area of their "Judea." They have no responsibility beyond their locale until they have successfully fulfilled their local mission. Unfortunately this never happens! The

Great Commission is often interpreted as applying to whatever a church happens to do in its local programs of witness and ministry, ignoring the fact that the mandate of our Lord is to the *pante ta ethne.* Certainly God wants us to witness to the lost where we live and minister to the needs of those around us, but it doesn't exempt the church from responsibility for the mission of God to the ends of the earth. If a church sees responsibility for the mission of God as a sequential set of concentric circles, they will never move beyond the narrow core and will forfeit the privilege of being a part of what God is doing among the nations.

This attitude is reflected in the church seeing the denomination, or combination of mission agencies, as responsible for fulfilling the mission of God to the nations on their behalf. This is parallel to a modern-day trend that is decimating the effectiveness of many churches in relegating ministry and witness to professional staff. However, only as the entire church, the body of Christ, is equipped in applying each member's unique giftedness to the work of ministry is it healthy, growing, and effective in impacting its community and transforming society. Despite the effectiveness of many specialized mission agencies and the ability of many to send and channel support for full-time missionaries, only as the massive grassroots potential of God's people is mobilized to engage His mission will the task be accomplished.

If every church that acknowledges the uniqueness of Jesus Christ as the only way of salvation for a lost world, that recognizes all who have yet to come to Him in repentance and faith are lost and bound for an eternity in hell, and would be committed to the Great Commission of discipling the nations, the mission of God could be readily fulfilled, even in this generation. But Satan does not want to see that happen, so he convinces churches to be content with their provincialism and limited local focus.

Moses reviewed a little history to remind the tribes of Reuben and Gad why God had brought them to this place and of the mission before them. But then he offered a solution in response to their request: "If you do this—if you arm yourselves for battle before the

LORD, and every one of your armed men crosses the Jordan before the LORD until He has driven His enemies from His presence, and the land is subdued before the LORD—afterwards you may return and be free from obligation to the LORD and to Israel. And this land will belong to you as a possession before the LORD. But if you don't do this, you will certainly sin against the LORD; be sure your sin will catch up with you" (Num. 32:20–23).

He made clear that no one is exempt; everyone has an obligation in fulfilling the mission. Yes, some of God's people are called to missionary service. They are to plant their lives in an incarnational witness among the peoples throughout a lost world. But those not called to be missionaries and permitted to live in their comfortable American culture are not exempt from the mission of making Christ known among the nations. As Moses said, all of God's people are to arm themselves and engage the battle. The task will be accomplished only when every church and every believer finds their place in God's mission. Note the consequences of neglecting this obligation. As most translations say, "Your sin will find you out."

This expression is quoted a number of times in the Bible, but this is the original text. We think of this in the context of sinful living and the consequence that must be paid. But what sin is it that we are in danger of catching up with us, or coming back to haunt us for which judgment will be exacted. It is the sin of omission— failure to engage in God's mission and being negligent in what God has called us to do as His people. James 4:17 puts it another way: "So, for the person who knows to do good and doesn't do it, it is a sin."

We have often used the admonition in Ezekiel to warn the wicked as an impetus for personal evangelism and to put people on a guilt trip for not witnessing as they should. "I have made you a watchman over the house of Israel. When you hear a word from My mouth, give them a warning from Me. If I say to the wicked person: You will surely die, but you do not warn him—you don't speak out to warn him about his wicked way in order to save his life—that wicked person will die for his iniquity. Yet I will hold you responsible for his blood" (Ezek. 3:17–18). This is not a reality just in regard to personal evangelism; Israel was to be a witness to the nations, just as we are to be as the people of God. Nations and peoples are dying in their sin and wickedness without any warning from us. And surely God will hold us responsible.

But God goes on to say, "I will display My glory among the nations" (Ezek. 39:21). He proclaimed through the prophet Habakkuk, "Look at the nations and observe—be utterly astounded! For something is taking place in your days that you will not believe when you hear about it. . . . He gathers all the nations to himself; he collects all the peoples for himself" (Hab. 1:5; 2:5). Zechariah added, "Many nations will join themselves to the LORD on that day and become My people" (Zech. 2:11). God is looking forward to that day when "the earth will be filled with the knowledge of the LORD's glory, as the waters cover the sea" (Hab. 2:14). He is moving in power and providence through global events to be exalted among the nations. This is not just an eschatological reality but God's plan throughout the ages. He has called us as His instrument to "proclaim His salvation from day to day. Declare His glory among the nations, His wonderful works among all peoples" (1 Chron. 16:23–24) that all the ends of the earth would sing His praise.

We are fortunate in having heard and responded to the gospel. We know that our salvation and eternal destiny are secure. One day we will don our robes of white when our Lord returns and prepare to enter His eternal glory. It will be a great day of celebration and rejoicing. But across a great chasm will be a multitude of people with bowed heads, slumped shoulders, and sad countenances. Being judged for their sins, they will be filing into an eternity of torment in hell. I believe they will look across that chasm at us with a look of envy that will say, "You knew. You knew the way to heaven, but you never came and told us."

But sadder still will be the eyes of Jesus, in one of those paradoxes of the Christian faith. Even as He welcomes us into His eternal glory, His eyes will betray a sadness that so many never knew He had come and died for them. I think His eyes will meet ours, much as they did Peter's on that night of denial, and without a word will say, "I told you to go. I promised you My power and assured you of My grace. But you chose to stay at home and follow your own will. Now it is too late."

Or we can choose to trust God, resist the evil one, stand firm in the faith, and go on mission to proclaim the glory of God among every tongue, tribe, and nation. Then we will be able to live out our faith confidently in the One who deserves our love and obedience, as He receives glory, honor, and praise. At the final day we should be counted as those who led the peoples of this world to worship the Christ, the Son of the living God.

Going Deeper

1. What difference should it make in our lives to realize the resurrection of Jesus Christ was not just to assure us of salvation but to empower us to fulfill His mission?

2. Realizing that you live in a unique era of history when God is moving to fulfill His mission, what does it mean to you personally to be among those called into the kingdom for such a time as this?

3. What are the consequences and judgment of God on His people who fail to be obedient to His purpose?

NOTES

Chapter 1

1. Dr. James B. Slack, A "Ta Ethne" *Ethnolinguistic People Group Focus as Seen in the Scriptures* (2003), 9.

2. Paul M. Lewis, ed., *Ethnologue: Languages of the World, Sixteenth edition* (Dallas, TX: SIL International, 2009). Online http://www.ethnologue.com.

3. John Piper, *Let the Nations Be Glad!* (Grand Rapids, MI: Baker Books, 1993), 1.

4. Ibid.

Chapter 2

1. Barbara Singerman, *Beyond Surrender* (Garland, TX: Hannibal Books, 2003), 52–53.

Chapter 3

1. John Piper, *Let the Nations Be Glad!* (Grand Rapids, MI: Baker Books, 1993), 41.

2. Christian Schwarz, *Natural Church Development: A Guide to Eight Essential Qualities of Healthy Churches* (Carol Stream, IL: ChurchSmart Resources, 1996), 68.

Chapter 5

1. Neil Cole, *Organic Church: Growing Faith Where Life Happens* (San Francisco, CA: Jossey-Bass Publishers, 2005), 149.

2. Patrick Johnson, *The Church Is Bigger than You Think* (Great Britain: Christian Focus Publications, 1998).

Chapter 6

1. John Foxe, *Foxe's Book of Martyrs*, Harold J. Chadwick, ed., (Gainesville, FL: Bridge-Logos Publishers, 2001).

2. Susan Bergman, ed., *Martyrs: Contemporary Writers on Modern Lives of Faith* (Marynoll, NY: Orbis Books, 1998).

3. Paul Marshall, "Present Day Persecution of Christians," *Evangelical Review of Theology* 24, n. 1 (2000), 19–30.

4. Ken Anderson, *Bold as a Lamb: Pastor Samuel Lamb and the Underground Church of China* (Grand Rapids, MI: Zondervan, 1991).

5. Nik Ripken, "A Missiology of Suffering: Witness and Church Planting in the Midst of Persecution," (unpublished paper, 2006), 8.

6. C. S. Lewis, *The Screwtape Letters* (Uhrichsville, OH: Barbour Publishing, 1990).

Chapter 8

1. C. S. Lewis, *The Screwtape Letters* (Uhrichsville, OH: Barbour Publishing, 1990).

2. Bob Logan and Sherilyn Carlton, *Coaching 101: Discover the Power of Coaching* (St. Charles, IL: ChurchSmart Resources), 23.

Chapter 9

1. Jonathan Dienst and Michael Clancy, *Madoff Gets the Max: 150 Years in Jail,* Copyright Associated Press/NBC New York, June 28, 2009.

Chapter 10

1. Bob Roberts Jr., *Transformations: How Global Churches Transform Lives and the World* (Grand Rapids, MI: Zondervan, 2006), 48–49.

2. David T. Olsen, *The American Church in Crisis* (Grand Rapids, MI: Zondervan, 2008), 176.

Chapter 11

1. Samuel Moffett, *The History of Christianity in Asia, Volume I* (Marynoll, NY: Orbis Books, 1998), 506.

2. Philip Nations and Ed Stetzer, *Compelled by Love* (Birmingham, AL: New Hope Publishers, 2008).

Chapter 12

1. George Barna, *Revolution: Finding Vibrant Faith Beyond the Walls of the Sanctuary* (Carol Stream, IL: Tyndale Publishers, 2005), 31.

2. Robert S. McGee, *The Search for Significance: Seeing Your True Worth through God's Eyes* (Nashville, TN: W Publishing Group, 1998), 95.

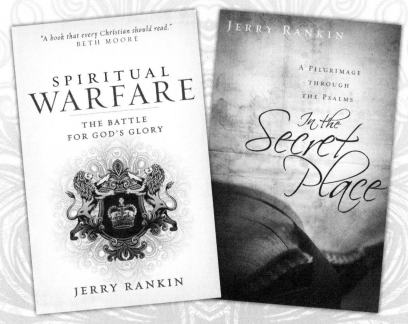